Patriotic Education in a Global Age

The History and Philosophy of Education Series

EDITED BY RANDALL CURREN AND JONATHAN ZIMMERMAN

THE COLOR OF MIND: WHY THE ORIGINS OF THE ACHIEVEMENT
GAP MATTER FOR JUSTICE *by Derrick Darby and John L. Rury*

THE CASE FOR CONTENTION: TEACHING CONTROVERSIAL
ISSUES IN AMERICAN SCHOOLS *by Jonathan Zimmerman and Emily Robertson*

HAVE A LITTLE FAITH: RELIGION, DEMOCRACY, AND
THE AMERICAN PUBLIC SCHOOL *by Benjamin Justice and Colin Macleod*

TEACHING EVOLUTION IN A CREATION NATION
by Adam Laats and Harvey Siegel

Patriotic Education in a Global Age

RANDALL CURREN AND
CHARLES DORN

The University of Chicago Press
Chicago and London

The History and Philosophy of Education Series is published in cooperation with the Association for Philosophy of Education and the History of Education Society.

The University of Chicago Press, Chicago 60637
The University of Chicago Press, Ltd., London
© 2018 by The University of Chicago
Published 2018
Printed in the United States of America

27 26 25 24 23 22 21 20 19 18   1 2 3 4 5

ISBN-13: 978-0-226-55225-5 (cloth)
ISBN-13: 978-0-226-55239-2 (paper)
ISBN-13: 978-0-226-55242-2 (e-book)
DOI: https://doi.org/10.7208/chicago/9780226552422.001.0001

Library of Congress Cataloging-in-Publication Data
Names: Curren, Randall R., author. | Dorn, Charles, author.
   Title: Patriotic education in a global age / Randall Curren and Charles Dorn.
   Other titles: History and philosophy of education.
   Description: Chicago ; London : The University of Chicago Press, 2018. |
Series: The history and philosophy of education series
   Identifiers: LCCN 2017040697 | ISBN 9780226552255 (cloth : alk. paper) |
ISBN 9780226552392 (pbk. : alk. paper) | ISBN 9780226552422 (e-book)
   Subjects: LCSH: Patriotism—Study and teaching—United States. |
Nationalism—Study and teaching—United States.
   Classification: LCC LC1091 .C97 2018 | DDC 372.83—dc23
   LC record available at https://lccn.loc.gov/2017040697

For
LeRoy E. Dorn
and
Harold Wechsler
in memoriam

CONTENTS

The central question for this book is whether schools should attempt to cultivate patriotism, and if so why, how, and with what conception of patriotism in mind. The promotion of patriotism has figured prominently in the history of public schooling in the United States, always with the idea that patriotism is both an inherently admirable attribute and an essential motivational basis for good citizenship. It has been assumed, in short, that patriotism is a virtue in its own right and that it is a foundational aspect of civic virtue more generally. Assumptions have also been made concerning the capacity of schools to inspire patriotism and the educational means by which virtues in general, and patriotism in particular, can be cultivated. Different conceptions of these educational means have been advanced in connection with competing visions of civic virtue and patriotism, so assumptions about which varieties of civic virtue and patriotism are most admirable or desirable have also shaped educational practices.

In order to assess these assumptions and answer the questions that concern us, we must consider the *nature* of virtue and consult research findings in motivational psychology that can help us understand what sustains civic responsibility. We must ask whether there is a genuinely virtuous form of patriotism and, if so, what relationship it may have to an educationally responsible form of civic education.

In order to define an educationally responsible form of civic education we will begin by framing and defending an understanding of what defines responsible education generally. On that basis we will then derive a general account of responsible civic education. These accounts of education in general and civic education in particular will incorporate views on the nature of virtue and the nature and acquisition of virtuous motivation. We will argue on the basis of these views that there surely is a virtuous form of patriotism, and we will argue that an inclusive and enabling just school community may contribute to its development in some valuable ways. Saying that there is a virtuous form of patriotism does not imply that patriotism is a virtue, however. We will argue that civic virtue is what schools should aim to cultivate, and that civic education should be organized around three components of it, namely, civic intelligence, civic friendship, and civic competence. We show how each of these can be motivationally significant in sustaining civic responsibility. We also hold that appropriate responsiveness to a country's value is the motivational core of civic virtue with respect to a country, and that virtuous patriotism is responsiveness of this kind involving commitments of membership permitted by obligations of universal morality and global justice.

An important aspect of our view of virtuous patriotism is that it would be compatible with civic responsibility in all the spheres of civic life in which cooperation is desirable, from the local to the global. The importance of global cooperation and perceived tensions between global cooperation and patriotism lead us to finish with an account of global civic education.

There has been a resurgence of interest in patriotic education in recent years, but we are not aware of any book that adopts the kind of methodically foundational approach that we do. We are even more certain that no previous work on this topic brings history and philosophy into direct conversation to ensure that the ethical analysis of what is educationally appropriate is informed by a strong and ethically attuned understanding of what schools have done in the name of patriotism. The philosophical and historical aspects of this work are both much different from what they would have been without the other.

Our project is strongly anchored in the practices of patriotic education in the United States and the debates surrounding those practices, but much of what we have to say should be of interest to readers everywhere. This should be the case given the generality of the questions we pose and the wide applicability of our approach to answering them. It is also likely that the United States has not been alone in adopting the kinds of pedagogical practices it has and that our nuanced assessment of these practices will resonate in significant ways with many national traditions. Finally, whatever one's national traditions, it should also be clear that international cooperation is an urgent necessity and one we must learn to harmonize with devotion to the countries we call our own. Our closing chapter on global civic education speaks to the common interests we all share, wherever we live.

This book is the product of a seven-year collaboration between a philosopher (Curren) and a historian (Dorn). We began with open minds about the conclusions we would reach, hoping but not knowing that we could bridge the differences between our two disciplines, learn from each other, and reach agreement on a common thesis. We ask readers to engage this work with similarly open minds, knowing that it is because the topic of this book is important that we have made every effort to understand it and articulate a responsible view of what we owe our children and each other. We do not write as partisans.

As scholars, our work is judged primarily by the scholarly standards of our respective fields, where careers are made and destroyed by strength of evidence, soundness of reasoning, validity of constructs, tireless investigation, theoretical insight, good judgment, and exquisite attention to detail. So we must hope that colleagues in our respective fields of study will approve the work we have done. This is a short book by design and written for a wide audience, so scholars and any others with an eye for scholarly rigor may need to consult the related works we cite to be satisfied that this book advances a scholarly understanding of patriotic education in important ways. Readers with scholarly interests in patriotism and civic education should also understand that this book is neither a comprehensive investigation of patriotism nor a comprehensive investigation of civic education; it confines itself to the intersection of these topics and refers only very selectively to the rich and wide-ranging philosophical literature on patriotism.[1]

Writing for a wide audience, we have written not only as scholars but also as citizens of our own country and the world. We have done so in the interest of a more informed, reasoned, and mutually respectful public conversation—one that is sensitive enough to evidence and the value of what is at stake in our collective existence to have some chance of seriously addressing and solving the problems we face.

Theresa May, who became Britain's prime minister in the wake of the June 2016 Brexit vote, famously remarked that "if you believe you are a citizen of the world, you're a citizen of nowhere. You don't understand what citizenship means."[2] We agree wholeheartedly with the sentiment that identification with "international elites" at the expense of "fellow citizens down the road" is incompatible with civic responsibility, but the position we take in this book is in other respects sharply at odds with May's assertion.[3] The fates of ordinary people across the world are simply too interconnected, interdependent, and imperiled for us to have much chance of preserving the conditions of a desirable future for any of us if we do not master an art of global civic cooperation compatible with justice for everyone closer to home. The families whose children cannot find work in rural England and America can no more be ignored than the climate refugees made destitute by water scarcity and encroachment of deserts.[4]

The development of this work benefited from the invitations, advice, and comments of many people, numerous encounters with colleagues whose work has shaped the literature on patriotism and education, and opportunities to teach and present the topic of this work in a variety of venues over the span of many years, including the Katholische Universität in Eichstätt, Germany, in April 2014; Oriel College, Oxford, in January 2016; and Illinois State University in April 2016. The colleagues to whom we are most indebted are Danielle Allen, Sigal Ben-Porath, Jason Blokhuis, Harry Brighouse, Eamonn Callan, Arun Gandhi, Michael Hand, Meira Levinson, Ian MacMullen, Daniel Perlstein, Emily Robertson, Richard Ryan, Mitja Sardo, Gina Schouten, Krassimir Stojanov, David Tyack, David Walker, Danielle Zwarthoed, and above all Jonathan Zimmerman and Harold Wechsler. This book and the History and Philosophy of Education series of which it is a part would not have existed without Harold's vision and guidance. We are also indebted to our editor, Elizabeth Branch Dyson, for her keen editorial eye and unwavering support, and to the anonymous referees who offered valuable guidance for revisions.

For the financial assistance that enabled us to present our work in progress at a series of three workshops, we are grateful to New York University, the Spencer Foundation, and the Humanities Project of the University of Rochester. Early stages of Curren's work on this book were completed during his residence at the Institute for Advanced Study (IAS), in Princeton, New Jersey, as the Ginny and Robert Loughlin Founders' Circle Member for 2012–13. He is grateful to the Institute, its School of Social Science, and the Loughlin family for providing ideal circumstances for research. Curren also owes thanks to the University of Rochester for facilitating his IAS residency and for a university research award that enabled him to conduct a related study of motivation, well-being, and civic responsibility with psychologist colleagues Richard Ryan and Laura Wray-Lake, from July 1, 2014, to December 31, 2015.

Fragments of the following articles by Curren appear with revisions in chapters 4 and 5 with the permission of the publishers: "Aristotelian Necessities," *Good Society* 22, no. 2 (2013): 247–63; "A Neo-Aristotelian Account of Education, Justice, and the Human Good," *Theory and Research in Education* 11, no. 3 (2013): 232–50; "Motivational Aspects of Moral Learning and Progress," *Journal of Moral Education* 43, no. 4 (2014): 484–99. Chapter 6 is a revised version of Curren's paper, "Global Civic Education," in *Philosophy of Education—Main Topics, Disciplinary Identity, Political Significance*, ed. Michael Spieker and Krassimir Stojanov (Tutzig: NOMOS, 2017), published here by prior arrangement with Spieker, Stojanov, and NOMOS.

Dorn is grateful to the Spencer Foundation and Bowdoin College for the financial support that facilitated the research and writing of chapters 1, 2, and 3. He is also extremely appreciative of the opportunity to interview individuals who were students during the World War II era (the recollections provided through just a few of those oral histories are directly related in chapter 3). Dorn benefited from conversations about schooling and patriotism with students enrolled in a number of his courses, including Contemporary American Education, Democracy's Citadel, and The Educational Crusade. He is indebted to them for their thoughtful insights and suggestions. Finally, he would like to thank Veronica Fyer-Morrel, Alec Morrison, and Molly Porcher for their research and editorial assistance.

Introduction

O, yes,
I say it plain,
America never was America to me,
And yet I swear this oath—
America will be!

—Langston Hughes[1]

"A time comes when silence is betrayal," Dr. Martin Luther King declared, addressing the Clergy and Laymen Concerned about Vietnam and echoing its executive committee's recent statement.[2] "I come to this platform tonight to make a passionate plea to my beloved nation. . . . To my fellow Americans who, with me, bear the greatest responsibility in ending a conflict that has exacted a heavy price on both continents."[3] With these words, King identified himself as a patriot whose love of country moved him to not betray it—to not stand by in silence as it betrayed its own ideals abroad and at home—and it was in this context that he quoted the lines above from Langston Hughes's poem "Let America Be America Again." Delivered at Riverside Church in New York on April 4, 1967, this speech opposing the Vietnam War led to King being widely condemned as anti-American and recklessly irresponsible. Unyielding in the face of mounting death threats, he was assassinated one year later, on April 4, 1968.

What does it mean to say, as Hughes and King did, that "America will be"? To affirm this as an article of faith and commitment? It is surely not a disinterested prediction, nor an idle expression of hope. To "swear" this "oath" is to pledge or commit oneself to the fulfilment of an ideal—the fulfillment of American ideals—not just anywhere but in America itself. To say that "America never was America to me" is to observe that these worthy ideals are not yet fulfilled. It is, indeed, to protest that they fall far short of being fulfilled in the conditions of one's own life and the lives of many others. Yet, it is more than this. It is also, and importantly, a public affirmation of the value of America as an ideal and as a country that embraces that ideal. Saying "America will be" as a swearing of oath is also evidently to pledge oneself to advance this worthy object of attachment and aspiration. It is to take a stand from which one cannot retreat without shame, and to invite others to do the same, in defense of an America not yet fully realized.

King emphasized early in the address the ironic betrayal of American ideals entailed by

> taking the black young men who had been crippled by our own society and sending them eight thousand miles away to guarantee liberties in Southeast Asia which they had not found in southwest Georgia and East Harlem. So we have been repeatedly faced with the cruel irony of watching Negro and white boys on TV screens as they kill and die together for a nation that has been unable to seat them together in the same schools.[4]

In stark contrast to the country's history of using public schools to integrate and "Americanize" newly arriving immigrants, the racial integration of schools had been strenuously resisted. Alabama governor George C. Wallace had declared only four years earlier in his 1963 inaugural address, "I draw the line in the dust and toss the gauntlet before the feet of tyranny and I say segregation now, segregation tomorrow, segregation forever."[5] By "tyranny" he evidently meant enforcement of Fourteenth and Fifteenth Amendment constitutional guarantees of equal citizenship and the 1954 US Supreme Court ruling, in *Brown v. Board of Education*, that segregated schooling is unconstitutional. King also recounted Vietnam's 1945 declaration of independence from France, which quoted the American colonies' Declaration of Independence from Britain and the United States' subsequent ironic role in aiding France's attempts to recolonize Vietnam. Unspoken was the irony in the FBI's illegal wiretapping of King's hotel rooms and attempt to blackmail him into committing suicide in 1964 as he was about to receive the Nobel Peace Prize.[6] Although it would remain invisible to the American public until the release of FBI internal documents in 1971, King had been the victim of illegal government spying for years and would soon be subject to ongoing surveillance by US military intelligence. The Southern Christian Leadership Conference and other peaceful civil rights and antiwar citizen and student organizations were also targets of FBI spying and hostile infiltration—as similar organizations are now in the post–September 11 era.[7]

King frames his patriotism as heartfelt, but reaching "beyond national allegiances" to embrace a brotherhood of man that is entirely consistent with fidelity to the ideals that have defined what America has been understood to be:

> Now, it should be incandescently clear that no one who has any concern for the *integrity* and life of America today can ignore the present war. . . . [America] can never be saved so long as it destroys the deepest hopes of man the world over. So it is that those of us who are yet determined that America *will* be are led down the path of protest and dissent, working for the health of our land.[8]

What could the word *integrity* mean in this context but being true to oneself, to the commitments that make one who one is, make a country what it thinks it is or intends to be? This is what integrity would most obviously mean in the context of affirming that "America *will* be." Yet it could, and evidently does, also signify being both true to oneself—one's best self—*and* doing what is right or exhibiting moral rectitude.

King frames his dissent as patriotic, and some may conceive of patriotism and patriotic dissent as grounded solely in a country's ideals, while others would insist that virtuous patriotism is answerable to moral standards that transcend, and may in some places and times override, a country's ideals.[9] King seems to hold the latter view and to think that it is by exemplifying independently important moral ideals that a country's own ideals and actions provide the basis for a healthy, well-functioning society. The word *integrity* may indeed signify a kind of functional integrity or healthy functioning of a society that could be severely undermined by persistent betrayal of norms of equal respect, justice, and opportunity—ideals on which societies and their governments typically stake their claims to legitimacy. King's religious convictions would have led him to think that the health or good of all countries requires fidelity to such ideals of natural justice and that to confront and overcome injustice is to promote a country's good, its health, and its functionality.[10] By this measure, realizing America would entail the realization of its morally sound ideals of liberty, equality, and opportunity not only at home but abroad, that America would not "[destroy] the deepest hopes of man the world over," by sponsoring dictators and waging ruinous, unnecessary wars. Patriotic devotion to a country's good would begin with what is good for its people, but virtuous patriotism would not pursue domestic advantage in ways that wrong others elsewhere.

A *legitimate* government is one whose relationships with citizens are normally mediated by an honest give-and-take of reasons.[11] A government's equal respect for its citizens as rationally self-determining members of a cooperative society is the heart of legitimacy, and it entails norms of transparency, liberty, and noncoercion. The rational and informed cooperation of citizens can only be procured on the basis of terms of cooperation that are perceived as good enough or the best that can be reasonably expected, and it is in this (extended) sense that the legitimacy of a particular government may be staked on the promise of such things as equal economic and cultural opportunity. In the context of enduring and invidious segregation, denial of voting rights, and systematic violent intimidation of black citizens, the civil rights movement was a struggle for the wider legitimacy of government in the United States and an embodiment of constitutional renewal. It did not simply aim to bring about a more legitimate relationship between black Americans and government, but enacted for its part a relationship that was more legitimate and more worthy of human dignity, one that was reasoned, respectful, and courageous in affirming justice in the face of intransigence.

King had insisted in this address that "these are days which demand wise restraint and calm reasonableness," and he had undertaken a monumental labor of keeping alive the hope of achieving the equal citizenship long promised through persuasion and enactment, and without violence.[12] It was predictable that his death would trigger riots across the United States and that the struggle for racial justice would subsequently take a more violent turn, matching violence with violence rather than embodying for its part the legitimacy and justice it sought. When he insisted that "our lives must be placed on the line if our nation is to survive its own folly," he meant that Americans in 1967 would have to overcome the unreasonableness and intransigence of racial and global injustice by putting themselves in harm's way, without harming others:

> in the ghettos of the North over the last three years . . . As I have walked among the desperate, rejected, and angry young men I have told them that Molotov cocktails and rifles would not solve their problems. I have tried to offer them my deepest compassion while maintaining my conviction that social change comes most meaningfully through nonviolent action.[13]

There are obvious advantages to keeping alive the democratic hope of being a society of equal citizens who solve their problems by reasoning together and with their elected leaders in a spirit of mutual respect and receptivity to evidence. Yet, how will reason triumph if some acknowledge and others do not that the legacy of slavery and Jim Crow apartheid has not been fully overcome, that the fear of communism could not justify treating peoples of the global South as expendable pawns, that the tide of economic growth does not "lift all boats" without policies to ensure it benefits the poor of coastal cities and rural interior alike, or that human-induced climate disruption is a problem too serious to ignore? How will it triumph if we live apart from each other in such different circumstances that we perceive each other as being radically dissimilar, do not trust each other, and have no experience of cooperation? Faced with intransigence, the aim of nonviolent resistance is to make the necessary conversations unavoidable, to withhold one's cooperation in unjust social arrangements and foreign ventures, and to do so in such a way as to elicit wide recognition that one is in the right. In this context, putting one's life on the line has meant exposing it to violent injustice that would be visible to a world that would recognize it as such.

Is dissent sometimes compelled by patriotism, as King insisted? It would seem that it is, though we will not offer a definitive answer to this question until chapter 5. For now, let us consider some basic aspects of patriotism.

Patriotism is sometimes defined simply as love of one's country, but a more complete definition would identify two further characteristics: a concern for the good of one's country and experiencing membership in it as an aspect of one's identity.[14] Devotion to the good of one's country is often framed as loyalty and fulfillment of the obligations of citizenship. These features of patriotism are mediated by conceptions of what is and is not part of the country, and efforts to inspire patriotism have often been focused on national unity, especially when smaller civic units are joined into new and larger wholes. Societies have long devised symbols and rituals of unity at the time of their unification, as affirmations of inclusion, belonging, and equal justice. Images of the deities representing the family clans of ancient Athens were erected together at the city's courts, signifying a commitment to a common good and impartial justice, and lawgivers and moralists from Solon to Socrates reaffirmed this commitment in their portrayals of Athenian law itself as an impartial codification of divine wisdom. Gandhi and Nehru conjured images of a pluralistic India's common struggle for self-rule and were aided in this by Rabindranath Tagore's song "Jana Gana Mana," which became the country's national anthem. Its addressee is similarly an immortal personification of moral law—"You who bring in the unity of the people!"—and its words evoke the breadth and beauty of India's landscapes and regions, people, and traditions.[15] The United States has a more militant national anthem focused on war as a necessity of self-rule, of course, but also a popular tradition of patriotic song much closer in spirit to "Jana Gana Mana."

Best known in this regard is "America the Beautiful," with its references to the beauty and bounty of natural features—waves of grain, purple mountains, and fruited plains—stretching "from sea to shining sea."[16] Woody Guthrie's "This Land Is Your Land" refers similarly to the redwood forest, wheat fields, and sparkling sands stretching "From California to the New York island," but also the 1930s Dust Bowl and "my people; As they stood there hungry" at the relief office, when their farms were obliterated by windswept mountains of dirt.[17] The first of these songs is celebratory, the second cautionary, but both evoke the full extent of the country of which all Americans are a part, whatever their differences and regional loyalties; and both evoke images of the basis of opportunity in the natural features of a *land* worthy of love and protection. Both songs knit these images together with ideals of liberty, justice, and unity, and aim to inspire related emotional attachments: to morally worthy ideals, to one's compatriots whatever their differences, and to the full extent of land within the country's jurisdiction— the land that is both a home and the natural basis of opportunities to live well as members of a cooperative society.[18]

"The House I Live In" shares many of these features but is more explicit in its references to national symbols, democratic institutions, and an American identity that encompasses different races, religions, and national origins. Lewis Allan's lyrics, recorded in 1947 by Paul Robeson, open and close with these words:

> What is America to me?
> A name, a map, of a flag I see
> A certain word, democracy
> What is America to me?
>
> . . .
>
> The house I live in, my neighbors white and black
> The people who just came here or from generations back
> The town hall and the soap box, the torch of liberty
> A home for all God's children
> That's America to me.
>
> The house I live in, the goodness everywhere
> A land of wealth and beauty with enough for all to share
> A house that we call freedom, the home of liberty

But especially the people, that's America to me
But especially the people, that's the true America.[19]

Much could be said of the movement in this song from representations of the whole country to the aspects of the country itself to which Americans should feel a special attachment and devotion: our civic ideals and institutions, but most of all each other. Sung by a black man, it evokes a promise of inclusion and equal citizenship in a whole made up of diverse parts. It also commends such democratic institutions as the "town hall and the soap box" as objects worthy of patriotic attachment.

If the "true America" is especially the people whose well-being is at stake, these songs collectively evoke the moral, institutional, and natural bases of our ability to live well together, and they suggest that to love America is to love *all* of these things.[20] They defend an understanding of patriotism that conspicuously rejects nationalism, in the sense of an orientation or ideology that focuses identity and loyalty not on a country but on a nationality or identity defined by culture, language, religion, or race.[21] They also evoke a patriotism of liberty or constitutional patriotism that embraces the institutions of a constitutional system that give voice and protection to free and equal citizenship.[22] Finally, they suggest a form of patriotism that incorporates a land ethic that is not an entitlement to a land "of our fathers"—there being no one land from which Americans arrived—but a commitment to protect the land on which we depend and make a home.

Set against these ideals of unity and justice is the unfortunate reality that there are forms of patriotism and nationalism that subvert justice because they are shaped by race, religion, or regional sensibilities in ways that exclude many who are by all rights part of the very country patriots profess to love. There are forms of patriotism and nationalism that reject norms of international justice, and there are forms of nationalism that embrace populist movements that attack democratic institutions. The German nationalists of Austria set aside both patriotism and international justice when they favored absorption into Hitler's Germany at the expense of Austrian self-rule in the 1930s, while Emmanuel Macron committed himself to both patriotism and justice when he declared in April 2017 that if elected he would be the "president of patriots, to face the threat of nationalists."[23] Macron evidently meant that he would be a president for all of the diverse loyal people of France and would defend the institutions of democracy that protect minority rights, in opposition to nationalist (e.g., ethnic, cultural, and religious) criteria for who is truly French and in opposition to (nationalist) populist threats to liberal democratic institutions. Assaults on the strength and independence of the courts, press, universities, and other institutions are typically carried out by populist leaders in order to consolidate authoritarian power that allegedly gives true democratic voice to "the people"—an idealized national group conceived as the true and morally pure Hungarians, Turks, Poles, Russians, or Americans who are denied fair representation by "corrupt elites" who must be swept away.[24]

There are also forms and manipulations of patriotism that undermine legitimacy by inducing positive regard for governments and policies whose merits do not warrant the respect they enjoy. Exclusionary and manipulated patriotism tend to converge in times of war, when dissent is least welcome yet potentially most valuable in averting costly errors—the costs of war being immense, and irrationality in the face of danger being common. As Jane Addams observed following World War I, instincts of self-preservation make it natural "to dislike, to distrust and finally to destroy the individual who differs from the mass in time of danger."[25] This may explain how Americans could be attracted to proposals to ban the immigration of Muslims in an era of domestic mass killings overwhelmingly committed by white, non-Muslim men. President Obama might have been paraphrasing "The House I Live In" when he observed in response, "Muslim-Americans are our friends and our neighbors, our co-workers, our sports heroes."[26] The iconic and beloved Muslim American sports hero Muhammad Ali, embraced as a friend by Donald Trump, offered his own criticism of those who mischaracterize Islam for political gain.[27]

Cassius Clay was eighteen years old when he regaled the press with this patriotic rhyme after winning a gold medal in boxing at the 1960 Rome Olympics:

> To make America the greatest is my goal
> So I beat the Russian and I beat the Pole
> And for the USA won the medal of gold.
> The Greeks said, You're better than the Cassius of Old.[28]

Yet he had also begun to make sense of his disturbing experiences of racial injustice through the Nation of Islam (NOI) teachings of Elijah Muhammad, having encountered the Muslims in Atlanta in 1958 and in Chicago in 1959. Having narrowly escaped failing English in his senior year of high school when his teacher was alarmed by the ideas expressed in his paper about the NOI, he kept his developing religious beliefs and associations hidden for some years.[29] In 1964, the day after he defeated Sonny Liston to become the new heavyweight-boxing champion, he announced his membership in the Nation. When he then took the name Muhammad Ali, outrage at his NOI affiliation was conjoined with refusal to refer to him by his chosen name. A black ex-champion, Floyd Patterson, soon challenged Ali, declaring,

> This fight is a crusade to reclaim the title from the Black Muslims. As a Catholic I am fighting Clay as a patriotic duty. I am going to return the crown to America.[30]

The American male's exposure to patriotic messages occurs overwhelmingly in the context of spectator sports, a setting sure to convey that patriotism is fulfilled in "us" dominating and beating "them." But who is "us" and who is "them" in Patterson's rendering of the fight? How could defeating an American, Ali, "return the crown" to an America that was never exclusively Christian or white? Patterson's insistence that he was an American, implying that Ali was not, evidently rested on the idea that an American cannot be a Muslim.[31] Ali yelled in response during the fight: "Come on, America! Come on, white America. . . . What's my name? Is my name Clay? What's my name, fool?"[32]

When Ali was drafted for service in the US armed forces in 1966 and persisted in refusing to serve, he was sentenced to five years in prison and stripped of his heavyweight title for conduct "detrimental to the best interests of boxing."[33] Yet his principled stand proved to be a watershed event. "I will not disgrace my religion, my people or myself by becoming a tool to enslave those who are fighting for their own justice, freedom and equality," he told a reporter from *Sports Illustrated*. "If I thought the war was going to bring freedom and equality to 22 million of my people they wouldn't have to draft me, I'd join tomorrow."[34] When Martin Luther King announced his own opposition to the war at a 1967 press conference, he cited Ali's view that "we are all—Black and Brown and poor—victims of the same system of oppression."[35]

Did Ali ever fully embrace the idea of national "greatness" as something established through athletic triumphs? It seems unlikely that he did, but the language of greatness and the psychology of national pride, patriotism, and prevailing on a global stage are often interwoven. Americans bask in the reflected glory of their Olympic victors and chant "We're number one!" with much more than athletic victory in mind. Civic leaders include impressive stadiums and successful National Football League (NFL) teams on their checklists for being a "great" city, and political candidates invoke the language of winning and losing in their promises to "make America great again." While there are many forms of achievement that could warrant national pride and substantiate claims of "greatness"—an ill-defined attribute, at best—the shaping of American patriotism by boxing and football encourages a belligerent form of citizenship that excludes, suppresses dissent, and polarizes international relations at the expense of peace, cooperation, and the national interest.[36]

Recounting the NFL's embrace of war and patriotic ritual, its euphemistic celebration of "hits" that cripple and shorten the lives of players, and evidence that even in high school players may routinely sustain irreversible brain damage, Steve Almond writes that "football . . . reinforces conformity and desensitizes us to violence. It militarizes the way we think and feel."[37] He quotes an NFL player, Paul Younger, explaining that

> my inspirational speech was when they played the national anthem. . . . It always fired me up and I wanted to go and hit somebody. . . . When they sang *o'er the land of the free and the home of the brave*, I'm ready to go knock the hell out of somebody.[38]

Knocking the hell of out of people is evidently enjoyed both personally by players and vicariously by the game's most ardent fans. Michael Strahan, a famous NFL player turned television personality on *Good Morning America*, explains that "it's the most perfect feeling in the world to know you've hit a guy just right, that you've maximized the physical pain he can feel. . . . You feel the life just go out of him."[39] Inaugurating the era of "overt collaboration between the NFL and the military," President George H. W. Bush launched his 1991 aerial assault on Iraqi military and civilian infrastructure a few days before Super Bowl XXV was aired as a five-hour patriotic extravaganza. It featured Bush in a halftime address to the nation in which he described the war as his Super Bowl—inviting the fantasy that war is a "winnable contest" fair to all concerned.[40]

Honoring the "oath" in Hughes's poem by standing one's ground in defense of American ideals and their fuller realization would seem to be no less an act of patriotism than what a good soldier does in standing his ground in battle. Both defend the country in ways that often require courage, and in neither context—civic nor military—could we rightly speak of true courage unless it is virtuously motivated and reflects good judgment.

In the days after the September 11, 2001, attacks on the World Trade Center and Pentagon, ABC cancelled Bill Maher's 2002 contract for his show

Politically Incorrect in response to his controversial suggestion that the hijackers were "not cowardly" and the US military's practice of "lobbing cruise missiles from two thousand miles away" was cowardly.[41] The hijackers had overcome fear of death to do what they thought was right, and this might seem to define courage (as Maher supposed), but it does not *fully* define it. In this context, President George W. Bush's frequent references to our "brave" men and women in uniform were clearly predicated on the idea that the members of our armed forces, who invaded Iraq in 2003 on his orders, were not just facing danger in the belief that they were doing the right thing. Calling them brave presupposed that their belief was true—the belief that an invasion of Iraq was necessary to protect the American "homeland" against Saddam Hussein's alleged determination to attack it with weapons of mass destruction (weapons the UN inspectors could not find, because none existed).[42] If being right about the worthiness of one's cause did not matter in describing someone as courageous or brave, then the American public would have had no reason to deny that the hijackers were courageous or to implicitly predicate the courage of US forces on the belief that the invasion of Iraq was just and prudent.

The moral understanding of patriotic courage this implies is incompatible with an "America, right or wrong" understanding of courage or patriotism. It implies that true or virtuous courage is animated and guided by a well-informed devotion to what is genuinely good. By this measure, patriotic courage would necessarily be courage motivated by what is genuinely valuable in one's country and guided by sound judgment about how to protect it and act well in circumstances in which other things of value may also be at stake. One could scarcely fault soldiers whose primary motivation in war is loyalty to their fellow soldiers, but what is valuable and worth preserving in a country would surely revolve around what is celebrated in the tradition of popular song noted above: the people and the moral, institutional, and natural bases for them living well together.

Virtuous patriotism would be similarly responsive to what is valuable both in and beyond one's own country. Yet, the motivational texture of actual patriotism is undoubtedly more complex than this and often at odds with it. Being or identifying oneself as American is an aspect of one's identity that typically has motivational significance. There is a natural tendency to experience as one's own the fates of the larger social and political entities to which one belongs, being pained by misfortune, experiencing pride in accomplishment, and denying or feeling shame in the recognition of shameful exposure or wrongdoing. We feel shame when we allow ourselves to acknowledge America's failings *because* we are American and we are implicated in those failings, and shame can in this way serve to motivate dissent and reform. National pride may similarly play a useful—some say necessary—role in civic engagement and exertion.[43] To the extent that belonging to a country is an important part of our own identity and a source of pride, it may also be a potent deterrent to acknowledging wrongdoing, which is to say a source of denial or resistance to evidence that wrongdoing is occurring. A more detached stance toward one's country might be more conducive to the clear-eyed understanding and balanced perspective that true virtues require, but detachment and patriotism seem to be mutually incompatible. On the other hand, a genuine concern for the good of a country might motivate diligence in seeking to know its limitations. Whether patriotism inherently involves self-deception is a matter we will address in due course.[44]

It is especially in times of war and of influxes of new immigrants whose loyalty is questioned that patriotism is colored not by courage but by fear, suppression of dissent, and solidarity that is often racialized; and it is at such times in American history that schools have felt most compelled to cultivate patriotism. This compulsion was most recently evident in the United States in the years immediately following the terrorist attacks of September 11, and it has been evident in response to anxieties about Muslim immigrants in both Europe and North America. Even without the often misleading and counterproductive invocation of a "clash of civilizations"—an imagined geopolitical struggle between the Christian and Muslim worlds—the arrival of immigrants poses questions about how they do or do not come to share the values most essential to becoming full participants in a cooperative society whose constitutional principles may be antecedently unfamiliar or uncongenial. What role should schools play?

Ideals of patriotism have been invoked not only in times of war and large-scale immigration, but also to affirm ideals and civic virtues of racial and economic justice, as they are in Langston Hughes's poem "Let America Be America Again." In the period since the 2008 financial collapse, patriotism has been invoked in criticizing American citizens who evade taxes by moving their wealth offshore while continuing to enjoy the rights and privileges of US citizenship and residence. This compares interestingly with a more pervasive and nonpartisan conversation in the United Kingdom about the bad behavior of bankers and fund managers that contributed to the collapse. Concern about such behavior continues to be invoked in support of strengthening character education, in a national context in which patriotism has had a bad name and teachers are loathe to embrace it.[45] Putting uneasiness about a history of misguided patriotism and empire aside, why should selfish indifference to the fate of one's fellow citizens and country not qualify as unpatriotic and as a fit object for educational redress? If such indifference were remedied through character education focused on the virtues of justice and friendly respect for others, would that be a vindication of patriotism? Or would it show that patriotism is motivationally superfluous?

We will see in the pages ahead that the imagined closing of the American frontier had consequences that invited a reconceptualization of civic education and American patriotism, shaped by the idea of cooperation to solve the social problems associated with burgeoning urban populations of poor immigrants. The idea of such cooperation is unavoidably tied to the idea of fair terms of social cooperation and a civic—perhaps patriotic—obligation to accept those terms; terms that might limit the extremities of inequality and disparities of opportunity. The ramifications of this mythical frontier closing and America "turning back on itself" are in important respects parallel to those addressed by Plato and Aristotle in the aftermath of the Peloponnesian War that cost Athens its empire, and are parallel to the present global realities of the expansion of humanity having turned back on itself, so that it is now faced with problems it cannot export and can only solve through global cooperation. And, in this context of global interdependence we are compelled, as educators in the Progressive Era were, to reconceptualize civic and patriotic virtue and the role of schools in cultivating it.

Why is it useful to address patriotism in schools now and in connection with civic education? One answer is that patriotism and civic education have had a continuous and inevitable presence in American schools, the demoralizing effects of our present high-stakes testing regimes notwithstanding. Educators will encounter patriotism and should understand it when they do. This is true not only with respect to the civic education schools plan for but when conflicting expressions of patriotism thrust themselves upon schools, as they did in the autumn of 2016 when student athletes across the United States followed Colin Kaepernick's example and knelt in protest during the playing of the national anthem.[46] A second answer is that there are reasons to regard education for global citizenship as a vital necessity to which educational institutions at all levels should contribute, and the relationship between global citizenship and patriotism is fraught with controversy. Understanding how they are compatible will be important to educational practice for the foreseeable future. A third answer, for those who can think of priorities that are more urgent for the near term, is that it is better to prepare for challenges before we face them. The best time for educators to think through the relationships between patriotism and civic education is when schools are not already swept up in the emotional contagion of perceived security threats or the heat of war.

Are the hazards of patriotism so great as to overshadow its potential benefits? Is patriotism essential to national unity, to sustaining vigorous commitment to just institutions, or to motivating national service? Is there a genuinely virtuous form of patriotism that societies and their schools should strive to cultivate? These questions are so empirically and normatively complex that it is not clear they can be fully answered. To make progress in answering the question that fundamentally concerns us, we will need to focus on the subquestions that are foundational to the rationales on which patriotic education has been predicated. As we noted in our preface, the question we aim to answer is whether schools should attempt to cultivate patriotism, and if so why, how, and with what conception of patriotism in mind.

We begin in chapters 1 through 3 by detailing the aims and rationales that have guided the inculcation of patriotism in American schools, the methods by which schools have sought to cultivate patriotism, and the conceptions of patriotism evident in those aims, rationales, and methods. These chapters are organized around a sequence of methods of instruction or forms of learning, rather than a sequence of historical periods or chronological narrative. Chapter 1 is concerned with the teaching and facilitation of patriotism through curricular content that is to varying degrees explained, justified, and examined. We find here both skills, such as English language competence, and knowledge, such as knowledge of US history, but also tensions concerning indoctrination and the purposes with which history is taught. The competing claims of traditional history instruction and Progressive Era social studies figure importantly in this chapter. Chapter 2 concerns the presentation of heroes and the involvement of students in rituals, both of which move beyond skills and cognition, preparing students to act in the national interest. We show how the presentation of fictional or fictionalized heroes to admire and emulate has been used to induce sentiments of national solidarity and reverence, and how civic rituals, such as the pledge to the flag, have habituated students to act in unison. The McGuffey's Readers' lessons in moral and patriotic virtue, celebration of America's Founding Fathers, and legal challenges to the Pledge of Allegiance are considered in some detail. Chapter 3, on the militarization of schools and mobilization of students, considers forms of experiential learning in which students engage not simply in activities of learning, or symbolic acts of national unity and commitment, but engage in the very kinds of acts that civic virtues characteristically engender: acts of public service. The role of Junior Reserve Officers' Training Corp (ROTC) units in high schools, Junior Red Cross, direct involvement of students in funding the country's "arsenal of democracy" through war stamps and bonds during World War II, and Future Farmers of America receive special attention. Education is a sphere of human practice in which motivation is fundamental both in the facilitation of learning and as an outcome of learning, so we have designed these historical chapters to illuminate the ways in which schools have sought to engender patriotic motivation.

The conceptions of patriotism, rationales, and methods detailed in chapters 1 through 3 are examined in chapter 4 in light of recent scholarship on patriotic education and a philosophical understanding of justice, education, and human flourishing. We open with the argument that patriotism provides the essential motivational basis for civic responsibility, sketch a basic ethic of respect for persons as rationally self-determining individuals, explain some implications of this ethic for political legitimacy and education, and offer a brief account of just institutions and the education that justice requires. On that basis, we go on to outline a philosophical theory of education that will serve as the basis for an account of responsible civic education in chapter 5. The relevance of motivation research to motivation-focused arguments for patriotic education is clear, but ignored, so we explain the role of psychological needs in motivation and some implications of research in motivational psychology for responsible citizenship and traditional and Progressive approaches to patriotic education. We argue that contemporary research on motivation undermines key assumptions on which rationales and methods for inculcating patriotism have often rested, while providing the basis for a more complex view of the motivation that can sustain civic responsibility.

Chapter 5 considers whether there is a virtuous form of patriotism and if so what role it might play in the scheme of civic virtue and civic education. Building on the foundations laid in chapter 4, we offer an account of the nature and cultivation of civic virtue. We conceive of civic virtue as having three components— civic intelligence, civic friendship, and civic competence—corresponding to the civic fulfillment of three basic forms of human potential, and we identify virtuous patriotism as a central aspect of the motivational architecture of civic virtue with regard to one's country. We clarify the nature and ethical structure of a country—matters widely overlooked in discussions of patriotic education—and we place devotion to the good of a country within the wider context of this ethical structure and the need for civic virtue at all levels of civic life, from the local to the global. The motivational core of civic virtue at any of these levels is a civic-minded responsiveness to the public interest or value of all that the community in question entails. Virtuous patriotism is thus a state-level counterpart of the civic-mindedness at the heart of civic responsibility in local, regional, or global civic affairs, and no more or less inherently desirable than civic-mindedness in any of these other spheres. We outline the basic elements of education for civic intelligence, civic friendship, civic competence, and virtuous civic motivation, emphasizing features of a just school community; the disciplinary foundations of public reason, understanding, and judgment; discussion; problem-based cooperative and experiential learning; and a global perspective.

We identify a country as a geographic region within the jurisdiction of a common constitutional structure and the society of persons committed to living in that region within the terms of that constitutional structure. We also argue that virtuous devotion to the good of one's country is targeted and proportionate, protecting what is good and opposing what is bad. Virtuous patriotism would normally be expressed both in defense of what is valuable in a country, or conducive to its members living well together across generations, and in loyal dissent in the interest of that value at home and abroad. Virtuous patriotism would be compatible with fair terms of global cooperation and with respecting others around the world as moral equals. Countries have a moral obligation to negotiate such terms of cooperation in the circumstances of unavoidable globalization and interdependence we now face—circumstances of a civilization that is in many ways global and critically dependent on the health of an atmospheric and oceanic system that defies national borders. We conclude in chapter 6 with a defense of global civic education as a focus of higher education. In doing this, we aim to overcome widely perceived tensions between patriotism and international cooperation, as well as doubts about the very idea of global citizenship and the possibility of global civic friendship.

ONE

Americanizing Curricula

In October 1917, six months following the United States' entry into World War I, the *New York Times* reported on the ways city schoolteachers and the mayor's "defense committee" had "systemized training" in "our language and customs."[1] Characterizing America's "immigration problem" as "a many-sided thing," the paper claimed that the war created "a vigorous new interest" in responding to an influx of immigrants into New York City. "The men and women who are working for Americanization are emphatic in the statement that it is 'not war work,'" the paper reported. "The war has a good deal to do with it, and it has a good deal to do with the war. But, they explained, the city is awakening to a need that has long existed, that will go on existing, and that must go on being met." That need, according to local officials, was the fashioning of "good citizens" out of the "foreign-born" through education in American history, government, and especially the English language. "People can't fulfill the duties of citizenship unless they speak the language of the country," the *Times* reported. "It is a most important thing for the nation. Mere ignorance of the language tends to create segregation, and in this state of isolation the foreigners live."[2]

Between 1890 and 1930, over 22 million immigrants arrived into the United States. Settling largely in urban areas, the newcomers came to comprise between one-half and three-fourths of residents in cities such as New York, Chicago, Milwaukee, and Boston.[3] Among them were 3 million children who filled city schools to capacity. Indeed, in the fifteen years between 1899 and 1914, New York City public school enrollments alone increased by 60 percent, while the city turned away between sixty and seventy thousand students per year due to overcrowding.[4]

During this period, immigrants increasingly arrived to the United States from southern and eastern Europe—namely, Poland, Italy, and the

Balkans—regions with which most Americans lacked familiarity. Consequently, many came to believe that the demographic transformation these immigrants wrought undermined the nation's social norms and values. Leading schoolmen such as Stanford University School of Education dean Elwood P. Cubberley highlighted ethnic differences by contrasting the newcomers with previous immigrants from northwestern Europe, describing these "new" immigrants as "illiterate, docile, often lacking in initiative, and almost wholly without Anglo-Saxon conceptions of righteousness, liberty, law, order, public decency, and government."[5]

As historians such as Paula Fass have observed, broad political and economic transformations such as the United States' transition from an agrarian to an industrialized nation as well as transportation advances that permitted increased immigration from greater distances both preceded and catalyzed this period of social change in America. Of the era, Fass concludes, the "industrial crisis of the late nineteenth century had also become a cultural crisis," one that revolved around "the meaning of American identity and state loyalty."[6] With educators such as Cubberley disparaging immigrants' ethnicity and journalists such as Jacob Riis documenting "how the other half lives," it is hardly surprising that Americanization—by proposing to teach students both the knowledge and behaviors necessary for good citizenship—provided a popular response to the "immigration problem."[7]

Americanization, however, was not encompassed by a single, coherent educational program. A variety of occasionally conflicting ideas and approaches comprised the effort to assimilate immigrants into the American way of life. Some educators believed that the values and customs immigrant students contributed to American society—their so-called cultural gifts—should be maintained and integrated, while others argued that foreign traits had to be eradicated before students could become proper Americans.[8] Nevertheless, as historian Patricia Graham notes, while some teachers and administrators considered "the interests and welfare" of their students, "the force behind their effort was the national perception that these youngsters must grow up as patriotic Americans."[9] The work of assimilation was thus inherently tied up with the schools' efforts to teach students to become patriots. As one delegate to a National Education Association (NEA) meeting declared at the end of the Civil War:

> Our schools must teach our children to love their country, by acquainting them with its geography and history, the blessings derived from its form of government, the great men it has produced and the great deeds it has done. . . . Above all, our schools must teach our children that that patriotism

is not genuine which is bounded by corporate limits or state lines, but that only is genuine which holds as its own and would fight to protect every foot of land belonging to the United States of America. Let teachers remember that a monarchy may exist for ages among a hostile people, but that a republic must die if the love of its citizens for it once grows cold.[10]

Conceiving of love of country as arising from an acquaintance with the country's merits, this delegate's patriotism was nationalistic in the sense that it embraced the entire jurisdiction of the United States—the word *nation* being sometimes used interchangeably with the word *country*. Patriotism and nationalism may also be distinguished, however, as George Orwell observed in an essay published at the end of World War II. Orwell identified patriotism as "a devotion to a particular place and a particular way of life, which one believes to be the best in the world but has no wish to force on other people." He identified nationalism, in terms inspired by the Nazi's embrace of Nietzsche, as "inseparable from the desire for power" and placing one's nation "beyond good or evil."[11] "The abiding purpose of every nationalist," Orwell wrote, "is to secure more power and more prestige, *not* for himself but for the nation or other unit in which he has chosen to sink his own individuality."[12]

Perhaps no American at the turn of the twentieth century better symbolized Orwell's description of a nationalist than Theodore Roosevelt. Seeking to establish the United States as a world power, Roosevelt worked energetically as assistant secretary of the navy to expand the US naval fleet, which he believed essential to projecting an image of American might around the world (he would later, as commander in chief, order this "great white fleet" to literally circumnavigate the globe). The president was also an outspoken advocate of imperial expansion, a policy in which he personally participated in 1898 when he led the Rough Riders in the Battle of San Juan Hill during the Spanish-American War.[13] In addition, Roosevelt expressed a tenacious loyalty to the United States throughout his life, especially when he issued such unwavering declarations as, "We will fight for America whenever necessary. America, first, last, and all the time. . . . America against the world; America, right or wrong; always America."[14] Yet as Orwell recognized, Roosevelt's nationalism conflicted with forms of patriotism demonstrated by many of his leading contemporaries, including William James (Roosevelt's former Harvard professor), John Dewey, Jane Addams, and W. E. B. DuBois.[15]

Although these "cosmopolitan patriots," as historian Jonathan Hansen calls them, were all devoted to their country, they did not share Roosevelt's uncritical attitude toward the United States. Indeed, on more than one occasion Roosevelt and James challenged each other directly on the issue of national loyalty. In late 1895, James wrote a letter to his congressman, which he also submitted to the *Harvard Crimson*, strongly criticizing US president Grover Cleveland's hawkish response to a border dispute between Venezuela and British Guiana. "We have written ourselves squarely down as a people dangerous to the peace of the world," James claimed. Roosevelt responded with his own letter to the *Crimson*, challenging James's betrayal of "the honor and dignity of the United States."[16] "James," Hansen concludes in relation to the exchange, "insisted that the nation's strength derived from the deliberations of an active citizenry; Roosevelt equated national power with military might."[17]

With such widely differing conceptions of patriotism informing Americanization, it is hardly surprising that schools adopted a wide range of policies and prescriptions designed to transform students into patriotic citizens. Of the many elements of the school curriculum that contributed to this educational project, however, Americanization advocates identified and then promoted three as essential: instruction in the English language, instruction in civics and citizenship, and instruction in social studies, particularly US history.

Language, Civics, and Social Studies

Throughout this era, many Americans—natural born and immigrants alike—came to view fluency in English as a marker of citizenship. Consequently, they claimed that schools should teach students solely in English, a dramatic departure from earlier in the nation's history when school subjects were often taught in the dominant language of the local community.[18] Given the large influx of German immigrants into the Midwest, for example, in 1839 the Ohio General Assembly gave legal authority to the already common practice of using German as a language of instruction in public schools. Louisiana followed suit with French in 1843, and seven years later New Mexico legislated Spanish-English bilingual education. These laws reflected America's multilingual society, with the early national government, for instance, publishing documents such as the Articles of Confederation in three languages: English, German, and French.[19]

By 1920, however, xenophobic reactions to US involvement in World War I combined with prewar Americanization efforts to lead many states to either reverse previous statutes regarding foreign language instruction or write English language requirements into law for the first time.[20] Such legislation may have been unnecessary. According to historian Jonathan Zimmerman, immigrant parents desired and even demanded that their children learn English, sometimes openly opposing immigrant community leaders who declared that students should study native tongues in order to maintain ethnic identities.[21] In fact, many immigrant parents studied English at the same time as their children, with employers frequently supporting their efforts by allotting employees time to attend language classes during the workday. As a result of such widespread support as well as imposition, knowledge of the English language became a central part of what it meant to be an American.

Since then, and especially when Americans have perceived their "way of life" as under threat, proficiency in English has increasingly been interpreted as a sign of loyalty to the United States. Not only was German rejected as a "cultural gift" during World War I, for instance, President Woodrow Wilson characterized it as a "sinister tongue" that indicated treasonous intentions on the part of its speakers. Some states, such as Ohio, which had legally protected the use of German as a language of instruction in the state's public schools, responded to America's declaration of war by prohibiting its use. The primary result of these policies was a severe decline in the number of students studying German as a foreign language, from approximately 324,000 in 1915 to 14,000 by 1922. A related outcome was the overall decline in the number of students studying any foreign language, from 73 percent of secondary school students in 1915 to 22 percent by 1948.[22] Throughout the rest of the twentieth century and up until the present, foreign language study has remained a minimal part of the public school academic program.

Coinciding with the push for English language instruction, many educators during this period supported the inclusion of civics or citizenship as a distinct subject in schools. When established in the 1830s and 1840s, the public schools—initially known as "common" schools because of the common educational experience that students were meant to share—taught a curriculum consisting primarily of literacy and numeracy. It was through these subjects that teachers sought to inculcate the traits necessary for students to become competent citizens.[23] As historian Carl Kaestle has observed, antebellum educational reformers agreed that schooling should emphasize "unity, obedience, restraint, self-sacrifice, and the careful exercise of intelligence," all of which were considered characteristics of virtuous and moral citizens as well as necessary for the republic's survival.[24]

Using curricular materials rich in moral lessons and exemplars, schoolteachers instilled these virtues through instruction in reading and writing. The *New England Primer* provided one such text during the colonial period, while during the first half of the nineteenth century students frequently recited from Noah Webster's *Spelling Book*. Of these various resources, however,

William Holmes McGuffey's texts were probably the most well-known. Selling over 122 million copies between 1836 and 1922, McGuffey's Readers have been described as containing "moral lessons designed to teach appropriate behavior in a developing industrial society with increasing concentrations of wealth and expanding social divisions between the rich and the poor."[25] Sales of McGuffey's Readers peaked between 1870 and 1890, with 60 million copies sold during these decades. Simultaneously, however, courses in the history of the United States and civil government began to be taught widely at the secondary level. A steady decline in the readers' sales ensued, as many educators determined that a more intrusive and explicit form of civics education was necessary to Americanize students to become patriotic citizens.

In addition to accelerating rates of urbanization, industrialization, and immigration, political corruption and scandal characterized America in the decades following the Civil War. Figures such as Boss Tweed of New York City's Tammany Hall became symbols of profiteering, fraud, and misconduct at all levels of government. Educators responded by seeking to establish courses intended to reaffirm traditional notions of civic virtue while emphasizing aspects of citizenship that clearly drew upon the attributes of many Progressive Era reforms. Among many others, these included an increasing trust in trained experts to develop appropriate public policies as well as the need for the state (especially its educational institutions) to play a more assertive role in the lives of Americans, particularly the foreign born.

Of the efforts to construct a distinct course in citizenship education during the Progressive Era, "community civics" provided the greatest departure from previous approaches to citizen formation. Whereas courses in US history and civil government had begun to appear at the secondary school level during the latter half of the nineteenth century, relatively few students attended school past the age of fifteen, leaving a large majority of public school students receiving little or no explicit instruction in civics. Proponents of community civics, therefore, designed their curricular program to be taught beginning at age six and continuing through age eighteen.[26]

Equally innovative was the way that community civics redefined the "good citizen" in American society. Although community civics courses had been taught in a variety of forms for several years, their curriculum became formalized in 1915 through the work of the NEA's Commission on the Reorganization of Secondary Education. Appointing a special committee on community civics, the commission issued a report that defined the good citizen as "a person who habitually conducts himself with proper regard for the welfare of the communities of which he is a member, and who is active and intelligent with his fellow members to that end." Emphasizing citizens' dependence on "social agencies" as well as their need to cooperate with others toward "desirable social ends," committee members contributed to refashioning the role of the citizen from that of an individual who exercised political rights and fulfilled political responsibilities to a community member who acted in concert with others to meet community needs. As conceived in community civics curricula, the patriotic American acted in the "interest of others" or "upon a common interest."[27]

In redefining the good citizen, committee members drew on ideas circulating among the era's many social reformers. Perhaps most importantly for schools, this redefinition expanded the citizenry to include children, who could be taught at a young age to act in ways that would contribute to achieving desirable social ends. As historian Julie Reuben describes, "By de-emphasizing voting and extending citizenship to children, the new civics courses claimed to define citizenship in terms 'broader' than politics. . . . Educators who designed community civics thought that older political ideals that emphasized minimal government and maximum individual liberty and initiative were not well suited to industrial, urban society."[28]

To accomplish their goals, community civics proponents borrowed from the work of John Dewey and other Progressive educators in identifying personal experience as the most authentic context for student learning. Between the ages of six and twelve, for instance, children were to begin their studies by exploring how people in their neighborhood, "the grocer, the iceman, the policeman, the postman, and many others," were "interdependent" and contributed to the community's welfare. Proponents also acknowledged the value of previous approaches to instilling civic virtue when they suggested that young children "form ideals of loyalty and of personal honor and integrity" through studying "appropriate literature" and "noble characters of history." Committee members maintained this approach to civics instruction for students between the ages of twelve and fifteen by proposing the study of "elementary history." Moreover, they advocated cultivating among students an "instinct" of "social feeling, social thought, and social action," permitting students to learn to fulfill their civic responsibilities in age-appropriate ways. For instance, the committee suggested that students could act in the common interest by "avoiding waste from water taps" (thus conserving their community's water supply) and by shoveling their sidewalks following a snowstorm.[29]

Through examples such as these, committee members discouraged students from challenging authority figures, a behavior they generally deemed contrary to good citizenship. "It is hardly appropriate for a child to reprove the milkman for carelessness in handling milk," the committee claimed, "but he may exert influence in securing proper care of milk and milk bottles in the home." Similarly, in the example of the snow-covered sidewalks, committee members encouraged students to investigate why so many sidewalks were left unshoveled. After learning that a city ordinance required residents to keep their sidewalks clear, students proposed speaking directly to the law's offenders. The committee, however, decided "that to do so would be slightly officious and perhaps offensive to older citizens."[30] As a course of study, then, community civics placed clear limits on the actions that students could take as responsible citizens in contributing to their communities' general welfare.

For students who continued their schooling following age fifteen, committee members proposed including community civics within "social studies," a collection of subjects that encompassed civics, history, and economics. This "entire group" of courses, wrote the committee, "should have for its immediate aim the training of the good citizen." The committee's report warned, however, that many previous courses in civil government failed to educate for citizenship because they focused students' attention "upon the machinery of government" rather than "the elements of community welfare for which government exists." "That is," they wrote, "they familiarize the pupil with the manipulation of the social machinery without showing him the importance of the social ends for which this machinery should be used. Consequently, the pupil, upon leaving school, uses his knowledge for ends which are most evident to him, namely, his own selfish interests."[31] Committee members accordingly proposed that instruction in social studies be designed to "cultivate a motive" consistent with good citizenship among students. "This motive," the report concluded, "is to be found in the *common interest*, which includes *his* [the student's] interest, at least until such time as an ideal altruism may lead to the placing of the interest of others and the community above the interest of self."[32]

By affirming the place of social studies in the public school academic program, the members of the NEA special committee on community civics inserted themselves into a curricular dispute that had been ongoing for several years. The debate, between the advocates of traditional history and civil government courses and Progressive Era social studies, had begun as early as 1896 when the American Historical Association appointed (at the NEA's request) the "Committee of Seven" to provide guidance in developing history curricula for public schools. The committee's final report stressed the importance of historical study in "fitting" students for "good and useful citizenship" and recommended a sequential course of study in "four blocks," including (1) ancient history, (2) medieval and modern European history, (3) English history, and (4) American history and civil government.

In the ensuing years, public schools throughout the United States adopted the four blocks sequence, which became the standard history curriculum in most US public secondary schools through the 1930s.[33] Citing a variety of reasons for traditional history's resilience, Ronald Evans has noted, "History instruction, like civil government, was aimed at developing the good, patriotic, and obedient citizen." "Likewise," he observes, "history is frequently a conservative discipline, focused, by definition, on the past, and often imbued with explicitly patriotic purposes."[34] These purposes fit well within an era of dramatic social, political, and economic change, especially during the First World War. On the other hand, Progressive educators, including the advocates of community civics, argued that a more dynamic curriculum—one that linked academic study to students' personal experiences and took community welfare as its central concern—provided a more appropriate and effective course of study. Nevertheless, both traditionalists and Progressives identified fostering patriotism among students as a central goal of their work.

The Story of Harold Rugg

The timing of the release of the 1917 subcommittee report on community civics could not have been worse for the NEA. Just months later, the United States declared war on Germany. With jingoism on the rise during the First World War and many Americans equating "good citizenship" with nationalism as Orwell defined it, several years passed before elementary and secondary schools began implementing a social studies curriculum on a broad scale. When they finally did, many schools adopted the one conceived primarily by Progressive educator Harold Rugg.

As with many of his colleagues at Columbia University's Teachers College, Harold Rugg believed that the social, political, and economic arrangements developing in the United States to serve an expanding system of laissez-faire industrial capitalism threatened American democracy—a conviction for which he and others later believed they found irrefutable evidence in the onset of the Great Depression.[35] Concluding that a "child-centered" school concerned with "social needs" was the only appropriate cure for a society experiencing increasing social unrest, war, and class stratification, Rugg committed himself to theorizing a problem-based curriculum and implementing a "reconstructed" social studies program.[36] "Not the learning of *texts*," Rugg urged, "but the solving of *problems* is what we need. Our materials must be organized around *issues*, problems—unanswered questions which the pupil recognizes as important and which he really strives to unravel."[37]

Developing elementary and secondary social studies curricula designed to introduce students to the "insistent problems of the present," Rugg and his research team wrote twenty-five thousand pages of printed material—a body of work that was reportedly read by several million students between the ages of eight and eighteen.[38] Contracting with Ginn and Company in 1926, Rugg published his series, previously known as Social Science Pamphlets, under the title Man and His Changing Society.[39] The series was a huge commercial success, making Rugg one of the best-selling textbook authors since William Holmes McGuffey.

Peaking in 1940, Rugg's textbook sales plummeted 90 percent over the next four years.[40] One reason for this decline involved the negative press the texts received in the context of World War II. Although as early as 1935 a Washington, DC, citizens' group labeled Rugg's secondary school text, *An Introduction to American Civilization*, "communistic" and insisted it be banned from district schools, the city's school board rejected the demand after a "special textbook investigating committee" found there was "no mention of communism in this textbook, not even a suggestion of it."[41] Nevertheless, reactionary groups throughout the 1930s continued to label Rugg's texts as "un-American." In 1939, the intensity of the attacks increased when the American Federation of Advertising (AFA) took offense to a passage in one of Rugg's books in which he claimed that "advertising costs were passed on to consumers."[42] Objecting to the author's criticism of corporate marketing practices, the AFA notified its membership of what it considered numerous inaccuracies and misrepresentations in the texts. Through a newsletter bluntly entitled "Facts You Should Know about Anti-Advertising Propaganda in School Textbooks," Alfred T. Falk, director of the AFA's Bureau of Research and Education, charged Rugg with insinuating that the cost of advertising unnecessarily drove up the cost of consumer products and that advertising was a dishonest line of work.[43]

Criticism of Rugg's work quickly escalated, receiving national attention when Bertie C. Forbes (owner and publisher of *Forbes* magazine) used his position on the Englewood, New Jersey, Board of Education to urge the books' removal from schools in his district. Forbes, who also wrote a column for Hearst newspapers, had previously published scathing commentaries on Rugg in his popular business magazine. Labeling the texts "viciously un-American," Forbes declared that their author was "in love with the way things are done in Russia" and that he distorted "facts to convince the oncoming generation that America's private enterprise system is wholly inferior and nefarious."[44] Intending to use his role as a school board member to have Rugg's books banned from his school district, Forbes wrote:

> I mean to battle against such poisoning of the youth of America. I plan to insist that this anti-American educator's text books be cast out. Moreover, I find this same fellow's outpourings included in a list recommended for inclusion in a school library. I am protesting. I would not want my own children contaminated by conversion to Communism. Therefore, I consider it my duty to protect the children of others against such insidious contamination.
>
> In my humble opinion, it is time for members of boards of education all over the continent to inquire more closely into what is being fed our offspring and to consider seriously what steps should be taken against teachers who have no use for Americanism, who want to see America ape Russia or other lands under dictatorships.[45]

With totalitarian dictatorships firmly established in Europe and Asia and Hitler's Wehrmacht igniting the Second World War in Europe by storming across the border into Poland, Forbes's attack capitalized on Americans' increasing anxiety over national security. Indeed, given this wartime context, it is hardly surprising that the most vocal and aggressive criticism of Rugg's work came from members of the American Legion. In "Treason in the Textbooks," a libelous article published in the *American Legion Magazine*, Legion member O. K. Armstrong named Harold Rugg one of the leaders of a conspiracy designed to undermine American society; "the most insidious attack of un-Americanism yet perfected by the Trojan horsemen," proclaimed Armstrong.[46] Illustrated with caricatures of a sinister-looking educator holding a "Subversive Textbook" while blinding his students with dark glasses, the article was reportedly read in over a million homes.[47] According to Armstrong, who asserted that Rugg and his colleagues were "trying to sell our youth the idea that the American way of life has failed," the textbooks were "a case for the personal attention of every parent who would like to preserve American ideals and institutions."[48]

School districts' responses to the attack on Rugg's texts were mixed, with some banning the books and others defending their continued use. That conservative opponents succeeded in having Rugg's texts banned in some districts during a period of national crisis should be expected; the United States has a rich history of politicized debate over public school textbooks.[49] It is also hardly surprising that Rugg's book sales declined following the controversy. Rugg authored most of his texts during the 1920s. With many of the books taking contemporary issues as their central concern, he had difficulty consistently supplying his publisher with timely revisions.[50] For many school officials during the war years, then, simply maintaining the outdated Rugg texts as reference books and replacing them with readily available alternatives was far less troublesome than confronting special interest groups demanding that they be eliminated from school classrooms and libraries. What is surprising, however, is the extent to which Rugg's opponents failed to mount a broader textbook censorship movement during World War II. Although reactionaries compiled lists of hundreds of books they deemed inappropriate for use in public school classrooms, the only leading texts banned between 1939 and 1945 were Rugg's.[51] Indeed, as sales for Rugg's books declined, those for a series of social studies texts authored by Paul R. Hanna and Isaac James Quillen, both self-avowed liberal school reformers, grew rapidly (Quillen would eventually serve as president of the National Council for the Social Studies). If members of the American Legion and other conservative organizations expected to eliminate even a handful of the thirty-eight books and magazines O. K. Armstrong identified as subversive, their efforts amounted to an almost complete failure.

The Pedagogy of Patriotism

In addition to illuminating the dispute between the advocates of traditional history and social studies curricula, the Rugg textbook controversy revealed a persistent tension in the United States over what body of knowledge—and how much of it—is necessary for students to acquire in order to become patriotic citizens. In the midst of the battle over Rugg's books in 1943, for instance, the *New York Times* published the results of a survey of seven thousand college freshmen suggesting that many had failed to master knowledge of their nation's history. The results received widespread attention, in part because they seemed to provide substantial evidence for a controversial claim made by respected historian Allan Nevins in which he argued that American youth were "all too ignorant" of their nation's history.[52] Advocates of traditional history immediately interpreted the survey results as an indicator of the failure of social studies to teach the historical knowledge necessary for students to become patriotic Americans. "Responsibility for the appalling neglect of American history in the high schools must go to the social studies extremists," wrote one US Office of Education official the day following the survey results' publication. "They have acted toward United States history instruction like the proverbial bull in the china shop."[53]

In the years that followed, the publication of survey and standardized test results claiming to demonstrate student "ignorance" of US history became routine, as did the handwringing accompanying them. Sam Wineburg has described the "stale headlines" and pejorative remarks many in the media have used to report on, what they claimed to be, students' ever-declining ability to accurately identify famous Americans. These include an article entitled "Kids Get Abysmal Grade in History: High School Seniors Don't Know Basics," a description of the nation's youth as "historical nitwits," and a characterization of students as "dumb as rocks."[54] Wineburg's work, on the other hand, aims to gain a greater understanding of what students indeed do know about US history rather than attempting to demonstrate their "ignorance."[55] In one particular study, Wineburg and colleague Chauncey Monte-Sano asked a national sample of two thousand eleventh and twelfth graders to respond to the following prompt: "Starting from Columbus to the present day, jot down the names of the most famous Americans in history. The only ground rule is that *they cannot be presidents*."[56] Given sixty years of rhetoric regarding student ignorance, it is perhaps not surprising that even the teachers and administrators Wineburg and Monte-Sano interviewed for their study expected student lists to be dominated by the names of pop stars, athletes, and celebrities. Instead, students overwhelmingly noted historical figures, with Martin Luther King Jr., Rosa Parks, Harriet Tubman, Susan B. Anthony, and Benjamin Franklin comprising the top five individuals named. Only two celebrities, Marilyn Monroe and Oprah Winfrey, made it into the top ten.[57]

Wineburg and Monte-Sano's "ground rule" makes it difficult to know how many US presidents students would have listed had they been permitted. Nevertheless, students' choice of three African Americans among the top five individuals identified reveals yet another element of America's century-long history debates.[58] During the second half of the twentieth century, as the controversial claim that social studies curricula resulted in students' declining historical knowledge slowly withered, it was replaced by the claim that a growing number of "multiculturalists" who sought to use history classes to promote racial, ethnic, and gender identity were undermining, if not usurping, traditional history. As during the first half of the century, critics decried changes to the traditional history curriculum, again claiming that such changes were eroding schools' capacity to educate for patriotism.

Beginning in the second half of the nineteenth century, as historian David Tyack has observed, US history courses and the textbooks from which they drew their curriculum provided a "pedagogy of patriotism" through which students learned to celebrate America. "The narrative in this 'real' history," writes Tyack, "started with the 'discovery' of the New World and colonization, told the triumphant story of Independence and the Revolution, and celebrated the creation of the Constitution. The history textbooks then organized their story around the administrations of President after President."[59] Between 1960 and 1980, however, blacks, Latinos, and women (among other groups) insisted that "their" histories, previously excluded from (if not degraded in) the pageant that comprised most US history texts, be included. Consequently, a market for "integrated" texts emerged in major US cities, leading publishers to produce books that incorporated racial and ethnic minorities as well as women into the prevailing celebratory narrative.[60]

Simultaneously, professional historians increasingly began to pursue investigations previously relegated to the periphery of their fields. Social historians such as Howard Zinn produced "people's histories" that took as their central concern the workaday lives of "ordinary" Americans, while scholars such as Ronald Takaki wrote "multicultural histories" of the United States that questioned America's "march of progress."[61] When the National Center for History in the Schools included elements of these historical interpretations in a set of history standards the Center published in 1994 at the request of the National Endowment for the Humanities (NEH), conservative defenders of traditional US history objected. Led by NEH head Lynn Cheney, conservatives rejected the standards, labeling them "politically correct" and lambasting them for representing America's history as "grim and gloomy" rather than celebratory. Occurring in the context of a conservative reaction against the election of President Bill Clinton two years earlier, controversy over the national history standards provided a lightning rod for veterans of the nation's culture wars, culminating in the US Senate passing a resolution (on a procedural basis only) to reject the standards.[62]

In contrast to the fight over the history standards, some federal officials, such as Senator Robert Byrd of West Virginia, sought to foster students' greater understanding of American history through federally supported teacher professional development. Claiming that "those who teach and those of us who purport to serve the public in some capacity have a special responsibility to make others sensitive to the importance of every citizen's role in preserving our freedoms," Byrd proposed establishing the Teaching American History (TAH) program as part of the 2001 congressional reauthorization of the Elementary and Secondary Act.[63] Eventually becoming the largest federal history education program in the United States, TAH allocated nearly $1 billion to teacher professional development activities between 2001 and 2012 for the primary purpose of "upgrading the content knowledge" of teachers of American history in kindergarten through twelfth grade.[64] School districts applied for three- to five-year grants in collaboration with a partner institution or organization with "content expertise," including colleges, universities, museums, and libraries. Averaging almost a million dollars each, the program's grants funded intensive summer institutes, mentoring programs, colloquia, field studies, and curriculum development. By 2005, the TAH program had fifty active grants throughout the United States, Puerto Rico, and the Virgin Islands.[65]

Despite Byrd's efforts, as well as the reported success of the TAH program, over time public school history curricula went from being the subject of congressional controversy to receiving relatively little attention. As accountability reform measures such as No Child Left Behind drove educators to focus their energies on improving student performance in reading and math, little class time remained for the study of US history and civics in any form. National figures such as Sandra Day O'Connor (retired associate justice of the Supreme Court) and Roy Romer (former governor of Colorado and superintendent of the Los Angeles Unified School District) responded by encouraging schools to maintain their historical commitment to educating students for patriotic citizenship. In a 2006 *Washington Post* op-ed, O'Connor and Romer, after wringing their own hands regarding twelfth-grade students' failure to achieve on a national civics assessment, wrote, "A healthy democracy depends on the participation of citizens, and that participation is learned behavior; it doesn't just happen. . . . That means civic learning—educating students for democracy—needs to be on par with other academic subjects."[66]

Proclamations such as O'Connor and Romer's had little effect. Although many educators hoped the Obama administration would lower the stakes associated with student performance on standardized tests of literacy and numeracy, just the opposite occurred. Secretary of Education Arne Duncan's Race to the Top reform program rewarded states that demonstrated a willingness to tie teacher performance evaluations to reading and math test scores.[67] As a 2012 *Education Week* headline declared regarding a federal budget compromise involving educational initiatives, "Literacy Wins, History Loses in Fiscal '12 Federal Budget."[68] It came as little surprise to many educators when, within two years of Senator Robert Byrd's death in 2010, Congress eliminated funding for the TAH program.

As long as powerful incentives remain in place for teachers to direct their time and students' attention to subjects other than US history, government, and civics, those studies will be kept on the periphery of most schools' academic programs. On the other hand, since the turn of the twenty-first century, two educational ventures have claimed to place patriotism and citizenship at the core of student learning. The first is the creation of programs

seeking to train students for a place in the nation's homeland security appa-
ratus. The second is the establishment of charter schools that promote civic
engagement and/or military service.

Schooling Patriots

Americans have frequently enlisted education as a strategy for addressing national crises. Whether offering aviation instruction in secondary schools during World War II, implementing new science curricula following the launch
of the Soviet Sputnik satellites, or providing AIDS education to combat the
spread of HIV, Americans have expected public schools to contribute to
resolving the nation's political, economic, and social problems. Quite frequently, however, educators' actions in response to national crises have been
extremely controversial. September 11 offers a useful example. Less than a
year following the terrorist attacks, critics assailed the NEA for promoting
a "blame-America" approach toward teaching about the events of that day
through a series of lesson plans posted on the organization's website.[69] The
Thomas B. Fordham Foundation responded to what it labeled the NEA's "diversity and feelings" approach to teaching about September 11 with what
it claimed to be a "constructive and hard-hitting" report addressing "what
schools should teach and children should learn" about the attacks. Although
the "leading educators and experts" who contributed to the report provided
no lesson plans for teachers to use, they did include proclamations with titles
such as "Teaching Students to Count Their Blessings," "Celebrating American
Freedom," and "Teaching Young People to be Patriots."[70]

In 2003, educators at Joppatowne High School in Joppa, Maryland, responded to September 11 in a similarly controversial way when they developed a program designed to train students for careers in the then-dramatically
expanding homeland security industry. Educators designed the Homeland
Security Emergency Preparedness Program to offer students the option of
following one of three pathways beginning in their sophomore year. The
Homeland Security Sciences pathway offers courses in chemical and biologi-
cal threat identification and protection, scientific writing and research, and a
career exploration/internship project. The Law Enforcement/Criminal Justice
pathway includes courses in criminal law enforcement, evidence collection
and analysis and, again, a career exploration/internship project. The Informa-
tion/Communications Technology pathway offers training in geographic information systems (GIS) and remote sensing, culminating in GIS technician
certification and "job shadowing opportunities."[71]

Although Joppatowne's Homeland Security Emergency Preparedness Program has received national attention as well as substantial external funding from organizations such as the Maryland Emergency Management Administration, a number of observers have questioned whether the program is engaging in education, indoctrination, or simply early job training.[72] In typically provocative fashion, and in reference to the hit television show *24*, *Mother Jones* magazine described Joppatowne High as "the first school in the country dedicated to churning out would-be Jack Bauers."[73] The school's administrators, however, claim that their educational objective is to provide students with "access to career pathways in homeland security studies," to offer "a better education," and to provide "more choices to allow them to provide services back to the community."[74]

Although Homeland Security Emergency Preparedness is offered as an elective program in the context of a mainstream public school, administrators hope to convert Joppatowne High into a magnet school. Similarly, charter school organizers have used national security, and especially military preparation, as a framework for establishing academic programs that claim to take citizenship, patriotism, and service as their central goals. In 2001, for instance, the California State Board of Education approved the charter of the Oakland Military Institute (OMI), a grade six through twelve school located in Oakland, California. With then-mayor Jerry Brown serving as a vocal proponent of the school's establishment, OMI adopted Brown's "vision" for a school that held "high expectations for student achievement, conduct, character, patriotism, and leadership."[75] The school identified its mission as providing "a structured and rigorous academic program where cadets [the title given students] develop as leaders, scholars, critical thinkers and citizens." To assist in achieving this goal, OMI borrowed its "cadet creed" from the Junior ROTC (the history of which is examined in chapter 3). A federal program that includes among its contemporary objectives promoting patriotism, developing "informed and responsible citizens," developing "respect for constructed authority," and promoting community service, the Junior ROTC's "cadet creed" includes the following declarations:

I will always conduct myself to bring credit to my family, country, academy, and corps of cadets.
I am loyal and patriotic. I am the future of the United States of America.
I do not lie, cheat, or steal and will always be accountable for my actions and deeds.
I will work hard to improve my mind and strengthen my body.

I will seek the mantle of leadership and stand prepared to uphold the Constitution of the United States of America.[76]

In part because of the indoctrinating quality of such a creed, some have questioned OMI's educational purpose. War veteran Dave Ionno, for instance, who frequently addresses student groups on the realities of war, has claimed that it is "immoral" to locate military charter schools in urban areas where children from poor families are more vulnerable to "exploitation."[77]

In an effort similar to Jerry Brown's, Charles Baldwin, a retired US Navy command master chief, and Jack Wintermantel, a US Army National Guard colonel, established Delaware Military Academy in 2003 with the mission of providing "a healthy mental and physical environment" for students that uses military training as "a requisite for a better understanding of the obligations of citizenship and self-discipline."[78] This grade nine through twelve school, which is open to all Delaware residents through an application process, is designated a Navy Junior ROTC unit.[79] As with Joppatowne's Homeland Security Emergency Preparedness Program and the OMI, there is controversy over the degree to which Delaware Military Academy—a public school that maintains direct ties with the US armed forces—is engaged in education or indoctrination.

Since the beginning of the twenty-first century, educators have also established charter schools that have little or no relationship to homeland security or the military yet maintain the goal of educating for citizenship. Democracy Prep Charter School opened in Central Harlem in 2006 with the goal of educating "responsible citizen-scholars for success in the college of their choice and a life of active citizenship."[80] Rather than modeling the school on the military, this grade six through ten school adopted what it considered the five guiding principles of the "no-excuses" school reform movement: academic rigor, data-driven decision making, a strong school culture, more time to learn, and exemplary teachers. In addition, and as the school's name suggests, Democracy Prep claims a special commitment to fostering "civic knowledge, civic understanding and civic disposition" among its students.[81]

To fulfill this commitment, Democracy Prep implemented a civic engagement program that required student participation in community service activities, attending state legislative sessions, taking part in speech and debate competitions, and encouraging students' families to register and vote.[82] As with many charter schools that compete for students with mainstream public schools, however, Democracy Prep relies on standardized test scores to demonstrate its educational effectiveness. Consequently, the school scaled back its civics curriculum in order to provide teachers with more time to instruct students in English language arts and mathematics, two core subjects tested as part of New York State's grade three through eight standardized examinations. Nevertheless, Democracy Prep joins the Delaware Military Academy, the OMI, and Joppatowne High School's Homeland Security Emergency Preparedness Program in continuing America's historic effort to employ academic curricula to foster patriotism, civic competence, and citizenship.

Whether Americanizing immigrants through English language classes, teaching students to cooperate toward common social ends, or constructing new school programs entirely, educators over the course of the twentieth, and now the twenty-first, century have sought to strongly influence, if not impose upon, students' understanding of their role in a democratic society. This chapter has focused on educators' attempts to shape students' understanding of that role though civics, social studies, and history curricula, and to equip students with a common language, fitting them for active citizenship and a common American identity. We have also begun to see how these curricula have looked beyond the acquisition of understanding and abilities to the acquisition of sentiments of loyalty and dispositions to act in the ways that good citizens have been expected to act. Chapter 2 will address educators' attempts to cultivate patriotic sentiments and dispositions through readings that present moral exemplars or heroes for emulation, celebration of "noble characters of history," and rituals of civic loyalty and solidarity.

TWO

Heroes and Rituals

In October 1935, Jehovah's Witness member Walter Gobitas told his ten-year-old son, Billy, and eleven-year-old daughter, Lillian, that they no longer needed to recite the Pledge of Allegiance in their Minersville (Pennsylvania) public school classrooms. Energized by efforts that the Witnesses had taken in court to challenge the forced recitation of the pledge as a violation of the freedoms of speech and religion, Gobitas told his children that pledging allegiance to the flag was an offense toward God. When Billy arrived at school the following day, he refused to join in the flag salute. The next day, his sister did the same. Weeks later, Billy submitted a handwritten statement to the Minersville School Board explaining his refusal. "I do not salute the flag," he wrote, "because I have promised to do the will of God. That means that I must not worship anything out of harmony with God's law." After quoting Exodus (20:4–6), in which God warns against bowing down to graven images, Billy concluded, "I do not salute the flag not because I do not love my country but I love my country and I love God more and I must obey His commandments."[1] The following day, the Minersville School Board summarily expelled Billy and Lillian.[2]

The Pledge of Allegiance and its accompanying flag salute serve as a century-long example of public schools' use of rituals to instill patriotic devotion and solidarity. Beginning at a young age, students have been taught to stand and recite the pledge in unison while maintaining a prescribed posture—arms and hands held in specified positions—during the recitation. Schools have devoted much time and attention to this activity, yet teachers rarely discuss with their elementary school students the pledge's complex vocabulary (including terms such as "allegiance," "republic," and "indivisible") or investigate with their secondary students the pledge's complicated history. The point of leading students in the Pledge of Allegiance is evidently not that they should understand, let alone examine, its literal meaning but that they should participate in a ritualized public affirmation of faith.

Sociologists Carl Bankston and Stephen Caldas describe public education in America as a kind of "civil religion" composed of many characteristics of established faiths, including belief systems, rituals, and worship.[3] As in established faiths, students have been expected to regularly profess the beliefs comprising an American "civil religion," and in both spheres participation in rituals of affirmation have one eye on belief and one eye on engagement in service to a community or nation. In both spheres, the beliefs are often communicated through stories that present models of virtue for emulation or imitative learning (as they have been for ages), through pageants and holidays that enlist initiates in celebrating the faith or nation's exceptionalism, and through pledges of faith and allegiance. Generally accepted as conventional features of the school program, these practices have not gone unchallenged. Indeed, precisely because these practices have sought to influence students' values and beliefs, Americans such as Walter Gobitas have contested them in courts of law, eliciting public scrutiny.

The challenges have occurred mostly in the twentieth century, however. Throughout much of the nineteenth century, teachers encountered few objections when they instructed students in reading and writing using primers, spellers, and readers that sought to inculcate civic and moral virtues. Of these resources, William Holmes McGuffey's were especially popular. Selling over 122 million copies between 1836 and 1922 (placing the book series in the same sales category as *Webster's Dictionary* and the Bible), McGuffey's Readers were used in schools throughout the United States, providing one of the nation's first standardized curricula and a central component of the public school academic program.

The Case of the McGuffey Readers

Born in 1800 and raised on the Ohio frontier, William Holmes McGuffey received his early education at a local school run by a Calvinist minister.[4] Excelling in his studies, McGuffey established a school of his own at the age of fourteen, tutoring pupils from surrounding farm families.[5] He later attended Greersburg Academy in Pennsylvania before enrolling at Washington College (present-day Washington and Jefferson College).[6] While a college student, McGuffey met the Reverend Robert Bishop, president of Miami University of Ohio, who was so impressed with McGuffey that he offered him the position of professor of ancient languages following his graduation. McGuffey accepted the offer and spent the next ten years teaching at Miami

University before becoming president of Cincinnati College in 1836. He would eventually serve as president of Ohio University and professor of languages at Woodward College before being offered the position of professor of moral philosophy at the University of Virginia in 1845.[7]

Ten years earlier, McGuffey had contracted with Cincinnati publishers Truman and Smith to compile a primer, a spelling book, and four school readers; the first and second of the readers were published in 1836, and the third and fourth in 1837. McGuffey had begun collecting material for the books as early as 1830, testing the lessons and taking notes on their successes and failures.[8] An immediate financial success, the readers led Truman and Smith to seek to contract with McGuffey for additional volumes. Having assumed the obligations of Cincinnati College president, however, McGuffey turned the writing of the next two readers over to his brother, Alexander.[9] Further readers would eventually be published under McGuffey's name, although he had no hand in authoring them. They did, however, maintain the pedagogical model McGuffey had established, using didactic stories to instill moral and civic virtues.

McGuffey's revised *Second Eclectic Reader* reveals the pedagogical approaches the series encouraged teachers to take with their students. Through progressively more challenging passages, students learned new vocabulary as well as the proper way to pronounce words using diacritical marks. One of the book's earlier passages, entitled "At Work," for instance, introduced students to the terms, "washed, hours (ours), pre'cious, game, harm, a'ny (en'y), brushed" and "end."[10] Regarding the articulation of the new vocabulary, the reader advised teachers, "Thorough and frequent drills on the elementary sounds are useful in correcting vicious habits of pronunciation and in strengthening the vocal organs."[11]

Illustrating the series' primary instructional methods, "At Work" also provides an example of the way in which the readers sought to impose values in the context of literacy instruction. Taking as its subject a young boy who enjoys playtime while also understanding the virtue of hard work, it reads:

AT WORK.

1. A little play does not harm any one, but does much good. After play, we should be glad to work.

2. I knew a boy who liked a good game very much. He could run, swim, jump, and play ball; and was always merry when out of school.

3. But he knew that time is not all for play; that our minutes, hours, and days are very precious.

4. At the end of his play, he would go home. After he had washed his
face and hands, and brushed his hair, he would help his mother, or
read in his book, or write upon his slate.

5. He used to say, "One thing at a time." When he had done with
work, he would play; but he did not try to play and to work at the
same time.[12]

The narrator of this passage tells the reader directly that "we should be glad
to work," and casts a favorable light on the boy in asserting that "he knew"
that time is precious—an attribution that presupposes what he "knew" is
true, thereby affirming by implication a second normative claim. He is portrayed as a happy ("merry") boy but also wise, and one to emulate as the
reader contemplates his virtues of cleanliness, helpfulness, and efficiency.
By emphasizing the virtuousness of hard work in daily life and the happiness that such work brings, the passage reflects a central characteristic of
the so-called Protestant ethic in early New England culture by which the
faithful obtained grace and salvation through hard work and discipline. It is
also consistent with the guidance on stories of heroes and gods laid down
by Plato, in his implicit criticism of Homer's *Iliad* and *Odyssey*: that heroes
and gods should be invariably portrayed as virtuous, and virtue should be
invariably depicted as foundational to happiness.

Stories such as "At Work," which communicate moral ideas in the context of literacy instruction, recur throughout the reader. A second illustra-
tive passage uses the story of an older boy's resistance to the temptation
of deceiving his younger brother to teach the importance of the virtue of
kindness. It reads:

A KIND BROTHER.

1. A boy was once sent from home to take a basket of things to his
grandmother.

2. The basket was so full that it was very heavy. So his little brother
went with him, to help carry the load.

3. They put a pole under the handle of the basket, and each then
took hold of an end of the pole. In this way they could carry the
basket very nicely.

4. Now the older boy thought, "My brother Tom does not know
about this pole."

5. "If I slip the basket near him, his side will be heavy, and mine
light; but if the basket is in the middle of the pole, it will be as heavy
for me as it is for him."

6. "Tom does not know this as I do. But I will not do it. It would be wrong, and I will not do what is wrong."

7. Then he slipped the basket quite near his own end of the pole. His load was now heavier than that of his little brother.

8. Yet he was happy; for he felt that he had done right. Had he de-ceived his brother, he would not have felt at all happy.[13]

Here again, we see a boy of notable virtue cast in an admiring light, as a model for emulation, and the narrator directly states that acting well made him happy and acting badly would have made him unhappy. In another context, such passages might serve as points of departure for engaging students in the examination of moral ideas, but the pedagogical focus in this context was not capacities of moral reflection but mastery of vocabulary and pronunciation. The communication of moral ideas and models for emula-tion is incidental to such mastery, but clearly no accident. What is evident in these passages is both a communication of moral beliefs that students are expected to accept, and child-size exemplars of virtue designed to inspire students to embrace the beliefs and act well.

McGuffey's Readers continued to seek to instill virtues of kindness and diligence long after William Holmes McGuffey ceased authoring the books. By the late nineteenth century, however, as historian Richard D. Mosier ob-serves, the series took on a more explicit patriotic character. "The inspiration of America's glorious past," Mosier writes of the readers' contents, "while no doubt potent enough to arouse the patriotic sentiments, was buttressed with a considerable emphasis on America's mission in the future. The doc-trine of the American mission may be traced, with more or less precision, from the earliest readers to the latest; but it is clearly in the decades fol-lowing the Civil War that this pattern becomes purified and sharpened in the McGuffey readers."[14] Partly the product of post–Civil War reunification and partly the rise of American imperial expansion, the "sharpening" that Mosier describes took the form of reader passages infused with patriotic sen-timent. In the *New McGuffey Fourth Reader*, published in 1901, for instance, a passage entitled "Our National Banner" followed the printing of "The Star-Spangled Banner." Written by renowned orator and politician Edward Everett, "Our National Banner" revered the American flag, with an opening that read, "All hail to our glorious ensign! Courage to the heart and strength to the hand, to which, in all time, it shall be intrusted! May it ever wave first in honor, in unsullied glory and patriotic hope, on the dome of the Capi-tol, on the country's stronghold, on the tented plain, on the wave-rocked topmast."[15]

Pageants and *The Promised Land*

While American reunification and expansion in the decades following the Civil War influenced the contents of McGuffey's Readers, a dramatic influx of immigrants into the United States catalyzed Americanization efforts. As examined in chapter 1, these immigrants originated in regions not traditionally associated with migration to the United States, such as southern and eastern Europe, becoming the focus of assimilation efforts during the late nineteenth and early twentieth centuries. David Glassberg has deftly demonstrated how public pageants and dramatic performances, which used imagery, oration, and reenactment to convey a sense of shared history, became a cultural phenomenon during this period at least in part because of the pageant's capacity to foster national sentiment. As Glassberg observes, however, pageants changed over time. Beginning earlier in the nineteenth century as community-based civic celebrations emphasizing local history, entertainment, and recreation, pageants eventually became spectacles of national pride.[16] Especially during World War I, the pageant attempted to unify "diverse towns, regions, and peoples," according to Glassberg, "into a single body instantaneously and completely identifying with the nation's present concerns."[17]

Although community-based pageants slowly declined in popularity following the First World War, schools nevertheless adopted pageant-like celebrations as a method through which to Americanize immigrant students. In 1926, for instance, public schools in New York City, which served as an entry point for millions of new immigrants, celebrated America's Founding Fathers through "Patriots' Week." Although designated a weeklong event, the celebration lasted from February 12 to February 22 in order to encompass the birthdays of both Abraham Lincoln and George Washington. Moreover, although 1926 marked the 150th anniversary of the signing of the Declaration of Independence, the Fourth of July fell during summer vacation, denying schools the opportunity to stage a celebratory event on the appropriate day.[18] Undeterred, Patriots' Week organizers not only included a sesquicentennial celebration of the declaration in their event but also organized a pageant marking the centennial anniversary of Thomas Jefferson's death.[19]

Patriots' Week activities included ringing bells, singing "patriotic songs," and, according to the *New York Times*, integrating "subjects of patriotic interest throughout the regular classwork."[20] The highlight of the week's festivities, however, involved students' recitation of the "Patriot's Pledge of Faith." Written by committee members of the Thomas Jefferson Memorial Foundation in honor of the centennial of Jefferson's death, the Patriot's Pledge proclaimed, "I do hereby pledge and declare my sincere belief and devout faith in the fundamental ideals of my country so bravely proclaimed to the world by the immortal signers of the Declaration of American Independence; and in their words and noble spirit we pledge to each other our lives, our fortunes and our sacred honor to the support of those ideals."[21] Unlike the "Pledge of Allegiance," which emphasized fidelity to the American flag and Republic, the Patriot's Pledge of Faith focused students' attention on the ideals enshrined in the Declaration of Independence as well as the "immortal" qualities of America's Founding Fathers. Indeed, public schools throughout the United States frequently used the civil-religious "worship" of national heroes, including Washington, Jefferson, and Lincoln, to inspire patriotism in students. The story of Mary Antin, a young Jewish girl who immigrated with her family to Boston in 1894, reveals the extent to which this element of the curriculum could influence students' convictions.

Arriving to America from Russia with her mother and sisters (her father had departed for the United States three years earlier), Mary Antin was thirteen years old when she enrolled in her local public school. The opportunity to attend school thrilled Antin; she later remembered that her heart was pulsing with "joy and pride and ambition" on her first day of class.[22] Although placed in what she called the "baby class" because of her weak English, Antin made enough progress in her first week of school to move up to second grade.[23] By the middle of her second year, she had reached the sixth grade.[24] As successful as she was in school, however, Antin later recalled that it was when her class learned about, and her school celebrated, the life of George Washington that she had an almost mystical experience.

In *The Promised Land*, in which she recorded her memories of immigrating to America, Antin described the profound effect that studying Washington had on her embrace of an American identity. Detailing the experience she had in class one day, Antin wrote in characteristically extravagant prose, "When the class read, and it came my turn, my voice shook and the book trembled in my hands, I could not pronounce the name of George Washington without a pause. Never had I prayed, never had I chanted the songs of David, never had I called upon the Most Holy, in such utter reverence and worship as I repeated the simple sentences of my child's story of the patriot."[25] Although Antin later acknowledged the role that nostalgia played in her recollections, her school experience nevertheless genuinely moved her. Confessing humility in learning about "the noble boy who would not tell a lie to save himself from punishment," Antin described how she acquired a "sense of dignity" when realizing that she and Washington were "related," not through kinship but by citizenship.[26] "Undoubtedly," she claimed, "I was a Fellow Citizen, and George Washington was another. It thrilled me to realize what sudden greatness had fallen on me; and at the same time it sobered me, as with a sense of responsibility. I strove to conduct myself as befitted a Fellow Citizen."[27] Antin goes on in *The Promised Land* to describe her "adoration" of America's Founding Father in emotional detail, providing a spirited illustration of the capacity of the "cult of George Washington" to influence children's beliefs.[28]

Washington's Birthday was only one of several "holy days of the state" celebrated in public schools throughout the United States.[29] Other such days, including Thanksgiving, Armistice Day (the forerunner of Veterans Day), and Decoration Day (the forerunner of Memorial Day), also sought to instill a sense of American exceptionalism in students. Public schools, for instance, have historically taught students to associate the story of Thanksgiving with America's founding by the Pilgrims, who—in their schoolteachers' telling—arrived to the New World on the Mayflower in search of religious freedom. Following a harsh winter, the surviving passengers, according to this narrative, established Plymouth Colony and, with the help of local Native Americans, prospered. Thankful for a successful harvest, the settlers held a celebratory feast along with members of the Wampanoag tribe, marking the first Thanksgiving and the birth of a new nation.[30]

As with Mary Antin's reference to learning of "the noble boy who would not tell a lie to save himself from punishment," Thanksgiving school celebrations demonstrate how academic curricula have occasionally been tailored to suit the needs of a patriotic pedagogy of hero worship and rituals of profession and solidarity. For well over a century, public schools celebrated the Plymouth founding narrative through art and craft projects as well as reenactments in which students dressed as Pilgrims and recited from the Mayflower Compact. Rarely, however, do these schools impart the history of the Jamestown Colony with equal prominence. Established in 1607, thirteen years *prior* to the Pilgrims' arrival at Plymouth, Jamestown was the first permanent English settlement in America. Founded by the Virginia Company of London as a profit-making enterprise, Jamestown's history is one of relative misfortune. Having settled on a narrow peninsula surrounded mostly by malarial swamp, many Jamestown colonists died of disease within their first year. Those who did not went hungry or starved due to their lack of experience with, if not elitist refusal to engage in, agricultural production. Moreover, although the colonists had reason to give thanks to the Native Americans who initially provided provisions, the relationship between the two groups was usually tense. Within two years of the settlers' arrival, the first Anglo-Powhatan War broke out.[31]

Given this dismal history, it is hardly surprising that the national holiday we call Thanksgiving has been linked to the story of Plymouth Colony rather than Jamestown. In addition to eclipsing the history of Jamestown, however, the Thanksgiving holiday itself has escaped the critical scrutiny that other topics in school history might receive. By the time Abraham Lincoln declared Thanksgiving a national holiday in 1863, cities and towns throughout the United States had been holding some form of a thanksgiving celebration for decades. Indeed, as early as October 3, 1789, George Washington issued a "Thanksgiving Proclamation."[32] Lincoln, however, had a specifically political purpose when he established Thanksgiving as an official national holiday. Seeking to rally the Union midway through the Civil War, Lincoln used his Thanksgiving Day proclamation to underscore how the United States flourished even in the midst of a devastating conflict, declaring,

> The year that is drawing towards its close, has been filled with the blessings of fruitful fields and healthful skies. . . . In the midst of a civil war of unequalled magnitude and severity, which has sometimes seemed to foreign States to invite and to provoke their aggression, peace has been preserved with all nations, order has been maintained, the laws have been respected and obeyed, and harmony has prevailed everywhere except in the theatre of military conflict; while that theatre has been greatly contracted by the advancing armies and navies of the Union. Needful diversions of wealth and of strength from the fields of peaceful industry to the national defence, have not arrested the plough, the shuttle, or the ship. . . . And the country, rejoicing in the consciousness of augmented strength and vigor, is permitted to expect continuance of years, with large increase of freedom.[33]

As with Washington's, Lincoln's proclamation makes no mention of Plymouth Colony or the Pilgrims. It does, however, assert a level of prosperity that most Americans living in the midst of the Civil War would have found highly questionable. Nevertheless, for most Northerners the link between the war's "unequalled magnitude and severity" and Thanksgiving Day was quite clear. Although Lincoln delivered his proclamation on October 3, the first observance of the new national holiday did not occur until November 26, exactly one week following Lincoln's dedication of Gettysburg National Cemetery.

Although Lincoln proclaimed Thanksgiving Day in 1863 and Americans celebrated war-memorial holidays such as Decoration Day beginning in the late 1860s, it was not until two decades later that schools began organizing patriotic activities to honor these occasions. The reason for this lag, as historian Stuart McConnell has observed, was that the "icons of American patriotism," including flying the American flag and singing "The Star-Spangled Banner," had a "relatively weak presence" in the United States prior to that time.[34] For most Americans throughout the nineteenth century, dedication to family and region took precedence over obligation to the nation. "Even when troops were raised to defend the Union or the Confederacy," McConnell writes, "they were raised and officered locally. . . . Northerners fought for Jacksonville, or Indianapolis, or Portland, as much as for an abstract Union."[35] Consequently, it was not until the period of Reconstruction, as Northerners and Southerners stumbled toward reunifying a country devastated by four years of bloodshed, that native-born whites sought to establish a new understanding of what it meant to be "American." Yet even then, as David Glassberg again shows, the Southern "religion of the lost cause" developed "its own pantheon of heroes, rituals, and holidays" with many Southern towns holding pageants in commemoration of Confederate Memorial Day (observed on June third—Jefferson Davis's Birthday—rather than Decoration Day) and Robert E. Lee's Birthday instead of Abraham Lincoln's.[36]

The American Flag

The effort to redefine what it meant to be an American gained significant momentum during the latter part of the nineteenth century when patriotic societies such as the Grand Army of the Republic (GAR) and the Woman's Relief Corps (WRC) led a crusade to place a flag in every schoolhouse in America.[37] The GAR and WRC were extremely successful in introducing military drill into schools for the purpose of instilling patriotic allegiance among students. Only older boys participated in drill, however, leaving younger boys and most girls without any form of patriotic training. The GAR and WRC sought to remedy this deficiency by cultivating an impassioned, nationwide veneration of the American flag oriented around public schools.[38] As Stuart McConnell observes, "Where previously the flag carried connotations of loyalty and familiarity," the GAR and WRC's crusade led to its being glorified "in almost mystical terms."[39] As evidence, McConnell quotes GAR commander-in-chief William Warner's address, delivered on the topic of public schools and flag veneration, to Union veterans in 1889. "The reverence of schoolchildren for the flag," Garner proclaimed, "should be like that of the Israelites for the Ark of the Covenant."[40]

What the GAR and WRC eventually accomplished in cooperation with newly formed hereditary groups such as the Daughters of the American Revolution (established in 1890) and organizations such as the American Flag

Association (established in 1894) did not fall terribly short of Warner's aim. Yet of the many participants in the "schoolhouse flag movement," Civil War veteran George T. Balch stands out due to his pivotal role in coordinating a program of flag-centered patriotic exercises in the nation's schools. A West Point graduate and skilled logistician, Balch served in the US Ordnance Office during the war years, where he was credited with keeping arms and munitions moving to the Union lines. Following his resignation from the army at war's end, Balch worked as auditor of the Erie Railroad Company before eventually taking a job in the office of the New York City Commissioners of Accounts, a position that afforded him significant influence in the city's public schools.[41]

In June 1889, the centennial year of George Washington's inauguration as president of the United States, Balch delivered an address before members of the New York City Children's Aid Society on the need for schools to instill patriotism in students, especially those who had recently immigrated to the United States. In the address, Balch proposed what he called "a practical plan" through which "the vast frame-work of our forty-nine state, territorial and district systems of public elementary education can be utilized and converted into a mighty engine for the inculcation of patriotism throughout the length and breadth of this land."[42] Distributing copies of his address to members of the New York City Board of Education, Balch was encouraged by Board President J. Edward Simmons to develop his talk into an instructional guide for teachers. Published the following year, Balch's *Methods of Teaching Patriotism in the Public Schools* catalyzed a movement that sought to direct public education toward the primary aim of schooling for patriotism through flag veneration.[43]

Balch's pedagogical strategies were, in fact, not terribly innovative; he claimed, for instance, that students would engage in prescribed behaviors if rewarded for doing so. What he proposed that was unprecedented, however, was integrating the American flag, in a variety of forms, throughout the school day. Balch described in remarkable detail the rewards students would receive for what he ambiguously deemed "good conduct" as well as the exercises and assemblies through which the awards would be "presented and surrendered."[44] After proposing, for instance, that each teacher present to the "best conducted pupil" in her class a reward called the Scholar's Flag, Balch thoroughly delineated the materials out of which the flag and its staff should be constructed. He then dedicated an additional four pages to describing, with even greater precision, the assembly at which teachers would present the awards.[45] One part of the ceremony, for instance, he described in this way:

Immediately after reading from the Scriptures . . . those scholars who for good conduct had been awarded the flags on the previous school-day, leave their seats and proceed with dignified steps to the front of the platform; arranging themselves in line and facing the class color-bearer and guard, leaving room sufficient for the Principal to pass between the lines easily, each one holding his or her flag erect, supported by both hands, in front of the center of the body. The simple act of leaving the seat, of moving forward to the position just indicated, the manner of holding and carrying the flag, and of surrendering it at the proper moment, can be made . . . at once graceful and dignified in action, elevating in their influence on both actor and spectator, and in entire harmony with the great purpose and object we have in view in all these exercises, namely that of impressing the child with a profound sense of the nobility and dignity of American citizenship.[46]

Continuing in this manner throughout his book, Balch proposed rewarding not only individual students but also entire classes through the presentation of the Class Flag, which he indicated should be saluted each morning at a similar school-wide assembly before being moved to the winning students' classroom.[47] In addition, Balch urged educators to adopt the flag as a symbol of American education by constructing a flagpole in the front of the school building and raising the flag each day school was in session. "It should occupy," Balch wrote of the School Flag, "the most prominent and conspicuous place, where it can be seen by every child, that it may form the center of attraction—the rallying point for every loyal heart."[48]

Balch's book was a huge success at least in part because many schools had already begun promoting patriotic Americanism. According to historian Cody Ewert, a "generation of educators" in the late nineteenth century believed they could strengthen public support for public schooling by embracing the teaching of "American ideas."[49] Although these efforts rarely resulted in significant changes to the school institution, teachers and administrators enthusiastically adopted what one scholar has characterized as the "high-profile, mostly symbolic activities" that comprised Americanization.[50] Consequently, organizations such as the NEA "heartily endorsed" the goal of instilling patriotism in students, which, it claimed, "finds expression in placing the national flag upon our schoolhouses, in the increased attention to school exercises which tend to a greater love and veneration for the flag, and in the observance of national holidays."[51] Over the next two years, the schoolhouse flag movement continued to spread; in public schools throughout the United States, principals raised flagpoles, teachers acquired

American flags for their classrooms, and students participated in patriotic pageants and assemblies.

In July 1891, the *Youth's Companion*, one of the nation's first weekly periodicals to target both adults and their children, reported on the effects of "the unfurling of the flag above so many schools."[52] "Has it stirred up in the breasts of boys and girls the hope of living to be brave men and good women?" the weekly asked rhetorically. "Has it begun to serve, with the children of the millions from abroad who inherit no love for our country, as a symbol around which will grow up a thoroughly American feeling?" Surveying teachers in classrooms throughout the United States, the weekly responded with an unqualified yes. "Eighty-six percent of my scholars were either born in other countries, or are the children of foreign-born parents," the weekly quoted one teacher. "The effect of the flag upon my school has been to make every one of my pupils enthusiastic Americans. If, for any reason, the flag is not raised for a day, they clamor for its raising. No more enthusiastic or patriotic . . . children can be found in the United States than those of my school."[53]

The exuberant tone with which the *Youth's Companion* reported on the status of the movement would have hardly surprised its readers. The weekly vigorously promoted the crusade in a number of ways, including selling flags at discounted prices and sponsoring a national essay contest on "The Patriotic Influence of the American Flag when raised over the Public School."[54] Indeed, the periodical's involvement marked one of the first times in US history that a company used modern advertising techniques to influence the public schools—and to profit from its efforts. With approximately a half million subscribers in 1891, the *Youth's Companion* was one of the most widely read weeklies in America and wielded considerable popular influence. For this reason, the magazine's decision to make public schools central to America's celebration of the four hundredth anniversary of Columbus's discovery of the New World proved a crucial moment in schools' efforts to intentionally promote patriotic values through a fusion of triumphalist narrative, national heroes and symbols, and rituals of "civil religion."

As Jeffrey Jones and Peter Meyer have observed, fostering a Columbian commemoration in public schools gave the *Youth's Companion* a chance to both "nurture patriotic awareness among the young" and, by linking its efforts to the World's Columbian Exposition already being planned in Chicago, "reap a promotional bonanza."[55] Enlisting the assistance of William T. Harris, US commissioner of education and celebrated former superintendent of Saint Louis public schools, the *Companion* garnered the support of the NEA and the National Association of School Superintendents. For their part, principals and schoolteachers, many of whom already used the celebration of national holidays to inculcate patriotic values, found another opportunity to do so through the *Companion*'s promotion of the Columbian quadricentennial.[56] Yet it was the work of a former Baptist minister whom the *Companion*'s directors put in charge of overseeing the project that ultimately gave the weekly's undertaking lasting historical significance.

The Pledge of Allegiance

Francis Bellamy came to the *Youth's Companion* after serving as a minister in Boston for eleven years. An outspoken supporter of the rights of the laboring classes, he held the position of vice president of Boston's Society of Christian Socialists and was a charter member of the city's Nationalist Club (an organization established to bring to fruition the socialist ideals that Edward Bellamy, Francis's cousin, expressed in his popular utopian novel *Looking Backward*). Bellamy promoted the social gospel, around which a movement formed in the late nineteenth and early twentieth centuries dedicated to ridding the United States of social, political, and economic injustice. As with the movement's leaders, including Josiah Strong and Richard T. Ely, Bellamy was profoundly concerned with the nation's rapidly changing racial and ethnic composition. Rather than opposing immigration, however, many promoters of the social gospel, including Bellamy, claimed that a "well-organized and patriotic public education system" would bring these newcomers into alignment with American ideals, beliefs, and behaviors.[57]

Foreshadowing his future career in advertising, Bellamy joined his experience as a preacher with the *Companion*'s promotional strategies to generate tremendous interest in the Columbian commemoration (with the *Companion* profiting from the sale of American flags throughout the lead-up to the celebration).[58] With the official commemoration date of October 21, 1892, approaching, Bellamy began developing a program for schools to follow, which the *Companion* published in its September 8 edition.[59] Along with parades honoring veterans, singing patriotic songs, and flying American flags in front of schools, the *Companion* urged that a scripted address entitled "The Meaning of the Four Centuries" be delivered at each community's celebration.[60] The address, which the *Companion* published along with its proposed celebratory program, explicitly linked the "memorable milestone" of Columbus's voyage with American progress as exemplified by the public school. In language that is difficult to imagine being used to describe public education in the United States in the twenty-first century, the address declared,

> We, therefore, on this anniversary of America present the Public School as the noblest expression of the principle of enlightenment which Columbus grasped by faith. We uplift the system of free and universal education as the master-force which, under God, has been informing each of our generations with the peculiar truths of Americanism. America, therefore, gathers her sons around the schoolhouse to-day as the institution closest to the people, most characteristic of the people, and fullest of hope for the people.[61]

According to the *Youth's Companion*, a student recitation or pledge in salute of the flag was to be the highlight of the Columbus Day celebration (as it would be during Patriot's Week over thirty years later). The United States, however, did not have an official pledge of national faith or allegiance. Instead, a variety of pledges existed. George T. Balch had penned one for students to recite during the first Flag Day celebration in 1885, which some schools had already adopted, making it an obvious choice for use in the Columbus Day program. It read, "I give my heart and my hand to my country— one country, one language, one flag."[62] Bellamy disliked it, however, calling it "pretty but childish," and claimed that students should recite something with greater "historical meaning."[63] Bellamy, therefore, composed his own pledge, which consisted of the following: "I pledge allegiance to my Flag and the Republic for which it stands, one nation, indivisible, with liberty and justice for all."[64]

Many years after schools across America had adopted the Pledge of Allegiance, Bellamy admitted writing it with an eye toward the ritual entailed in its recitation rather than children's understanding of the meaning. "When you analyze it you find a mouthful of orotund words," Bellamy acknowledged, "most of them abstract terms —a bunch of ideas rather than concrete names . . . this pledge would seem far better adapted to educated adults than to children."[65] Nevertheless, following the Columbian Celebration, school boards in towns and cities throughout the United States began sanctioning the pledge and compelling student recitation as part of a morning flag salute. In 1898, New York became the first state to legislate the requirement, passing its statute one day following the United States' declaration of war against Spain.[66] The following year, the GAR chose to give its sole endorsement to Bellamy's pledge while promoting legislation requiring American flags to be flown over all public schools.[67] By 1913, twenty-three states had

passed such laws.[68] Four years later, with the eruption of unbridled nationalism that accompanied the United States' entry into World War I, pledging
allegiance to the flag became a fixture of American public education.

Over the course of the next forty years, the pledge underwent three revisions. The first occurred almost immediately following the Columbus Day
celebration when Bellamy, unhappy with the rhythm of his original work,
inserted the word "to" before "the Republic." Between 1892 and the end of
World War I, this was the twenty-three-word pledge that many states wrote
into law. The second modification occurred in 1923 when the American
Legion's National Americanism Commission (which had assumed the
GAR's mantle) recommended that the US Congress officially adopt Bellamy's pledge as the national Pledge of Allegiance. Fearing, however, that
Bellamy's opening phrase—"I pledge allegiance to my Flag"—permitted
immigrants to pledge allegiance to any flag they desired, the commission
revised the line to read, "I pledge allegiance to the flag of the United States
of America." Over time, schools adopted the revision.[69] Finally, in 1954,
after the federal government included the pledge as part of the US Flag Code
during World War II, Congress reacted to the so-called godless communism
many believed was infiltrating US public institutions by adding the phrase
"under God" to the pledge.[70] This Cold War revision eventually served as
the basis for constitutional challenges to the pledge as violating the First
Amendment's establishment clause. Even prior to that moment, however,
and before Congress added "under God" to the salute, students and their
parents had disputed the pledge's legality over a dozen times, with perhaps
the most consequential test arising from Walter Gobitas's instruction to his
children, Billy and Lillian, to cease reciting the pledge at their Minersville
public school.[71]

Following Billy and Lillian's expulsion from school in 1935, the Jehovah's
Witness legal team, in cooperation with the American Civil Liberties Union,
enthusiastically pursued a court challenge on the grounds that pledging allegiance to the American flag was an act of idolatry strictly forbidden by the
Witnesses' faith. They argued that the pledge's forced recitation undermined
the children's religious freedom. The Witnesses and the ACLU were eager
to pursue the Gobitas case for two primary reasons. First, Pennsylvania had
never passed a statute requiring students to recite the pledge, meaning that
Billy and Lillian had been expelled for violating custom rather than state
law (the school board adopted a regulation requiring the pledge's recitation
on November 6, 1935, during the same meeting at which it expelled the
children). Second, southeastern Pennsylvania was home to a disproportion-
ately large number of antimilitarian Quakers.[72] The Witnesses assumed that

this demographic context would work to their benefit, an assumption that proved true when federal district judge Albert Branson Maris, a Quaker, was assigned the case.[73]

In 1938, Maris ruled in the Witnesses' favor, claiming, "While the salute to our national flag has no religious significance to me, and while I find it difficult to understand the plaintiffs' point of view, I am nevertheless entirely satisfied that they sincerely believe that the act does have a deep religious meaning and is an act of worship which they can conscientiously render to God alone."[74] A controversial ruling because of the authority it gave the plaintiffs to define a First Amendment violation, Maris's decision was undoubtedly affected by the social and political conditions of the time. With fascist regimes coming into power in Germany, Italy, and Japan, and Europe on the brink of war, Maris's decision emphasized the importance of fiercely protecting democratic liberties. "We need only glance at the current world scene," he wrote,

> to realize that the preservation of individual liberty is more important today than ever it was in the past. The safety of our nation largely depends upon the extent to which we foster in each individual citizen that sturdy independence of thought and action which is essential in a democracy. . . . Our country's safety surely does not depend upon the totalitarian idea of forcing all citizens into one common mold of thinking and acting or requiring them to render a lip service of loyalty in a manner which conflicts with their sincere religious convictions. Such a doctrine seems to me utterly alien to the genius and spirit of our nation and destructive of that personal liberty of which our flag itself is the symbol.[75]

The Minersville School District immediately appealed Maris's decision, and in late 1939 the US Court of Appeals for the Third Circuit upheld the ruling.[76] With the financial support of the American Legion, however, and growing public dissatisfaction with the case's outcome, the school board petitioned the US Supreme Court for review.

By the time oral arguments began in the case of *Minersville School District v. Gobitis* (a misspelling of the respondent's surname), Nazi armies had invaded Poland, swept through Belgium, and cornered the French and British Expeditionary Forces at Dunkirk. For this reason, the 8–1 opinion that Justice Felix Frankfurter authored for the Court's majority became known among that year's cohort of Supreme Court law clerks as "Felix's Fall of France" decision.[77] Ruling for the school district, Frankfurter claimed—in an affirmation of judicial restraint—that the Supreme Court was not "the school board for the country" and that it neither had nor would it assume the authority to "exercise censorship over the conviction of legislatures that a particular program or exercise will best promote in the minds of children who attend the common schools an attachment to the institutions of their country." Yet, he argued, the issue that the case presented was paramount. "We are dealing with an interest inferior to none in the hierarchy of legal values," Frankfurter wrote. "National unity is the basis of national security." Frankfurter then addressed the question at the center of the case: "Did the mandatory flag salute infringe upon liberties protected by the First and Fourteenth Amendments?" The Court responded:

> The preciousness of the family relation, the authority and independence which give dignity to parenthood, indeed the enjoyment of all freedom, presuppose the kind of ordered society which is summarized by our flag. A society which is dedicated to the preservation of these ultimate values of civilization may in self-protection utilize the educational process for inculcating those almost unconscious feelings which bind men together in a comprehending loyalty, whatever may be their lesser differences and difficulties. That is to say, the process may be utilized so long as men's right to believe as they please, to win others to their way of belief, and their right to assemble in their chosen places of worship for the devotional ceremonies of their faith, are all fully respected.[78]

Claiming that the Minersville School District had indeed respected the Gobitis children's "right to believe as they please," the Court decided in the district's favor, with Justice Harlan Stone providing the lone dissent.

Controversy immediately enveloped the decision. While some Americans debated its merits on the editorial pages of the country's leading newspapers, others vented their anger at the Witnesses through beatings, acts of arson, and even a case of tar and feathering.[79] In the midst of this violence, and perhaps partly because of it, three of the Court's members, Hugo Black, William O. Douglas, and Frank Murphy, began reconsidering their positions.[80] Following the Court's summer recess, Douglas informed Frankfurter that Black was having second thoughts about the ruling. Frankfurter responded by asking whether Black had been reading the Constitution. "No," Douglas replied, "he has been reading the newspapers."[81] Consequently, when the Court ruled against the Witnesses in a separate case involving the right to distribute proselytizing literature in June 1942, the three justices used their dissenting opinion to issue an unprecedented repudiation of their votes in *Gobitis*.[82]

With Black, Douglas, and Murphy joining Harlan Stone in criticizing the decision and newly appointed Justice Robert Jackson signaling his dissatisfaction with the ruling, the Witnesses sought a new case with which to challenge *Gobitis*. They found it almost immediately in West Virginia, where the state board of education had, following the announcement of the *Gobitis* decision, adopted a resolution requiring all public school teachers and students to pledge allegiance to the flag every day. When seven children from three Witness families residing in Charleston refused, they were expelled. With the Witnesses and the ACLU supporting the legal challenge, the families won in US District Court. The state board of education consequently appealed to the Supreme Court.[83]

The Court responded to *West Virginia State Board of Education v. Barnette* quite differently from *Gobitis*.[84] In a 6–3 decision, the Court ruled for the Witnesses. In an oft-quoted opinion delivered on Flag Day, 1943, at the height of America's involvement in World War II, Justice Jackson wrote for the majority, "If there is any fixed star in our constitutional constellation, it is that no official, high or petty, can prescribe what shall be orthodox in politics, nationalism, religion, or other matters of opinion, or force citizens to confess by word or act their faith therein. If there are any circumstances which permit an exception, they do not now occur to us."[85]

The Supreme Court's decision in *Barnette* held that students could not be forced to recite the Pledge of Allegiance. Nevertheless, the flag salute remained a mainstay of public school ritual throughout the United States. As such, legal challenges continued to arise, one of the most recent involving the inclusion of the phrase "under God" in the pledge. With the Supreme Court deciding *Elk Grove Unified School District v. Newdow* on standing grounds rather than addressing the establishment clause issue underlying the case, however, further religious freedom challenges are expected.[86] Similarly, *Barnette* did not address other pledge-oriented questions such as whether students need parental permission to opt out of the flag salute. Cases addressing this question, among others, continue to be argued.

The Pledge of Allegiance has played a significant role in schools' efforts to instill patriotism in students, and we have seen throughout this chapter how such rituals have been wed to the construction and celebration of national symbols, heroes, holidays, and triumphalist history. By promoting civic and moral virtues through early literacy curricula, inspiring a belief in American exceptionalism through celebrating national holidays, and promoting patriotic loyalty through pledges of faith and allegiance, schools have sought to overcome regionalism and foster a common American identity among students, especially those newly arrived to the United States. This educational project has not gone unchallenged, however, as parents during the twentieth century have opposed the pledge, in particular, as violating their children's constitutional rights. We turn in the next chapter to forms of learning in American public schools that moved beyond curricula of knowledge and skills, inspirations to virtue, and requiring students to participate in symbolic exercises. We will consider ways in which the circumstances of war and rural struggle, especially, led educators to develop cocurricular activities intended to inculcate patriotism and draw students directly into public and national service.

THREE

Militarizing Schools, Mobilizing Students

Just weeks following Japan's attack on Pearl Harbor on December 7, 1941, the US Educational Policies Commission issued "A War Policy for American Schools."[1] Having previously urged schools to "come to grips" with defense mobilization by "increasing the civic understanding, the loyalties and the intellectual competence of millions of citizens," the commission now issued a more fervent manifesto: "When the schools closed on Friday, December 5, they had many purposes and they followed many roads to achieve those purposes. When the schools opened on Monday, December 8, they had but one dominant purpose—complete, intelligent, and enthusiastic cooperation in the war effort."[2]

Seeking to foster patriotism, schools transformed their cocurricular programming to provide students with opportunities to become directly involved in the war effort.[3] From "militarizing" physical education (PE) classes to organizing students to sell war stamps and bonds, teachers during the war years brought to fruition a claim National Council on Education member Thomas J. Morgan made decades earlier, that "the American public school should be the nursery of American patriotism."[4] As with efforts during the Progressive Era to use the academic curriculum and rituals of "civil religion" to Americanize students, equip them for active citizenship, and instill patriotism, schools during the First and Second World Wars used the cocurriculum to influence students' patriotic values and behavior. Unlike that earlier period, however, which was characterized by an unprecedented increase in the number of immigrants arriving to the United States, cocurricular programs such as the Junior ROTC and the Cadet Corps grew out of America's involvement in war.

Junior ROTC and the Cadet Corps

During the last decade of the nineteenth century, the United States achieved the status of a world power as it made significant investments in military, especially naval, armaments. Joining in the imperial conquests of nations such as England, Germany, and France, America brought these investments to bear when, over a ten-week period in 1898, US forces brought an end to the Spanish Empire and assumed territorial control over Cuba, Puerto Rico, Guam, and the Philippines. Yet the Spanish-American War was only one of a number of US military operations during this time. In July 1898, for instance, President William McKinley authorized the annexation of Hawaii following the intervention of US Marines in deposing Queen Liliuokalani earlier in the decade. The following year, American warships confronted British and German naval forces in Samoa. Although shots were never fired (a typhoon destroyed most of the nations' vessels), the Tripartite Convention led to the division of Samoa, with the United States acquiring the region's easternmost islands. Similarly, the United States dispatched soldiers to Nicaragua in 1909, Mexico (Vera Cruz) in 1914, Haiti in 1915, and the Dominican Republic in 1916.

Simultaneously, a growing number of US interventionists and militarists, vociferously supported by President Theodore Roosevelt, insisted that America abandon its historic antipathy toward standing armies and develop a military force equal to that of the major European powers. Militarists' demands gained greater traction in 1914 when World War I plunged Europe into war and, less than a year later, a German submarine torpedoed the British passenger ship *Lusitania*, killing 128 Americans.[5] Ultimately, it was President Woodrow Wilson (reelected in 1916 partly because of the campaign slogan "He Kept Us Out of War") who approved a significant US military buildup.[6] Signing the National Defense Act of 1916 into law, Wilson secured congressional approval to enlarge the regular peacetime army to 175,000 men (300,000 in wartime), expand the US Military Academy, and increase the National Guard from 100,000 soldiers to over 400,000. He also obtained executive authority to assume control of the National Guard during periods of war or national emergency, thus permitting it to operate outside America's borders.[7]

Perhaps most importantly for schools, colleges, and universities, the National Defense Act gave the president authority to establish "in civil educational institutions" the ROTC for the purpose of preparing young men to serve as officers in the US Army. Four-year colleges and universities would host the ROTC's "senior division," while its "junior division" was to operate "at all other public or private educational institutions." The act set the minimum age for Junior ROTC participation at fourteen, required students to dedicate "at least an average of three hours per week per academic year" to the study of military tactics and drill, and authorized loaning secondary schools military equipment. Active duty military personnel were to serve as instructors.[8]

The Junior ROTC represented a significant extension of the armed forces into public education. In many ways, however, the program simply legislated at the federal level previous efforts to institute military training programs in public secondary schools at the local level. As early as 1862, for instance, the Bangor, Maine, City Council instituted military drill in its public high school. Established during the Civil War as the "Volunteer Drill Company," the organization engaged male students, who were responsible for obtaining their own uniforms and equipment, in military drill in the school gymnasium for two hours a week. When the group experienced a sudden increase in membership during the Spanish-American War, school officials reorganized and expanded the program under the banner "Bangor High School Cadet Corps."[9] Similarly, the first Junior ROTC unit in the United States traced its origins to a cadet corps established in Leavenworth, Kansas, one year prior to the Spanish-American War. The organization that would become the Leavenworth High School Junior ROTC began when students approached the commanding officer of the nearby army facility at Fort Leavenworth to request instruction in military subjects. Assigned the duty of teaching the students for one hour each morning, five days a week, an army captain drilled the students in the school hallways, with broomsticks substituting for rifles.[10]

Both of these communities' efforts aligned with work that the GAR and the WRC conducted during the 1890s in fostering martial patriotism in the nation's schools.[11] The first national veterans' group that counted officers as well as enlisted men among its members, the GAR wielded significant political and cultural influence in America.[12] Though it refused to admit women who served during the Civil War in a variety of capacities, the GAR supported the founding of the WRC as an auxiliary organization. The two groups, in addition to advocating a form of "patriotic education" that included a nationwide flag movement and school textbooks such as *The Patriotic Reader*, sought to introduce military drill into schools as a way to encourage patriotic allegiance and to prepare a new generation of citizen-soldiers. "The future of this government," claimed the GAR's chief patriotic instructor, "depends upon the patriotic teachings from the old soldier to the teachers and scholars of this beautiful land of ours which would never have been given to the rising generation had it not been for the Boys in Blue."[13]

As historian Cecilia O'Leary notes, the organizations' efforts were rewarded in 1895 when "16 regiments of 10,000 drilled boys, some 3,000 of whom were uniformed and armed," marched in a New York City Memorial Day parade.[14]

The GAR and WRC again proved influential in 1911 when California adjutant general Edwin Alexander Forbes established the first statewide voluntary program of military training in secondary schools. Modeled on the regular military, the California Cadet Corps claimed to prepare male students for service in the armed forces by marching and drilling them weekly and hosting a five-day summer encampment that involved physical training, field exercises, and target practice.[15] Regulations required members to maintain good academic standing and abide by the rules of "The Cadet's Glory," which read, "A high school cadet is a true gentleman. He stands for the high ideals of life. He loves peace and deplores war, but is always ready to defend his country in its hour of need. He respects authority. He obeys the law. He cultivates filial love, and strives earnestly to be an honor to his father and mother. He honors the Supreme Being in thought, word and deed."[16]

Yet compulsory, school-based military drill and Junior ROTC also provoked significant opposition. During World War I, for instance, as school districts across the nation increasingly adopted military programs, peace groups not only objected but put forth their own proposal for training in the form of PE. Although some schools began offering PE classes during the first half of the nineteenth century, peace advocates during the war years provided a sudden and nationwide justification for schools, districts, and states to adopt PE curricula. "We want not only to oppose the measure introducing military training which is sure to be presented this year," pronounced pacifist Eleanor Karsten in 1916, "but we also want to offer in its place a constructive measure of our own."[17] The movement led thirteen states to pass compulsory PE laws during the war, with another twelve adopting the laws by 1923. Although some consequently declined to adopt military training, many states implemented both, leading to pitched battles throughout the country between groups supporting military drill, such as the Daughters and Sons of the American Revolution, and those opposed, including the League of Nations Association.[18]

Although debates over school-based military training diminished during the decade of the Great Depression, they were rekindled in 1940 when America's first peacetime draft led the armed forces to issue a relatively high number of deferments due to recruits' poor physical conditioning. Placing the blame for the reportedly poor health of the nation's young men partly on high school PE classes, many Americans supported "militarizing" PE by transforming it into a preinduction training program.[19] Consequently, school districts that had previously opposed implementing programs such as Junior ROTC and the Cadet Corps began adopting them in schools following the US declaration of war against Japan in December 1941.

In 1940, the board of education of the city of Palo Alto, in northern California, responded to community members' claims that the Cadet Corps program was unnecessarily militaristic by unanimously rejecting a proposal to adopt the program in its high school. Board members, however, identified what they described as the need to "toughen up" potential recruits through rigorous PE courses.[20] Two years later, district officials tempered their opposition to direct military training as part of high school PE for boys, agreeing to include an obstacle course, calisthenics, and "basic marching tactics as set up by the army and navy."[21] As the national trend toward military training in high schools continued, the board eventually reversed its initial decision. Beginning in 1944, 307 Palo Alto High School boys put on brown khaki uniforms and gathered twice a week to drill under the command of army colonel R. E. Fletcher (retired).[22] With selected seniors serving as corps leaders, training included "calisthenics and cadence exercise" during the month of October, "organized games and runs" in November, "practice ceremonies and an obstacle course" in December, and "preparatory rifle marksmanship and tumbling" in January.[23]

Similarly, Berkeley High School in California's East Bay region sponsored a Cadet Corps that engaged students in physical activity designed to prepare them for enlistment. Berkeley's corps also served as a popular service and social organization. When the city of Berkeley had difficulty finding civic organizations to coordinate scrap metal drives held every few months as part of the community's war effort, Berkeley High Cadet Corps members volunteered their time. The students collected an average of eighty-five tons of scrap on each outing but did not go completely uncompensated for their efforts; the city paid them three dollars each for their day's work, which they turned over to the organization's quartermaster to fund social events.[24] Accordingly, the Berkeley High School newspaper, the *Berkeley Jacket*, reported in 1944, "Tonight the Social Hall will furnish the setting for the first military ball ever held at BHS and the first formal dance held here in ten years. . . . Entertainment for the evening includes presentation of the colors, a crack drill squad which will demonstrate maneuvers, the traditional grand march, introduction of honored guests, and awarding of gifts and door prizes. The playing of taps will close the dance at 11:45."[25]

As popular as the Cadet Corps was during the war years, many school districts, including Palo Alto and Berkeley, eliminated their programs following the war. Still, the Cadet Corps continued to operate in approximately fifty schools throughout California as of 2016, with almost six thousand student members. Claiming to have trained over a million students during the past one hundred years, the program has six primary objectives, including developing leadership, engendering citizenship, encouraging patriotism, fostering academic excellence, teaching basic military knowledge, and promoting health, fitness, and wellness.[26] In addition, some school districts, rather than eliminating their Cadet Corps programs entirely, transformed them into Junior ROTC units.[27] School officials in Bangor and Leavenworth followed this pattern when they adopted Junior ROTC programs in their schools following World War I.[28] Those programs also continued to function in 2016, along with Junior Army, Navy, and Air Force ROTC units in thousands of public schools across the nation. Almost a half million students currently claim Junior ROTC membership.

The issue of whether schools should maintain Junior ROTC as a cocurricular activity or require student participation as one element of the school program has been contentious for decades. Beginning with the founding of its Junior ROTC unit in 1919, for instance, Bangor High School instituted a two-year Junior ROTC graduation requirement for all male students. In 1957, the local school committee reduced the requirement to one year and, in 1972, dropped it altogether. More recently, the San Francisco School Board became embroiled in a politicized debate over whether to continue to grant PE credit to students participating in the district's Junior ROTC units. Controversy arose when a proposal to eliminate granting PE credit followed by a decision to phase out the program entirely passed in 2006.[29] Although the city school board ultimately voted to restore the program three years later, debate continues over whether the program meets the state standard for PE.[30]

Junior Red Cross

Although female students have been admitted to Junior ROTC units in recent decades, for most of the program's history it prohibited girls from participating. Many, therefore, chose to become members of the Junior Red Cross, which, as with the Junior ROTC, was established in response to defense mobilization during the First World War. Led by Vassar College president Henry Noble MacCracken, the Junior Red Cross (a partnership between the American Red Cross and the nation's public schools) was intended to direct "youthful patriotism" toward "service."[31] In September 1917, just five months following America's entry into World War I, President Woodrow Wilson gave the program a significant boost when he announced its establishment and then asked the nation's schoolchildren, "Is not this perhaps the chance for which you have been looking to give your time and efforts in some way to meet our national needs?"[32]

Junior Red Cross took the form of school auxiliaries to local American Red Cross chapters, with students or their schools paying a twenty-five cent per pupil annual membership fee to the national organization. Many communities responded enthusiastically to the program, so much so that by the end of its first year the Junior Red Cross claimed 8 million student members. During that period students participated in a range of projects, from collecting clothing for war victims to promoting food conservation and planting victory gardens. Junior Red Cross members were also "adept at ringing door bells and making collections," as American Red Cross historian Foster Rhea Dulles has observed, leading them to contribute over $3.5 million toward American Red Cross fund-raising efforts by the war.[33]

As important as was the organization's extraordinary membership rolls and fund-raising capacity, the Junior Red Cross promulgated a form of Americanism infused by "a world perspective."[34] Junior Red Cross leaders believed that education could be used as "a vehicle for improving world relations" and sought to use the public schools to provide students with that education.[35] During and following the war, Junior Red Cross officials promoted a classroom curriculum meant to be used in conjunction with organization activities that encouraged reciprocity and respect in global affairs and international friendship. Especially through "international interschool correspondence," one of America's first international pen-pal programs, Junior Red Cross leaders expected that children would gain a "sympathetic appreciation" for children across the globe. By directly communicating with peers in other parts of the world, claimed one Junior Red Cross staff member, the letter exchange would result in American children developing a "real appreciation of the life of the children and the people of these other countries, instead of merely feeling that America is the one grand country on earth, God's own country."[36]

Although the Junior Red Cross claimed as many as 11 million members at the end of the First World War, student involvement soon began to decline as the United States entered a period of isolation.[37] Throughout the 1920s and early 1930s, however, the organization maintained a following through youth-oriented publications such as *Junior Red Cross News* and by emphasizing public health programs and first aid.[38] Membership again began to rise with the onset of the Great Depression as students assisted in numerous relief projects. It was with America's entrance into World War II, however, that the Junior Red Cross experienced a spike in student interest and participation.[39]

Throughout the nation, the Junior Red Cross served as one of the few organizations dedicated to girls' participation in the Second World War. At Palo Alto High School, female students wrapped bandages at weekly meetings, represented the organization in their academic classes, and sponsored fund drives for Red Cross war services. In November 1943, the school student newspaper, the *Campanile*, reported that Junior Red Cross members raised $226.23 over the course of one week by challenging each classmate to contribute twenty-five cents.[40] With this money students carried out their "box-a-month" and "cake-a-week" war projects, sending cakes and boxes containing cigarettes, toiletries and other "comfort items" to servicemen recuperating from wounds suffered on the battlefield.[41]

Girls' involvement in the Junior Red Cross also occasionally influenced their future plans. One senior, for instance, claimed that she had hoped to become a director of religious education but that her experience with the Junior Red Cross led her to enroll in prenursing courses at nearby Stanford University.[42] Another student, Carolyn Field, reported that the battlefield death of her brother, along with her participation in the Junior Red Cross, led her to enlist in the Cadet Nurse Corps, a federal program designed to increase the number of nursing students in the United States. "It will be a proud day for me when I receive my R.N.," Field told a *Campanile* reporter, "and know that I can carry on the fight that took the life of my brother."[43]

The Victory Corps

As a "total war" involving the active participation of all citizens, including the young, World War II represented a unique moment in the history of American education. Perhaps the decision that most influenced secondary schools during the war years, however, was the lowering of the draft age from twenty-one to eighteen years of age in November 1942.[44] With the federal government forecasting that 80 percent of the country's 1.3 million male high school students between the ages sixteen and eighteen would enter the armed forces following graduation, the assistant secretary of war for air, Robert A. Lovett, and the US commissioner of education, John W. Studebaker, developed a program that aimed to ease the shock high schools were expected to feel when the government lowered the draft age.[45] By September, Lovett and Studebaker had established the "High School Victory Corps," with objectives that included

(1) Guidance of youth into critical services and occupations; (2) wartime citizenship training to insure better understanding of the war, its meaning, progress, and problems; (3) physical fitness; (4) voluntary military drill for selected boys; (5) competence in science and mathematics; (6) pre-flight training in aeronautics for those preparing for air service; (7) pre-induction training for critical occupations; (8) community service including training for essential civilian activities.[46]

According to historian Richard Ugland, the US Office of Education hoped that "the Victory Corps would give substance to the idea of the high school student as reservist."[47] Indeed, a conception of the high school as way station for young men prior to basic training was fully featured in the Victory Corps' characteristics. The program consisted of general membership and five special divisions: land, sea, air, production, and community service. Students within two years of graduation were permitted to join on a voluntary basis, although girls were encouraged to join the latter two divisions due to their probable nonenlistment in the armed forces.[48] Membership criteria included participation in a physical fitness program, involvement in at least one wartime service activity (such as assisting with child care or salvaging scrap metal), and enrolling in "subjects useful to the war effort."[49] Each division had its own insignia, and the program's guidelines encouraged members to wear the Victory Corps' uniform: a white shirt with dark trousers for boys, a white blouse and dark skirt for girls.[50]

Schools throughout the United States adopted the Victory Corps in a variety of ways. Some educators implemented the program as an additional cocurricular activity, while others used it to revise their entire school program. In July 1943, for instance, Dr. Sue Maxwell, chair of the Victory Corps steering committee at Ensley High School in Birmingham, Alabama, published a report in the *American School Board Journal* describing how teachers used the program as a model for reorienting Ensley High's activities to serve the war effort. "Our ideal," she wrote, "is to harness the potential strength of our sixteen hundred pupils for whatever national or community need it can best serve at any given time. . . . Under our plan, all curricular and extracurricular activities center about the Victory Corps."[51] In practice, this meant that Ensley High School's Land Division sponsored a "Victory Book Drive" that resulted in 1,800 volumes being donated to the armed forces, while the Community Division conducted a Red Cross fund drive. The Air Division collected silk and nylon stockings, which the school donated to the army to be made into parachutes and powder bags, while the Production Division planted victory gardens. Maxwell credited the program with boosting PE enrollments, although she also noted that the school had already "swelled the ranks" of its previously existing Junior ROTC unit in an effort to improve male students' physical fitness.[52]

As at Ensley High, many schools around the nation gave the Victory Corps a generally warm reception when it was initially announced. The NEA reported that just over half the schools it surveyed had adopted the program within one year of its inception, with California alone reporting that 17,450 students in eighty high schools claimed membership as early as February 1943.[53] Nevertheless, the Victory Corps soon came under a barrage of criticism, with student participation declining significantly following the end of the 1943 school year. By war's end, less than one-third of the nation's high schools had some form of the program in place.[54]

There are three primary reasons for the Victory Corps' rapid decline. First, the federal government charged harried state and local school administrators with adopting and managing the program. Although this was a pragmatic decision on the part of federal officials who resisted violating the tradition of local school control, it required local and state officials to commit to yet another civil defense responsibility. For some, this was one program too many.[55] Second, federal funding, promised when Lovett and Studebaker initially announced the program, never materialized.[56] Third, some Americans perceived the program's attempt to replicate the military hierarchy within the school as "artificial and unrealistic," while others thought it too "militaristic" and reminiscent of a "Fascist-type youth organization."[57] No less a literary luminary than E. B. White, whose son was about to enter high school at the time, issued a blistering criticism of the Victory Corps in *Harper's Magazine* and *Reader's Digest*. "If we prepare children at an early age for nothing but military triumph," White wrote, "direct their gaze steadily towards the infamous enemy, and indoctrinate them with hatred for opposing peoples, we shall endanger our own position. The best pre-flight training is a view of the whole sky, not a close-up of an instrument panel."[58]

The Victory Corps' overall significance is difficult to assess. Some have strongly criticized the organization as a "piece of wartime Washington folly," while others credit it with stimulating high schools to shift their cocurricular emphases to a greater wartime footing.[59] As Birmingham superintendent L. Frazer Banks observed, the Victory Corps served as "a peg" on which schools could "hang war activities."[60] Yet many schools throughout the United States, such as those in Denver and Salt Lake City, implemented Victory Corps–like changes in their schools without ever actually adopting the program.[61] Moreover, the most popular cocurricular activity during

World War II had nothing to do with the Victory Corps whatsoever and was one that did not belong to any single organization or club.

Stamps and Service

Americans seriously debated the question of how to most productively finance their nation's "arsenal of democracy" during World War II. Opinions ranged from dramatically increasing taxes on defense workers to replicating a system used during World War I that urged citizens to make voluntary long-term loans to the federal government. The Roosevelt administration adopted a modified version of the latter approach in the form of small denomination Series-E Bonds issued for sale to the public. The cost of these bonds was disaggregated into stamps, making an individual stamp affordable to almost every American.[62] US Treasury Department officials quickly recognized the role children and youth might play in marketing the stamps and developed a series of programs to actively involve them, including competitions, rallies, and even a songwriting project.[63] Students wrote songs and submitted them to the Music Educators National Conference (MENC—a professional association of school music teachers), which selected twenty for inclusion in a publication entitled "Songs for Schools at War." The Treasury Department's War Finance Division then issued over fifty thousand copies of the selections to schools across the country.[64] Indeed, the MENC received so many entries that the Treasury Department's War Finance Division published a second collection entitled "New Songs for Schools at War," which included the following, meant to be sung to the tune "Polly Wolly Doodle":

When Hitler started on his march
and took the Balkan land,
And Tojo bombed Pearl Harbor's shore,
amid the waves and sand.
Chorus:
Buy Bonds! Buy Bonds!
Buy Bonds to save our land.
Democracy must never die,
So help our Uncle Sam.
Our boys are fighting for our rights
They're found on every shore.
We must help out, for freedom's cause,
Must stand for evermore.[65]

In addition to participating in the songwriting project, students across the nation seized upon this opportunity to contribute to the war effort. The piano club at Berkeley High School, for example, required war stamps for admission to its "Noon-time Varieties."[66] At Palo Alto High School, students challenged their peers at nearby Sequoia High School to a "war stamp duel."[67] At the height of the competition, Palo Alto students purchased $350 worth of stamps and $125 worth of bonds in one day, with the *Campanile* reporting, "The number of bonds sold exceeded expectations . . . several classes went over the top with the entire class buying 100%."[68] Over fifty years later, Joan Manning remembered the stamp and bond sales and the central role the school played in them. "We all bought stamps and put them in a little book. They were sold through school. Sometimes it set a goal and we tried to meet it."[69] Peter Edmondson recalled both the stamps' value and the primary reason so many students participated: "$18.75 would get you a $25.00 bond," he explained, "and everyone bought them—you did it for patriotism."[70] Paula Minard remembered school rallies, which were held to encourage student involvement in buying and selling the stamps. "It seems to me," Minard recalled, "that there were monitors in the classroom who collected the money and handed out the stamps. There was a lot of enthusiasm."[71]

As enthusiastic as Minard and her classmates were, excitement over competing with a rival school diminished when students learned they could finance the acquisition of military equipment, including ships and planes, through yet another federal program designed to motivate war stamp and bonds sales. Once "purchased," students named the item and the US Office of Education sent the school its picture. Palo Alto High School students, for instance, began their first drive in 1943, seeking to raise $75,000 in stamp and bond sales toward the purchase of a pursuit aircraft. By the end of the first day, the local newspaper reported that students, "spurred by visions of a pursuit plane soaring through the skies with 'Palo Alto' painted across its nose" raised $14,750.[72] Before the end of the war, Palo Alto High School students would finance two pursuit aircraft as well as raise $175,000 to purchase a B-25 bomber. When a picture of "Palo Alto's" bomber arrived, students were thrilled to see the high school's name and "Li'l Viking"—the school's mascot—painted across its fuselage.[73]

As in Palo Alto, patriotism and competition motivated Berkeley students to buy and sell war stamps and bonds. On April 10, 1942, the *Berkeley Jacket* featured a student drawing of the Statue of Liberty with the words "KEEP IT BURNING" written in large letters next to it. The image's caption read, "How can Berkeley High students contribute to the cause of freedom? One way is by the purchase of United States defense stamps. So far 887 patriotic students have purchased stamps. You have until the end of this semester to do your part. Don't put it off."[74] Two weeks later, in an editorial entitled "You Can Do Your Part," one student chastised his classmates who had not been contributing regularly: "Hongkong, Manila, Guam, Burma, Sumatra, Malaya, Singapore—all are dead. Too little; too late. Not enough material or money; the folks back home didn't come through with the goods. Did you ever think it might have been the Defense Stamp you didn't buy that lost those citadels of Democracy? It's up to you whether or not we are going to win this war."[75] Again, as in Palo Alto, Berkeley students committed themselves to financing the purchase of military materiel. In a motivational stunt that proved terrifically successful, the Berkeley High student government arranged to have a P-39 Airacobra fighter plane placed on display in front of the school's academic building.[76] The resulting stamp and bond sales financed the acquisition of the $25,000 aircraft as well as the stern of a "Liberty" transport ship costing $30,000.[77]

Today, many Americans regard the cities of Berkeley and Palo Alto as unique, one for its history of radical protest and the other for its connection to Silicon Valley. In the 1940s, however, both communities typified emerging suburbs, with schools that supported students' patriotic efforts to become involved in the war. Yet as historian William Tuttle describes, not just in emerging suburbs but also in urban areas such as New York City, Los Angeles, Saint Louis, and Chicago, teachers and administrators urged students to demonstrate their patriotism by participating in the war effort.[78] Consequently, nationwide student involvement in buying and selling war stamps and bonds was so great that an award presented to Franklin Roosevelt in 1944 recorded the following: "To President Franklin D. Roosevelt, Commander in Chief of our Armed Forces, AMERICA'S SCHOOL CHILDREN are proud to present 13,500 PLANES, 44,700 JEEPS and other war equipment to the value of $510,000,000 through the purchase of War Bonds during the school year ending June 1944."[79]

This was no small contribution to financing America's war effort, and it succeeded in part because buying and selling war stamps and bonds was a simple and patriotic act in which children and youth could easily participate. Not all cocurricular activities were so straightforward, however. A more logistically complicated but equally important activity that schools urged older students to undertake was harvesting local produce. Throughout the war years, as the armed forces absorbed increasing numbers of able-bodied men into their ranks, fewer remained to work in the nation's fields and factories.[80] Moreover, following the implementation of US Executive Order 9066 in February 1942, Japanese internment resulted in tens of thousands of Japanese Americans who otherwise would have continued working in agriculture being forcibly removed from their jobs. Consequently, the labor shortage became a severe problem as defense plants scrambled to find workers and farmers pleaded with local and state governments for assistance in harvesting crops. As the labor shortage deepened, communities looked to the last abundant pool of cheap labor in the immediate vicinity: the student body.

Schools accepted responsibility for both coordinating access to student labor and rallying students to participate. In Seattle, for instance, schools organized boys and girls to harvest apples on the weekends, transporting them to outlying orchards where they either volunteered their time or received some minimal payment for their work.[81] In Illinois, too, schools served as "contact agents" to register youth and available adults to assist local farmers. In the town of Bethany, the local school board facilitated this process by altering the school calendar so that students attended school six days a week in winter, permitting the school year to end early enough for students to work full time harvesting crops in the spring.[82] In Palo Alto, high school administrators held a school-wide assembly to register students to work in the fields. Reporting on the event, the *Campanile* urged, "This story comes as an earnest appeal to the student body of this institution, loyal to their school and loyal to their country, to forget their football games, their dances, and their good time for just a short while, and devote themselves and their leisure time to the heaviest and most urgent task ever to confront a high school generation, that of saving the crops that feed America and the army defending it."[83]

Although the appeal was quite zealous, the description might not have been far from reality. Farmers in nearby rural communities such as Mountain View and Santa Clara frequently sought student labor to keep their crops from rotting on the vine. Years later, Sally Allen remembered her school sponsoring trips to the fields to pick the ripened fruit. "The yellow school bus came by the school and picked up the kids and took them to whatever orchard or berry farm, or whatever farm needed labor, because most of the labor was working in the factories or building ships."[84] Peter Edmondson remembered receiving seventeen cents a bucket for his labor, while Paula Minard recalled harvesting crops as a junior high school student. "I remember going out one day, getting up at dawn, and being transported to pick green beans! Backbreaking work! And then cutting apricots."[85] These students were not alone. In 1943, Palo Alto superintendent Charles W. Lockwood enthusiastically reported that 213 of Palo Alto High School's 779 students had worked to harvest crops during the previous year.[86] In fact, farmers in the San Francisco Bay Area became so heavily reliant upon student labor that State Senator Byrl R. Salsman introduced legislation into the state assembly proposing to waive PE class if students worked in the fields.[87]

Students seemed delighted to have the opportunity to contribute to the war effort and occasionally earn money (as well as skip PE) by working in local fields and orchards. As one Berkeley student wrote, "America has given us our chance to help. After all the times we high school students have been told that 'Modern Youth Is Soft,' we are being given a chance to prove otherwise. Our parents will have to hold their tongues from now on. So we're off to work, and I'll see you next summer."[88] For some students, however, especially those living in rural areas, working on farms and in orchards during the war years was not at all exceptional; it was a way of life. Through their schools, many of these students became members of the Future Farmers of America (FFA), another school-based organization that identified, among various goals, cultivating student patriotism.

Future Farmers of America

As with the Junior ROTC and the Junior Red Cross, the FFA's founding occurred earlier in the century—in 1928—with the roots of the organization's establishment reaching further back to the industrial and agricultural revolutions of the late nineteenth century. With the development of large-scale, single-crop agriculture in the United States, farmers in the post–Civil War era increasingly found themselves economically hobbled by the need to acquire expensive machinery and fertilizers. Going deeply into debt, farmers then suffered from their own successes as rising crop yields outstripped demand and an oversupply of grains, fruits, and vegetables led to lower prices. Combined with monopolistic practices of railroad and equipment suppliers, as well as the erosion of fertile soil through drought, flood, and overplanting, farmers became locked in a cycle of decline and young people lost interest in farming.[89]

Farmers responded to these challenges by banding together in fraternal associations dedicated to advancing favorable political and economic legislation. These associations, such as the National Grange of the Patrons of Husbandry (popularly known as the Grange), also formed youth organizations through which they sponsored a variety of activities, such as county fair crop and livestock competitions. Meanwhile, members of these associations began advocating the teaching of agricultural subjects in their children's schools, with the Grange launching what one scholar has called "a massive campaign to adapt public school lessons to farm life."[90] Over time, several states, including Virginia, North and South Carolina, and Georgia, passed laws encouraging schools to implement agricultural education curricula, while in 1888 Minnesota established the nation's first agricultural high school for the purpose of teaching students "scientific principles of agriculture," advanced farming methods, and better business practices.[91] Over the next twenty-five years, as farmers' alliances led a "populist crusade" committed to protecting rural ways of life, states established eighty more agricultural schools throughout the nation.[92]

Simultaneously, a parallel development occurred in the nation's urban areas among industrial interests. With America's rise as an industrial power at the end of the nineteenth century, organizations such as the National Association of Manufacturers and the National Society for the Promotion of Industrial Education joined with factory owners, educators, and unionists to implement vocational education programs in the nation's public schools. "Each interest group," historian Larry Cuban writes, "viewed vocational education as a panacea for the economic, social, and schooling problems of the day."[93] In part because of such broad support among a range of interests, vocational education's promoters actively sought financial support from the federal government, which until that time had been largely uninvolved in public schooling.[94] Rather than perceiving agricultural and vocational education as opposing forces, many reformers understood them as two elements of a single movement toward greater social efficiency, both in education and society at large.[95] As President Theodore Roosevelt claimed in a 1907 speech delivered at the fiftieth anniversary celebration of the Michigan Agricultural College (Michigan State University),

> For at least a generation we have been waking to the knowledge that there must be additional education beyond that provided in the public school as it is managed today. Our school system has hitherto been well-nigh wholly lacking on the side of industrial training, of the training which fits a man for the shop and the farm. This is a most serious lack, for no man can look at the peoples of mankind as they stand at present without realizing that industrial training is one of the most potent factors in national development.[96]

As historian Herbert Kliebard has observed, when Congress eventually responded to reformers' demands for federal assistance in 1917, it proceeded from the same position as Roosevelt had espoused ten years earlier by linking "the needs of industry and agriculture under the general aegis of the national interest."[97] The resulting legislation, the Smith-Hughes Act, provided funds for "vocational education," which it defined as occurring in classrooms as well as in youth organizations working in the schools.[98]

Agricultural youth organizations, however, such as the Grange's, had been in existence for decades prior to the passage of the Smith-Hughes Act. During the early 1900s, in particular, teachers established clubs in their schools to engage students' interest in studying agriculture and to promote vocational agriculture programs. The first of these were called "corn clubs" because teachers distributed seed corn to club members and held competitions to see which students could generate the highest yield.[99] Over time the "club movement" spread, with thousands of students participating in a youth corn exhibit at the 1904 Saint Louis World's Fair and a variety of states forming organizations to support school agricultural clubs.[100] In Virginia, officials worked with the state's agricultural teachers' organization to establish the "Future Farmers of Virginia" in 1925.[101] Two years later, South Carolina formed the "Future Palmetto Farmers."[102] These organizations, however, and many others like them, were racially segregated. In 1927, therefore, H. O. Sargent, the US agent for agricultural education for Negroes, and G. W. Owens, a teacher educator at the historically black Virginia State College, formed the "New Farmers of Virginia" to serve African American students. Over the next few years, several southern states formed "New Farmers" chapters, which eventually joined in 1935 to form a national organization, the New Farmers of America.[103]

During this time, white agricultural students representing state organizations had been participating in a national congress held each year in Kansas City, Missouri. They had yet to form a national organization, however, and so in 1928 thirty-three students from eighteen states met to establish the FFA.[104] In the ensuing years, many state agricultural youth organizations, such as the Future Farmers of Virginia and Future Palmetto Farmers, applied and received FFA charter membership.[105] With federal financial support provided through the Smith-Hughes Act, the FFA expanded rapidly. By 1935, the FFA claimed one hundred thousand members.[106]

FFA members participated in a range of activities at the local, state, and national levels. They studied "scientific methods of farming" in their vocational agriculture classes, worked on chapter-owned farms, prepared crop and livestock exhibits for state fairs, engaged in community service activities such as planting shelterbelts to control wind erosion, and sponsored a variety of leadership development and social events.[107] In Minnesota, FFA students participated in public speaking contests, formed musical groups and athletic teams, and toured various states as well as Canada for the purpose of giving the students, according to a local chapter advisor, "a broader view of life, to study the modes of agriculture in others states, visit and inspect places of interest, and for general recreation and education."[108] Describing the primary objectives of these activities, J. A. Linke, a regional agent for the Federal Board for Vocational Education, claimed that the FFA promoted scholarship, encouraged habits of putting ideals into practice, and developed "a love of country."[109] As for their educational effectiveness, one educator claimed in 1943 that the FFA "constitutes one of the most effective teaching devices discovered up to the present time."[110] Yet as historian D. Barry Croom has described, the FFA's place in local school agricultural programs was quite complex. State and federal employees administered the FFA, although it was a private organization, and agricultural students participated in FFA activities including field trips and summer camps, presenting local school boards with a host of liability issues.[111] Consequently, the organization sought and received a federal charter in 1950 that identified its several purposes, one of which was "to develop character, train for useful citizenship, and foster patriotism, and thereby develop competent and aggressive rural and agricultural leadership."[112]

Fifteen years following the receipt of its federal charter, the FFA merged with the segregated fifty-eight-thousand-member New Farmers of America. In 1969, the FFA officially granted women membership in the national organization (prior to this time, women participated as members of state and local chapters but were prohibited from membership in the national association).[113] By the late 1980s, in large part because of dramatic changes in agricultural production in the United States, the FFA transformed itself from an organization oriented around farming in rural communities to one dedicated more generally to youth development. Changing its name to the "National FFA Organization," it began welcoming student-members who had "diverse interests in the industry of agriculture, encompassing science, business and technology." In 1982, members elected their first female president and, in 1994, their first African American president (who was also the organization's first president residing in an urban area). Today, the National FFA claims over a half million members, 70 percent of whom reside in rural areas.[114]

School-based cocurricular activities have encouraged patriotism among students for well over a century. Especially during wartime, schools have sought to engage students in clubs and activities through which they could demonstrate their patriotic spirit and engage in civic acts that are not just symbolic and educationally formative but contribute directly and substantially to the public good. If wartime mobilization has reached directly into schools, not only to prepare students for military service but also to enlist an even wider number of students in civilian contributions to the war effort, national interest in economic power and farmers' interests in preserving the productive capacity of the land and their way of life came together in students' "patriotic" planting of shelterbelts to control erosion, state fair exhibits, and practice in "agricultural leadership." In this respect, the work of the FFA could be interpreted as a hybrid of the Progressives' vision of direct student-citizen involvement in social problem solving and Theodore Roosevelt's commitments to both land preservation and national greatness.

Indeed, the FFA club movement has features we can endorse as aspects of sound civic education. First, it grew out of cooperative grassroots networks that sought collective solutions to common problems, and it provided opportunities for active learning that prepared students to become leaders in such cooperative networks. Second, it promoted science-based, sustainable farm practices and wide—even international—networking to promote collective assessment and dissemination of best practices. Finally, it associated this conception of active and intelligent, problem-solving citizenship with the idea that patriotism can be manifested in efforts to collectively preserve and enhance a rural way of life and system of production that is foundational to the well-being of the wider society.

We have seen in this chapter and the previous two that attempts to teach patriotism in American schools have rested on a variety of rationales and conceptions of patriotism and civic virtue and have made use of several methods of instruction and forms of learning associated with different aspects of patriotism and virtues generally. We have also seen that attempts to cultivate patriotism have sometimes been controversial. In chapter 4, we will take a closer look at these historical roots of the current debate over patriotic education and address the most important enduring questions at stake. We argue that if the aim of patriotic education has been to motivate civic responsibility, then a serious examination of the merits of such education will not content itself with speculation about what is conducive to motivation in the civic, or any other, sphere.

FOUR

The Education We Need

Few individuals will come to embrace the commitments of liberal [i.e., freedom-respecting] society through a process of rational inquiry. If children are to be brought to accept these commitments as valid and binding, the method must be a pedagogy that is far more rhetorical than rational. . . . Civic education . . . requires a . . . noble, moralizing history; a pantheon of heroes who confer legitimacy on central institutions and constitute worthy objects of emulation.

—William Galston[1]

The city-states of the ancient Greek world conferred authority on their laws by attributing them to gods, and American public education in the late nineteenth century did something similar in constructing itself as an institution of "civil religion." We saw in chapter 2 how it did this by shaping the narrative and pedagogy of US history to enshrine national heroes and triumphs, instill national pride, foster an "Americanizing" sense of shared history or common identity, and cultivate obedient and loyal citizenship. It accepted a measure of mythology, worshipful reverence for the country's "immortal" Founding Fathers, and forced participation in ritual pledging of allegiance as part of an instructional approach modeled on religious practices designed to instill religious faith and inspire good deeds. It is safe to assume that in doing so it sacrificed opportunities to promote a sound understanding of historical processes, the country's failings, and how its problems might be remedied. In that era of US imperial expansion, military drill was also introduced into schools with the idea of instilling patriotism, and the indoctrinating character of the Junior ROTC's "cadet creed" was unmistakable: "I am loyal and patriotic. I am the future of the United States of America." What could this have meant if not a future of further imperial conquest, in which all citizens are equal but citizen-soldiers are even *more equal*?

What should we think of this model of patriotic education? Should we agree with the eminent political theorist William Galston that "few adults of liberal societies will ever move beyond the kind of civic commitment engendered by such a pedagogy"?[2] Can widespread civic commitment only be engendered through a mythologizing "rhetorical" or quasi-religious form of instruction? Many thoughtful commentators have focused on the distortions of history a mythologizing approach may involve and have insisted that such distortions are miseducational and should be avoided.[3] Others have defended a role for "mythic stories of heroism and nation building," sometimes arguing that historical narratives are inevitably selective and the omissions of moralizing history need not disqualify it as properly educational.[4] We think that misrepresentations should be avoided, and that they are unnecessary.

A larger concern of this chapter is that the instructional possibilities are scarcely exhausted by "rational inquiry" into the merits of democratic institutions and quasi-religious initiation into a national mythology. The aim of patriotic education has been to motivate civic responsibility, and a serious examination of the merits of such education would not content itself with speculation about what is conducive to motivation in the civic sphere or any other. It would consult the large and growing body of research on motivation and cast a wider net in considering the varieties and aspects of education that may be relevant to civic motivation.

Distortions of history aside, what should we think about the more indoctrinating aspects of a pedagogy of civil religion—rituals of hero worship, celebrations replete with unexamined messages, the Pledge of Allegiance, and the smuggling of moral doctrines and exemplars into elementary language arts? There is not one agreed upon analysis of what defines indoctrination, but requiring students to repeat morally charged formulas they are not expected to understand or examine is certainly one of its hallmarks.[5] What is objectionably indoctrinating can often be judged only in a wider educational context, however.

What is perhaps most importantly at stake in this regard is the matter of government legitimacy, which we addressed in the introduction to this book and will expand upon later in this chapter. Galston speaks of mythologized heroes as conferring legitimacy on civic institutions, but the perceived legitimacy so conferred might undermine the legitimacy essential to justifying government acts. Galston's suggestion is essentially that few people will ever comprehend or be moved by the actual merits of institutions that would justify supporting them, so it is acceptable to secure the public's support through myth that conveys the essential moral truth that the institutions are worthy of respect. This is not how the ideal of democratic self-government is supposed to work, however, and it is surely a violation of respect for students as developing rational beings to assume that they cannot comprehend or be moved by the actual merits (and deficiencies) of institutions.

A related worry is the understanding of loyal and obedient citizenship underlying rituals of reverence for national leaders and the flag. Obedience as such is not a virtue, and loyalty is at best a highly circumscribed virtue.[6] Loyalty among friends who are worthy of each other's devotion can be virtuous if it is reciprocal, autonomy affirming, and tempered by good judgment. We all value friends who stand by us in time of need, help us succeed, and do not try to control us.[7] By contrast, loyalty within hierarchies has often been understood to require the blind obedience of subordinates, which cannot be morally required because it is inconsistent with subordinates functioning as responsible moral agents. The loyal fulfillment of the duties of citizenship has often been associated with military service, and superior orders in the US armed services were regarded as absolutely binding until 1944, when the implications of this policy for prosecuting war crimes became obvious.[8] The notions of loyal and obedient citizenship in late nineteenth- and early twentieth-century US public schools may have transferred to the civilian sphere an idea that was problematic even in a military context.

Writing in June 1943 for the US Supreme Court majority that vindicated the Jehovah's Witnesses in their challenge to coerced pledging of allegiance to the flag, Justice Robert Jackson cited the "fast failing efforts of our present totalitarian regimes" as an example of the futility of "coercive elimination of dissent" that can only lead to the "unanimity of the graveyard." And it was Justice Jackson again who—on leave from the Court and serving as the chief US prosecutor at the Nuremberg Trials in November 1945—affirmed the individual responsibility of those who in the conduct of war violated common "ethical principles" that were ignored during the age of imperialistic expansion but enshrined in international law during the 1920s.[9] Together, these positions imply that absolute loyalty can be neither expected nor excused.

One of the Nazi officials whom Jackson succeeded in convicting of war crimes and crimes against humanity was Albert Speer. In the course of his twenty-year prison sentence, Speer evidently struggled with what he had done out of loyalty to Hitler and ultimately concluded that "there is only one valid kind of loyalty: to morality."[10] Should we agree that there is no uniformly or unconditionally virtuous form of loyalty but loyalty to morality as such—or to everything of value morality protects? Perhaps, but we could preserve the common intuition that loyalty is a virtue by insisting that loyalty to a person, government, or country is only virtuous if its devotion is limited by an overriding commitment to honoring the requirements of common morality in everything one does.

Another central and potentially separable feature of the quasi-religious form of US public education was the "Americanizing" of immigrants. By Mary Antin's own account, learning the story of George Washington elicited in her "a sense of dignity" and striving to conduct herself as a "Fellow Citizen" of Washington when she realized they were "related" to each other by common citizenship. Identity and pride are important features of this example, no less than emulation. US history textbooks invoke and encourage the sharing of a common American identity through reference to "our" country and heritage and what "we" Americans have done.[11] Although there may be distortions of that heritage, it is important to ask whether an educationally sound cultivation of a sufficiently inclusive, common civic identity is possible. To deny it is possible, one would have to think that countries normally lack objects of warranted national pride that could focus young citizens' aspirations for a future they might collectively attain. If most countries do have such objects of national pride, then cultivating a shared identity that grounds commitment to a "more perfect union" might be easily reconciled with honest history.[12]

To the extent that the cultivation of a common American identity facilitates civic-minded cooperation that transcends differences of language, national origin, and culture, one could see it as promoting a valuable form of civic friendship. Rituals and celebrations of solidarity that furthered this end might be legitimately educative and quite valuable, if they succeeded without compelling belief, undermining government legitimacy, or limiting the understanding essential to efficacious collective action. Before a democratic public can be motivated to cooperate in civically responsible collective action, it must conceive itself as a public that can solve problems through democratic cooperation. The perception of oneself as belonging to a public is inescapably a question of identity, and it is reasonable to assume that a sense of belonging or membership in a public is itself a source of motivation, as we noted in the introduction to this book. Identity is an essential aspect of patriotism, moreover. Scholarly questions about patriotic motivation often focus on love, but love of a country is not patriotism unless one perceives or feels the country is one's own.[13]

There may also be no good grounds for objecting to the exemplars of virtue portrayed in the McGuffey's Readers. These follow an ancient pattern still evident in a great deal of contemporary literature: a character exemplifies some virtue and is portrayed in an admiring light as suitable for emulation, and the idea that virtue is essential to happiness is illustrated and repeated. If what is exemplified *is* indeed a virtue and it is *true* that virtue is essential to happiness, there may be no harm in this form of moral instruction as long as students are later engaged, as suits their age and maturity, with literature and inquiry that advance their moral understanding and maturity beyond these most elementary lessons.[14]

The rationale for the dominant approach to patriotic education in US history has been, overwhelmingly, the perceived need to Americanize and integrate newly arriving immigrants, so as to prevent their social and civic isolation and ensure their loyalty, especially in times of war. How far these efforts were necessary or proved successful is hard to say, but one obvious effect of them was to create markers of loyalty—of who is "us" and who is "them"—that made Americans without those marks targets of persecution. Recall the movement to establish English as the singular language of instruction in public schools and description of German as a "sinister tongue," and the violent persecution of Jehovah's Witnesses following the 1940 Supreme Court ruling that upheld the constitutionality of making the pledge to the flag compulsory. A lesson of such examples is that efforts to motivate good citizenship should take care to minimize the potential for persecution. We will also press some basic questions about what patriotism is supposed to be and what motivates good citizenship. Is patriotism essential to motivating responsible citizenship? Can it be cultivated in schools effectively and with greater benefit and less risk than any available alternatives would provide?

We saw in chapter 1 how a different model of civic education emerged in the Progressive Era, one equally dedicated to the cultivation of patriotism, but based on a conception of the good citizen as "a person who habitually conducts himself with proper regard for the welfare of the communities of which he is a member, and who is active and intelligent with his fellow members to that end."[15] This Progressive "community civics" model reflected a less hierarchical and more cooperative conception of democratic citizenship and supplemented "appropriate literature" and "noble characters in history" with a problem-based curriculum and experiential, community-based learning that encouraged students to fulfill their civic responsibilities by investigating and working to solve actual problems—"unanswered questions which the pupil recognizes as important and which he really strives to unravel."[16] It also rejected imperialism and other assertions of national interest that were contrary to norms of international justice. The motivational core of good citizenship was conceived not as an attitude of reverence, national pride, or something of the sort, but as an instinct of "social feeling" or devotion to "the common interest." It is reasonable to ask whether "regard for the welfare of the communities" to which one belongs is a form of motivation that can be cultivated in schools. It is also reasonable to ask, as we will in chapter 6, whether a sense of membership in, and regard for the welfare of, a global community can be cultivated.

We saw in chapter 3 how schools not only facilitated military training during World War II, but also involved students in broader war-related public service: Junior Red Cross projects, funding America's "arsenal of democracy" through war bonds and stamps, and providing critically needed farm labor. We also saw how farmers' fraternal organizations and the agricultural club movement involved students in land preservation, community service, educational travel, and other activities to prepare them for patriotic citizenship and "competent and aggressive rural and agricultural leadership." The extracurricular club activities of the Junior Red Cross and the FFA, the community civics pedagogy, and the Bay Area students' extracurricular fundraising and farm labor were all similar in involving students in community service and problem solving in ways that developed their capacity to serve in responsible adult roles. The exercise and development of students' civic agency sets these experiences apart from most school learning and would have been motivating in ways that are often unrecognized in discussions of patriotic education. One aspect of such motivation is evident in the Berkeley High School student's remark that "after all the times we high school students have been told that 'Modern Youth Is Soft,' we are being given a chance to prove otherwise."[17] As we explain later in this chapter, there can be no doubting that experiences of competence, self-determination, and positive social connection play large motivational roles in sustaining civic engagement.

The task of the remainder of this chapter will be to sketch a general theory of the education we need, as a basis for understanding what could constitute responsible civic education and what role, if any, the cultivation of patriotism would play in such education. Is there a genuinely virtuous form of patriotism, one that is appropriately responsive to what is valuable not just at home but abroad, moves us to cooperate as widely as circumstances call for, avoids destructive racialized and authoritarian responses to perceived threats, offers and appraises dissent in the public interest on its rational merits, and faces challenges with courage, endurance, and restraint? If there is a virtuous form of patriotism, can it be taught or nurtured in schools? *Should* it be taught or nurtured in schools, and, if so, by what means?

We will begin by distinguishing the various ethically significant aspects of education that are at stake, identifying relevant principles, and sketching a view of the education that justice requires. We will identify understanding, virtues, and capabilities as the fundamental forms of personal development at which education should aim, and it is on this basis that we will define the basic components of civic virtue and civic education. We will argue that civic intelligence, civic friendship, and civic competence are the components of civic virtue that must be animated by the right motivation to sustain responsible citizenship. We will argue that there are educable forms of motivation strongly associated with the aspects of our acts corresponding to these components of civic virtue. We will also argue that the motivational core of civic virtue with respect to one's country consists of valuing the country's many valuable aspects. If it makes sense to identify virtuous patriotism as the motivational core of civic virtue with respect to a country, and if patriotic acts of civic virtue are motivated by caring about one's country, there are ways in which ethically responsible education can shape patriotic sentiment.

The Ethical Dimensions of Education

Education is a kind of governance of the activities of learners, and we can distinguish five different basic ethical questions about governance that concern education.[18] The five ethical questions about governance are, What are its proper aims? What authority does it rest on? What responsibilities does it entail? How, or in what manner, should it be conducted? What should its communicated content be? Corresponding to these ethical questions about governance are related subdivisions of philosophy of education pertaining to the *aims* of education and associated ideas about its nature; the authority to educate (its basis, limits, and distribution); the extent and assignment of responsibility to educate adequately and equitably; the conduct of teaching and of educational institutions generally; and curricular and noncurricular educational content. These questions mark off five forms of political justice and five corresponding divisions of educational philosophy in which questions of justice arise. The significance of these distinctions for defining responsible civic education is that there are five distinct ethical aspects of it to be addressed.

We must also face a perennial question of educational justice: To what extent can educating children for the common good be reconciled with educating them for their own good? Justice demands a reconciliation. It requires that educational institutions promote the good of all learners while simultaneously promoting the good of society. This was certainly the aim of John Dewey, Harold Rugg, and other Progressive educators. Writing with the devastation of World War I in mind, Dewey also recognized, however, that societies must strive—as a matter of both global justice and national prudence—for education that promotes both the good of individual students and the common good of humanity.[19] Here too, justice seems to demand that the two be reconciled, and prudence demands this as well in a context of global interdependence. Should students not be equipped with cosmopolitan moral sensibilities as "citizens of the world" who are ready to cooperate globally as well as nationally, in the interest of solving common problems? Are patriotism and cosmopolitanism fundamentally opposed, as some argue, or can they be reconciled?[20] If they cannot be reconciled, and justice and the future well-being of Americans can only be secured through greater global cooperation, then the case for abandoning patriotism as a goal of civic education would be simple.

Our view is that *virtuous* patriotism would be properly responsive to the value of one's country and properly responsive to the value of other countries as well. The fundamental boundaries of proper response would be determined in both cases by requirements of universal justice and respect for persons, and within those boundaries there must be some room for committing oneself to civic projects within different civic spheres. We hold, as many others have, that compliance with the requirements of universal morality and justice would leave room for limited patriotic partiality in advancing the good of one's own country, but we take a country's good to essentially involve and depend on commitments to both global and domestic justice.[21] Our immediate task is not to explain this view of virtuous patriotism, however, but to explain the philosophy of education on which our whole approach to civic education is based.

Universal Respect for Persons

An ethic of governance that encompasses all five of the ethical dimensions we have named would provide the basis for a comprehensive account of the ethics of education generally and the ethics of civic education in particular. With this in mind, we begin from the idea of an ethic of respect for persons as rational agents, by which philosophers mean the respect that persons owe each other as self-determining individuals who act in pursuit of things or "ends" they value.[22] This ethic has long been associated with the Golden

Rule, but in the world of moral theory it is usually attributed to Immanuel Kant, who argued that it grounds moral duties of nonviolence, noncoercion, truth telling, and mutual aid. The logic by which these duties can be justified is essentially this: Suppose first of all that morality is impartial in the sense that it accords all persons equal respect, and suppose that such impartiality is assured by considering only some very general facts about the human condition. Each of us should consider that we are rational agents who have ends we wish to fulfill, that we are finite agents who are vulnerable and have limited knowledge and capacity to fulfill those ends, and that there are a multitude of other finite agents whose aid could often enable us to better fulfill our ends at little cost to themselves. Kant argues that in light of these facts it is rational for us all to accept norms of self-restraint, mutual respect, and cooperation in sharing information and aiding each other when it is not too costly to do so.[23] The way Kant puts it is (roughly) that we could not choose to make it a universal law that beings like us would not cooperate in a variety of ways, if we realized that as finite rational beings we may have ends we will not be able to fulfill without the cooperation of others.

We should regard the duties of common morality justified in this way as authoritative in all spheres of human activity, and as such they will constrain the manner in which citizens and states deal with each other. What is required most obviously is what we have referred to as *legitimacy*: that the interactions between citizens and governments be transacted primarily through truthful and reasoned instruction, persuasion, and consultation, and only as a last resort through force or violence. These duties of common morality will also partially define the content of governance or laws that pertain to duties not to harm and the protection of basic rights. The content of law can be only partially determined in this way because natural moral duties are not enough to fully define the specific property rights people will have, or how much risk they may impose on each other, or how far they can go in withholding aid. To fulfill our basic duty to not harm the people with whom we interact, what we must do is join them in negotiating a social contract that defines mutually agreeable terms of interaction. The effect of entering into such a contract is to create a common rule of law and government with power to administer it.[24]

We can already see elements of this ethic of respect in the philosophy of Socrates, who envisioned a social and political order regulated by reason-giving. Following Socrates, a central theme of Plato's and Aristotle's moral and political thought was that an ethic of respect for persons as rational beings requires that societies be regulated as much as possible by truthful and reasoned persuasion and instruction and only as a last resort by force and violence. A basic question at issue was how this can be achieved. Socrates presented himself as able to induce the young men of Athens to rationally examine their beliefs and change their ways, however bad their prior education may have been. If this was intended as a model of how education could enable a society to reason together, Plato repudiates it in the opening lines of the *Republic*, through a depiction of an encounter between Socrates, walking with his companion Glaucon, and Polemarchus and his associates:

> Polemarchus said: It looks to me, Socrates, as if you two are starting off for Athens.
> Socrates: It looks the way it is, then, I said.
> Do you see how many we are? He said.
> I do.
> Well, you must either prove stronger than we are, or you will have to stay here.
> Isn't there another alternative, namely, that we persuade you to let us go?
> *But could you persuade us, if we won't listen?*
> Certainly not, Glaucon said.
> Well, we won't listen; you'd better make up your mind to that.[25]

Plato endorses Socrates's vision of a social and political order mediated by reason-giving and respect for persons as rational beings, rather than force and violence, but the point of this exchange is to pose the question of how this vision could be achieved without systematic investment in education that prepares people to be reasonable.

Plato and Aristotle both regarded such education as an inalienable public responsibility, because being rationally self-determining is fundamental to an individual's ability to live well, and because being reasonable and understanding the merits of a just system of law would prepare a society's members to accept the reasonable burdens of law in the only way that could be consistent with respecting them as (developing) rational beings.[26] If human rational self-determination and understanding are attributes that develop over time and with the aid of education, then it is also likely that what actually establishes a rule of law is not so much the threat of legal penalties but efforts to nurture a degree of civic understanding and moral self-determination sufficient for recognizing and responding to the reasonableness of reasonable laws.[27] A rule of law whereby individuals generally understand and comply with laws voluntarily is one that will therefore require a wide cultivation of powers of discrimination in matters of justice and the public interest. It will also require efforts to ensure the legal system is worthy of respect.[28] And what is true of cooperation with the law is true of civic responsibility more broadly. Education can lay foundations for a rational appreciation of the merits of a system of law and government, but as Justice Black wrote in his concurring opinion in *West Virginia State Board of Education v. Barnette*, "Love of country must spring from willing hearts and free minds, inspired by a fair administration of wise laws enacted by the people's elected representatives within the bounds of express constitutional prohibitions."[29]

Just Institutions

The deduction of principles of universal morality outlined above depended on only the most general aspects of the "human condition" or situation of finite rational agents. Anglo-American political philosophy since the 1960s has often pursued a similar strategy in order to construct an impartial specification of fair terms of social cooperation. The work that set this in motion and that has dominated discussion is John Rawls's 1971 classic, *A Theory of Justice*. It begins with the idea of a society as a "fair system of social cooperation over time from one generation to the next," the idea of citizens as "free and equal persons" who are open to finding and agreeing to fair terms of social cooperation, and the idea of principles of justice as a specification of those fair terms of cooperation.[30] Rawls offers a thought experiment in which there are representatives who must determine the principles of justice. They are to know the general truths of human nature and society, including "the basis of social organization and the laws of human psychology," but in order to ensure their impartiality they are not to know particular facts about themselves, their place in society, or those they represent.[31] He argues that from behind this "veil of ignorance" they will select principles of justice that guarantee equal and extensive rights and liberties (pertaining to speech, freedom of movement, and so on), fair equality of opportunity with respect to employment and election to offices, and limits on inequality.

Rawls identified self-respect as a *primary good* or all-purpose foundation for a good life, and he was sensitive to the impact of institutions on self-respect and opportunities to pursue divergent conceptions of a good life. Yet, his principles of justice are primarily concerned with the generation and distribution of wealth and income. His critics have suggested other aspects of the human condition as also having fundamental importance, such as the benefits of cooperative production and sharing of knowledge and the inevitability of physical and cognitive dependence early in life and often late in life and in between.

Our own approach is to take a step back from the question Rawls puts to representatives behind the veil of ignorance, and ask what the aims and guiding principles of society's major institutions should be.[32] Our conception of these aims, inspired by the idea of *eudaimonia* or living well in Aristotle's ethical writings, begins with the idea that people all want to live well—to live in ways that are satisfying and worthy of admiration. Because people all want to live well, despite having different ideas about what living well entails, representatives behind the veil of ignorance would agree that the institutions of a society would exist to enable all of its members to live well and should (as far as possible) provide opportunities sufficient to enable all of them to do so and thereby provide each other such opportunities. When representatives behind the veil of ignorance consider what institutions must provide in order for everyone to live well, they could consult what is known about basic human needs, including basic psychological needs.

It is now well confirmed cross-culturally and across the life span that there are universal basic psychological needs whose satisfaction is both essential to living well and strongly influenced by the way institutions function.[33] As it happens, they also play an important role in human motivation, regulating not only the direct impact of institutional designs on human well-being but also the impact of those designs on the quality of individuals' contributions to the fulfillment of institutional purposes. A workplace designed to be good for workers by facilitating the satisfaction of these needs in doing good work can expect better worker productivity than a workplace that is not good for workers. A school designed to allow teachers and students to fulfil their needs and experience competence, self-determination, and positive connections to each other in doing good work would similarly be more educationally productive than a school that is not good for them.

This is one illustration of a basic idea in self-determination theory (SDT), the most comprehensive body of theory and research on motivation currently available, namely, that subjective well-being or happiness is psychologically associated with fulfilling basic human potentials in "positive" or admirable ways.[34] The objective and subjective aspects of living well are, in other words, significantly related to one another through the satisfaction of basic psychological needs. Basic psychological needs theory (BPNT), a component of SDT, posits three innate, universal psychological needs associated with the satisfaction of human productive, intellectual, and social potentials: the need for *competence* or efficacy, the need for *self-determination* rooted in values with which the agent wholeheartedly identifies, and the need for *relatedness* or the experience of mutually affirming relationships. Frustration of these needs to fulfill personal potential is manifested in depressed affect, lack of energy and sense of purpose or meaning in engaging tasks, elevated error rates, and symptoms of stress and psychic conflict, such as headaches and sleep disturbances.

The evidence of hundreds of studies spanning diverse cultures and life stages suggests that the satisfaction of all three of these basic psychological needs is essential to, and a predictor of, the experience of happiness and related aspects of psychological well-being, such as a sense of purpose or meaning.[35] In addition, there is an important role for standards of success or excellence in the "positive" fulfillment of potential that is linked to satisfaction of these needs. The experience of competence will not reliably occur without efforts that are confirmed by others as measuring up to standards of competence or excellence, and the experience of success in self-determination typically requires the possession and exercise of intellectual virtues. A person is unlikely to experience competence as a cook, for example, if no one likes the food he prepares; and people with terrible judgment may experience a lot of frustration in making decisions for themselves. However, it is in the satisfaction of relatedness needs that the role of virtues of character is clearest. A person's psychic well-being is impaired not only by the failure of others to affirm her worth, but also by her own failures to affirm the value of others.[36] The importance of possessing virtue to being happy has been substantially vindicated, in other words.

Relying on these psychological findings, representatives behind the veil of ignorance would conclude that the fulfillment of basic human potentials in ways that satisfy related psychological needs for self-determination, mutually affirming relatedness, and competence is both sufficient for living well and compatible with a plurality of reasonable conceptions of a good life.[37] While there are aspects of existing cultures and institutions that hinder human flourishing, the diversity of forms of competence, mutually respectful relationships, and spheres of self-determination assures a wide scope for individual and cultural expression compatible with a public responsibility to ensure universal access to these essential goods. What should be impartially agreed upon is that living well requires the acquisition and exercise of virtues, development and use of powers or capabilities to act, and understanding what one is doing. These necessities for living well reflect the structure of human action. We act from our values and beliefs, making use of our capacities; and virtues, understanding, and capabilities are the corresponding forms of excellence required to act and live well. A person's success in acting requires that she be well equipped with respect to all of the fundamental dimensions of action, and to have virtues, capabilities, and understanding *is* to be well equipped with respect to the fundamental dimensions of action or forms of potential that come together in everything we do.

Recognizing that these are necessities for living well that people can only obtain in favorable circumstances, representatives behind the veil of ignorance would agree that a society's basic institutions should include educational ones, whose function is to promote forms of development conducive to living well. Moreover, they would agree that the arrangements and institutions of society should in general facilitate both the acquisition of personal qualities essential to living well and the expression of those qualities in the activities of a good life.

The Education That Justice Requires

If the foregoing is correct, then a defining attribute of just societies is that they provide all of their members with educational institutions whose basic function is to promote forms of development conducive to living well.[38] More specifically, these institutions will promote the acquisition of understanding, virtues of intellect and character, and capabilities, in circumstances favorable to expressing these developing attributes in rewarding and admirable activity.[39] The institutions will promote such development largely by coaching learners in structured activities through which their capabilities, understanding, perception, desire, and attachment to things of value develop, all in connection with acquiring related vocabularies, forming identities, and finding meaning and direction in life. Philosophers of education refer to this as initiating students into practices pertaining to goods.[40] A few examples of the diverse goods to which attachment becomes possible are powerful ideas; artistry in diverse domains of performance; qualities of craftsmanship; communities of civic, professional, or recreational practice; and aspects of the natural world. An introduction to a variety of such goods expands a student's understanding of value, while offering room for choice and resources and standards for critical thinking and judgment. Finding the activities of one's life meaningful is an essential aspect of living well, and such learning offers opportunities to live well in part by expanding the range of goods that might lend meaning to a life and doing so in conjunction with nurturing capabilities through which learners can relate to those goods in significant and productive ways.

We wrote in the previous section that the institutions of a just society exist to enable all of its members to live well and should (as far as possible) provide opportunities sufficient to enable all of them to do so and thereby provide each other such opportunities. Educational institutions should accordingly promote development that is not only directly conducive to students' acquisition of attributes essential to living well, but also instrumentally conducive to maintaining and strengthening the society's capacity to enable all its members to live well. The practices into which students are initiated should therefore include ones preparatory to sustaining the range of just institutions essential to a just society. There should be a variety of practices favorable to diverse children finding what is conducive to their own flourishing, but also a favoring of practices that are important to a functional, sustainable, and legitimate social, civic, and global order conducive to everyone living well.

Initiation into practices of inquiry, evaluation, and self-examination would be essential to the cultivation of both intellectual and moral virtues, inasmuch as good judgment is a defining aspect of true moral virtue and essential to competent self-determination in life and in many activities. The formation of good judgment has a long history of being considered a central or overarching aim of a liberal or general education, but it is an admittedly daunting task.[41] A variety of considerations and bodies of research suggest that the educational promotion of self-governance in accordance with good judgment should begin in forms of character education that orient children to thinking things through before acting. It would involve instruction in critical thinking and practice in analyzing case studies in judgment and choice. It would use integrated curricula and inquiry-based learning that provide experience in bringing the resources of diverse disciplinary and analytical frameworks to bear on matters of importance to students' present and future lives. It would ground all of this in school cultures favorable to such learning—school cultures that make learning meaningful for more students by "addressing their needs . . . establishing caring relationships with adults, maintaining positive and high expectations, and providing students with opportunities to participate and contribute."[42]

With regard to school culture, we know quite a bit about the role of basic psychological needs satisfaction in sustaining student effort, and the role of socially nurturing, autonomy-supportive, and optimally challenging school environments in meeting those needs.[43] Small schools can more easily function as cooperative learning communities that meet children's relational needs, and the strengthening of teacher-student relationships lends itself to educationally productive forms of character education and classroom management—ones that cultivate virtues of self-governance by engaging students in forms of self-reflection and self-management, rather than relying on regimes of control dominated by extrinsic rewards and punishments.[44]

Moral or character virtues are among the attributes we have identified as apt targets for education, and it is important to be clear about what they are and how they might be cultivated. Moral virtues are clusters of related dispositions of desire, emotion, perception, belief, conduct, and responsiveness to reasoning and evidence. Considered as merely habitual, they might be blind to relevant factors and lead people to act badly—as a person may do in acting out of loyalty and with insufficient regard for other important considerations. By contrast, a true moral virtue or virtuous state of character would be sensitive to the full range of ethically relevant factors in a situation and would be guided by good judgment. The moral motivation associated with true virtue is responsive to everything of moral value that is at stake in the situation in which a person acts, and this is only possible if a person is well attuned to everything of moral relevance. The heart of moral motivation is valuing what has moral value, beginning with persons and other sentient beings, their flourishing, and the necessities essential to their flourishing or living well.[45] Moral motivation disposes a person to be appropriately responsive to the goodness of what is morally good and the badness of what is morally bad in the world she inhabits.

How are true moral virtue and moral motivation acquired? The simple answer is that moral virtue and the motivation it involves are acquired through experiencing a nurturing and just social environment and through guided practice in acting well and becoming better.[46] The supervision and coaching of practice would call learners' attention to factors that are relevant to decisions, provide a related moral vocabulary and explanations, and guide them in exercising the forms of discernment, imagination, reasoning, and judgment on which good decisions are based. Moral motivation is *autonomously* responsive to what is good and bad, and reference to the psychology of motivation is essential to understanding how such motivation is acquired.

SDT conceives of human beings as having innate propensities to act, explore, learn, form relationships, and self-integrate or organize themselves as psychically integrated agents who act from coherent sets of values and goals they accept as their own. People don't need to be given reasons or externally motivated to do these things. Actions flowing from such propensities are intrinsically motivated and often accompanied by "inherently satisfying internal conditions" such as enjoyment, vitality, a sense of purpose, and satisfaction of basic psychological needs. Organismic integration theory, another key subtheory of SDT, distinguishes four grades of internalization or adoption of motivating goals and values that are not innate, ordered from least to most autonomous: controlled, introjected, identified, and integrated.[47] Action owing to controlled motivation is stimulated by an external force, such as a superior's direct orders, threat of punishment, or offer of a reward. Motivation is introjected when threats of such punishment, shaming, or other external sanctions are internalized and agents act so as to avoid these internalized threats, without accepting the value or goal as their own. Action arising from identified motivation is attributable to values or goals people identify with or accept as their own, on the strength of reasons and a perception that they are free to accept the reasons and embrace the values or goals or not, as they see fit.[48] SDT classifies this as a form of autonomous motivation. Further self-examination and self-regulatory striving yields integrated motivation in which the values a person identifies with form a more coherent whole and are more seamlessly deployed in response to the complex particulars of situations. A virtuous state of character would exhibit integrated motivation by the true value of everything that is touched by the actor's conduct.

SDT research has shown that "the satisfaction of the basic psychological needs for autonomy, competence, and relatedness is necessary for effective internalization and for psychological growth, integrity, and well-being."[49] Effective internalization yields identified motivation (self-regulation) in which "the individuals understand and accept the real importance [of something] for themselves" or have "identified with [its value] for themselves."[50] The "autonomy supportive" contextual factors identified as favorable to such motivation include the offering of a rationale that is meaningful to the learner, respectful acknowledgment of the learner's "inclinations and right to choose," and a manner of offering the rationale and acknowledgment that "minimizes pressure and conveys choice."[51] By contrast, it has been established through nearly one hundred experimental studies that the use of rewards and penalties as motivators diminishes intrinsic motivation and the experience of autonomy, yielding controlled motivation that is not characteristic of virtue and is less predictive of favorable engagement, quality of performance, and well-being.[52] SDT implies that for moral education to succeed on its own terms, it must be predicated on satisfying all three basic psychological needs. It commends an approach that is nurturing, promotes intellectual competence, and engages learners in moral inquiry that allows them to think through the moral landscape of their experience without pressure to adopt views they do not find reason to accept as their own.

The essence of moral motivation is autonomously valuing persons and other sentient beings, their flourishing, and what is essential to their flourishing. A value orientation of this kind is a predictable outcome for people nurtured in a needs-supportive social environment—an environment that models the valuing of persons and their flourishing, and that practices such valuing by providing sufficient opportunity for the satisfaction of autonomy, competence, and relatedness needs as children begin to explore and make their way in the world. Actions that are autonomous products of a virtuous value orientation are similarly rewarded by the internal satisfaction of those same basic needs.[53]

Rational Inquiry versus Moralizing History?

Considering what is actually known about human motivation and moral motivation in particular, the idea that civic virtue must be predicated on pa triotism cultivated through a moralizing history of mythologized national heroes is hard to sustain. Virtuous motivation is rooted in innate propensities to form relationships and function as psychically integrated agents, and in the inherent rewards of positive relatedness, competence, and being able to make sense of what we do. It is substantially a product of children's lived experience, but research in motivational psychology suggests that the reasons we are given for accepting new goals and values as our own, how we are given those reasons, and how well those reasons align with our needs and developing self-understanding all matter. If children perceive the communities in which they are embedded as protecting their interests, they will be strongly inclined to identify with those communities, feel loyalty to them, and accept their values as their own. Accepting values and integrating them into a coherent self or identity is motivationally potent, as we noted in the introduction.

The opposition between rational inquiry and moralizing history as educational bases for civic responsibility is thus a false dichotomy. It has lent undeserved credibility to an approach to patriotic education that undermines legitimacy and is incompatible with the purposes and methods of the just educational institutions we have described. Legitimacy rests on a sound understanding of a government's true merits, and such understanding is also often essential to effective civic action and the good judgment on which people depend in managing their own lives. We have argued that understanding is one of the fundamental aims of the education we need and owe our children, and that understanding, capabilities, and virtues are together the three fundamental developmental aims of education because they are foundational to living well. There is simply no basis in motivational research or educational ethics for arguing that these fundamental educational aims must be set aside or compromised in order to motivate civic responsibility.

The motivational core of civic virtue might rest on seeing the reasons why a system of government is worthy of respect and seeing what is valuable in everything else a country comprises—value one might learn to appreciate largely through direct experience. The motivational texture of *specific* acts of civic responsibility is nevertheless complex and powerfully shaped by the particulars of such acts and the contexts of their performance. Many acts of civic responsibility require an orientation to collective action and motivation to act in concert with specific others, using specific capabilities, in specific circumstances that may or may not lend themselves to experiencing success, self-determination, and positive connection to others. Acquired attributes of understanding, capability, and virtue will interact with the contexts of civic acts, and these interactions will mediate the satisfaction of basic psychological needs and influence the extent to which specific kinds of responsible civic actions will be performed and repeated.

The task of the next chapter is to build on this general understanding of education by defining a properly educative form of civic education and determining where patriotism might belong in it. The history of attempts to teach patriotism suggests that it has been perceived as a virtue, but we will argue that if virtuous patriotism is possible, it is not a virtue as such but the motivational core of civic virtue with respect to a country. We will examine whether there is a genuinely virtuous form of patriotic motivation that can play the role in civic virtue it is so often thought to play.

FIVE

Cultivating Civic Virtue

I will always be someone who understands the everlasting anguish of not belonging. We arrived in this country under the shield of the Red Cross, stateless, as refugees. Then Canada took us in.

It was in attending public school that I truly felt a sense of place in this country. . . . If we are going to accommodate newcomers into society, we must continue to have well-funded public education . . . where all children are treated as equal, regardless of income. That is how people really learn to belong. . . . We want people who will take their place in our society, but that means we must make sure there are no barriers to inclusion for people who come here.

—Adrienne Clarkson[1]

Born in Hong Kong, Adrienne Clarkson arrived in Canada as a refugee and received "endorsement to belong" from her seventh-grade teacher, Miss Bernice Jackson: "You weren't born here, but everything you do and will do prove[s] that you know what it is like to have been born here."[2] Clarkson may be rare in being a refugee who went on to become Canada's governor general, but the power of a teacher's affirmation is evident not only in her own personal narrative but in countless others the world over. Anyone whose teaching has made a difference to a student's life knows this and probably experienced it herself as a student. "You belong here." "You can do this." "You have something to contribute to this society." These are forms of affirmation all children need but not all receive.

Public school teachers represent a community and a country when they welcome children into their classrooms and affirm their belief in children's belonging, goodness, and potential. Classrooms and schools are microcosms of the society, especially if they reflect the latter's diversity. It is important both for children and for the wider society that they function as *just communities* in which children are accepted as equals and experience growth and progress in their lives and as contributing members. When Clarkson insists there be "no barriers to inclusion for people who come here," she is expressing a fundamental truth about the justice on which a cooperative society inevitably rests—a truth we ignore at our peril. Barriers to inclusion are the surest guarantee of economic hardship, social and civic isolation, and disaffection. We saw in chapter 4 that the satisfaction of needs for relatedness, competence, and self-determination are important to the internalization of norms, so the just classroom and school communities to which we welcome children must facilitate the satisfaction of these needs while nurturing children's aspiration and ability to lead admirable lives. We also saw that in the wider society voluntary respect for law rests substantially on a perception that it is fair or just, much as Justice Black affirmed in *Barnette*, that "love of country must [be] . . . inspired by a fair administration of wise laws."[3]

Anxieties about the integration and civic responsibility of immigrant and minority populations are now focused on terrorism and the fear that Muslim immigrants do not normally experience belonging in and loyalty to their new countries, even when the barriers to their integration are insignificant.[4] This is an unfounded fear, however. The evidence suggests that most Muslim immigrants do experience belonging and loyalty, and it suggests that opportunities at school play a significant role.

Newcomers tend to arrive optimistic about their prospects of a better life and with a great deal at stake in being contributing members of the communities and countries that welcome them. They also tend to arrive with vivid memories of difficulties they left behind and correspondingly greater appreciation for the merits of their new countries than many with less perspective might have. A 2011 study in Great Britain found that "British Muslims are *more likely* to be both patriotic and optimistic about Britain than are the white British community."[5] They "identify with the British nation in its current state and express support for the existing function of its institutions."[6] A 2005 study conducted by the US State Department after riots by immigrants in the Paris suburbs found similarly that "large majorities of Muslims in France voice confidence in the country's government, feel at least partly French, and support integrating into French society." This reported desire to belong is reflected in high rates of Muslims marrying, cohabiting with, and befriending non-Muslims, and a majority of Muslim women working outside of their homes, as other French women do.[7]

The desire to belong is often frustrated by barriers to opportunity, however. A 2011 comparative study of the integration of Muslim immigrants across nine countries demonstrates the significance of equitable educational and economic opportunity for integration. Canada scored highest in the measures used—employment, home ownership, and naturalization—and the United States was not far behind, but laws in many European countries were found to restrict educational and economic opportunities and full legal citizenship.[8] Faced with varying patterns of ethnic and religious discrimination,

> Muslim emigrants from the same countries of origin have very different fates depending on which countries they choose as their destination. In some places, they become fully integrated within a generation; in others, they and their children seem to become trapped on the margins. . . . For the most part, they exhibit no signs of any desire to become a "parallel society," either culturally or economically—but there are circumstances that could be creating one by default.[9]

In short, there is no reason to suppose that Muslims are any different from other immigrants who have become integral to American society, and Americans should be glad that the merits of inclusive and freedom-respecting societies continue to be recognized and valued by newcomers who are not held back by ethnic or religious discrimination. The research pertaining to the integration of Muslims into the societies of Europe and North America suggests that a critical role of schools in promoting civic responsibility is in enabling immigrants to experience belonging and take their place as contributing members.[10] Success in these inclusive and enabling roles is foundational to the education in civic virtue we will address in this chapter.[11]

Is there a virtuous form of patriotism? If so, what role might it play in the scheme of civic virtue and civic education? Building on the foundations laid in chapter 4, we offer an account of the nature and nurture of civic virtue. We conceive of civic virtue as having three components—civic intelligence, civic friendship, and civic competence—corresponding to the admirable civic fulfillment of human intellectual, social, and productive potential. With this in mind, we will identify virtuous patriotism as a central motivational aspect of civic virtue with regard to one's country. Patriotism that contributes to true civic virtue would embed a special commitment to the good of one's country within a wider responsiveness to the value of persons and prerequisites of their flourishing everywhere. It would constitute an aspect of an identity in which ideals of justice are psychically integrated and thus autonomously motivating. The civic virtue of which virtuous patriotism is a part would be responsive to reasoning and evidence, and thus attuned and responsive to failures of justice. Because civic virtue is manifested in acts of civic responsibility in which intellectual, social, and productive potential are all expressed, it will entail constituent excellences with regard to each of these forms of potential—the civic intelligence, friendship, and competence to which we have referred. Acts exhibiting these excellences will tend to recur, because they will typically be accompanied by the psychic gratification of basic psychological needs for autonomy, positive relatedness, and competence. Yet, the intrinsic gratification for which individuals may be equipped is also contingent upon circumstances favorable to the expression of these personal attributes in activity that is satisfying. Civic responsibility is important not just in the civic affairs of a country, but also in local, regional, international, and global civic spheres, and the motivational structure of civic responsibility in any of these spheres is complex. It is for this reason that we describe virtuous patriotism as a *central* motivational aspect of civic virtue *with regard to one's country*, and not the whole of motivation to engage in responsible civic acts even with respect to national affairs.

Our understanding of the motivational heart of virtue generally, and of civic virtue in particular, allows us to identify a form of patriotism that is compatible with legitimacy, patriotic dissent, and responsible global citizenship. In the spirit of the tradition of popular patriotic song noted in the introduction, we identify a country as a geographic region within the jurisdiction of a common constitutional structure and the society of persons committed to living in that region within the terms of that constitutional structure. Loving all that a country encompasses would be very different from loving its romanticized heroic founders or approving the policies of its present leaders, and much closer to the Progressive idea of devotion to the "welfare of the communities" to which one belongs. Virtuous love of a country requires a coherent grasp of the value of all it encompasses, how its parts and norms do or do not enable the persons comprising the society to live well together, and what is and is not alterable for the better. It follows that *informed* love of country should not be an impediment to legitimate governance.[12] It could surely motivate opposition to leadership and policies that are obstacles to the society's diverse members living well together. Virtuous devotion to the good of one's country is discerning and targeted, protecting what is good and opposing what is bad through loyal dissent and measured efforts to overcome bad decisions, laws, and institutional norms. Because virtuous patriotism would be the central motivational aspect of civic virtue with respect to one's country, and civic virtue would equip a person for civic responsibility in all the spheres in which civic cooperation is required or prudent, virtuous patriotism would also be compatible with cosmopolitan respect for people everywhere and with the fair terms of global cooperation that countries have a moral obligation to establish in circumstances of unavoidable globalization and interdependence.

We will elaborate on this conception of virtuous patriotism, and then outline the elements of sound civic education pertaining to civic intelligence, friendship, competence, and motivation. We take it as evident that if there is no genuinely virtuous form of patriotism, then patriotism cannot be a suitable object of educational cultivation. As we suggested in chapter 4, this will rule out some, but not all, of what has occurred in schools in the name of patriotism. And while civic virtue and its component virtues of civic intelligence, friendship, and competence would appear on a checklist of learning outcomes, we conclude that patriotism would not appear as a distinct item on such a list. We argue that love of country is a suitable goal of civic education *only to the extent* that it may be a product of an inclusive and enabling just school community that facilitates civic belonging and friendship, civic competence, and the accurately informed appreciation of the country's merits that is part of civic intelligence. What can be *taught* is the rational grounds for regarding various aspects of the country as valuable, whereas attachment, love, or devotion—hence patriotism or patriotic sentiment—is something that might be *inspired* by a student's experience of being a valued part of a just society and just school community.

Virtuous Patriotism

Scholars have sometimes begun by asking whether patriotism is a virtue.[13] By the standards of a true virtue, understood as an attribute of a person that is invariably good, or good without qualification, actual patriotism is often not very virtuous. It is combative, unjust in its favoring of one's own, racially exclusionary, tolerant of persecution and violations of civil liberties, intolerant of dissent, blinding in ways that undermine legitimacy and progress, and an obstacle to beneficial international cooperation. One might imagine a virtue of patriotism, defined as an ethically appropriate devotion to the good of one's country motivated by *caring about* one's country. This would not lend itself to a coherent cataloging of civic virtues, however. How are patriotism and civic virtue related?

To answer this, we must take a step back and consider a more abstract question: What is the basis for determining what is and is not a genuine virtue? A natural basis for doing so is to think of each social virtue as equipping a person to navigate a challenging form of human encounter: courage to face danger, compassion in the presence of suffering, generosity in sharing what one can afford to share, and so on. From this perspective, civic virtue equips a person for transactions in the civic sphere. It might be subdivided with respect to specific forms of civic transactions, different civic spheres, or with respect to its intrapersonal components, as we have done in distinguishing civic intelligence, friendship, and competence.

Is there a place for patriotism in any of these approaches to subdividing civic virtue? Patriotism pertains to one of several civic spheres, the national one, so one proposal would be that patriotism is simply civic virtue in that sphere. This is not very plausible, however. If the role of civic virtue in national affairs is to equip people to act responsibly in those affairs, then patriotic sentiment cannot qualify as a civic virtue. At best, it is a part of the motivational aspect of a virtue. The most plausible alternative proposal is that patriotism is not a virtue as such, but is rather an intrapersonal piece of civic virtue, namely, one piece of a larger civic motivation package. This larger motivational package must include motivation to act responsibly in all the other civic spheres besides the national one, as well as motivation sufficient to sustain specific forms of civic contribution.

So we begin not with the question of whether patriotism is a virtue and one that should be cultivated in schools, but by defining civic virtue as the educational target, and regarding virtuous patriotism as a central motivational element of civic virtue with respect to one's country—a responsiveness to the value of all that the country encompasses. The qualification, "with respect to one's country," recognizes that civic virtue pertains not just to acts of civic responsibility at a national level—in the national civic sphere—but at local, regional, international, and global levels, since civic responsibility in all of these spheres may be prudent and ethically obligatory. By framing virtuous patriotism within this wider context of civic virtue and responsibility, we recognize that a virtuous form of patriotic sentiment would play a limited if significant role in motivating acts of civic responsibility. The role would be significant from an ethical standpoint, because being moved by the value of what is at stake is the motivational heart of any virtue. When we address the education of civic intelligence, friendship, competence, and motivation, we will recognize that these apply across civic spheres and that virtuous patriotic motivation must be approached as something to be educationally reconciled with civic virtue and responsibility in all spheres. Why must patriotism be reconciled with civic virtue and responsibility in all spheres? The short answer is that cooperation in all the spheres in which we interact with others and encounter problems is not just prudent and rational, but is a correlate of the basic moral respect we owe each other. If patriotism has often revolved around common interests recognized in times of national unification and war, there is today no less need for a spirit of global citizenship focused on our common interests in avoiding war and protecting the overburdened planetary systems on which we all depend.

Patriotism is a devotion to the good of one's country, but what is a "country"? The Latin root of our words *patriot* and *patriotism* is *patria*, meaning father*land* or native country, though it is now widely accepted that a person can come to be a patriot of a country to which she is not native born, as Adrienne Clarkson did. This suggests that a country is a "land," in the sense of a geographical expanse, region, or district of a landmass, and one that is more or less bounded "in relation to human occupation," hence identifiable as a person's country of origin or native land. These are the first, second, and fourth senses of the word *country* identified by the *Oxford English Dictionary*, and the third and sixth are "the territory or land of a nation; usually an independent state or a region once independent and still distinct in race, language, institutions, or historical memories, as England, Scotland, and Ireland, in the United Kingdom" and "the people of a district or state; the nation."[14] In a legal context, to be tried by one's country is to be judged by a jury of one's peers, fellow countrymen, or compatriots, not by a representative of the king. The term *patriot*—which originally meant simply a compatriot or fellow countryman—has sometimes similarly signified a person who "supported the rights of the country against the King and court" or someone who is devoted to the public's "prosperity" or well-being.[15] The meaning of *patriotism* has been contested and appropriated for different purposes over the course of many centuries, yet its etymology and early English usage do provide some justification for regarding a region and its people as the primary objects of patriotic devotion.[16]

We have said that a country is a geographic region within the jurisdiction of a common constitutional structure and the society of persons committed to living in that region within the terms of that constitutional structure. What this adds to contemporary definitions of a country is essentially a specification of *who* qualifies as a fellow countryman or compatriot, namely, someone who is functionally a member of the society and committed to abiding by the terms of its constitutional structure—committed either by virtue of citizenship (de jure) or in fact (de facto). This accommodates the fact that not all of those who belong to a country are good citizens; some may be uncooperative citizens, and some may deserve citizenship but not be granted it. We also assume that the terms of a constitutional structure might or might not be codified in a constitutional document. The point of this is to include countries whose societies are regulated by customary norms and not by written political constitutions that define institutions, offices, powers, and procedures of government. Whether or not a society has a written constitution, it would have a constitution in a sense recognized in ancient Greek political theory and analogous to a person's constitution or health—the healthy or unhealthy state or norms of functioning of the society's "body politic."

Other scholars offer definitions of a country very similar to our own, but resist the terms of these definitions by writing as if loving a country—or the United States in particular—is, or should be, equivalent to loving its just institutions.[17] They have embraced forms of constitutional patriotism, in other words.[18] Our view incorporates constitutional patriotism within a wider conception of the focus of patriotic concern that also gives specificity to the universal values that should guide ongoing examination and improvement of the country's constitutional system. A passion for justice is properly anchored in what gives just institutions their value, namely, their contributions to enabling people to live well together. So a virtuous devotion to just institutions would be rooted in a wider concern for a country's people and what is conducive to their well-being. It is thus important to keep in mind what a country is, when one sets out to understand what devotion to the good of a country would be. Recognizing this, it is hard to quarrel with the tradition of American patriotic song that identifies the country as a "land of wealth and beauty" and "most of all the people," together with its institutions and ideals.

The ethical merit in this is that it allows us to make sense of the popular notion that patriotism is or can be virtuous. We sketched an ethic of basic moral respect for persons in chapter 4 and showed how it can ground ideals of free and equal citizenship and just institutions as bases of opportunity to live well. Within such a framework, virtuous patriotism would be *devotion to the good of a country's people, the land they occupy and from which they derive opportunities, and the institutions, traditions, and practices that shape their existence together in beneficial ways*. There is an *ethical structure* to a country that comes to rest in the intrinsic value of persons and other sentient creatures inhabiting the region or land it encompasses, together with the land, waters, climate, and living systems that constitute the most irreplaceable basis of opportunity for living well that a country provides. Built environments, institutions, traditions, and practices have instrumental value insofar as they create and preserve opportunities for people to live well together, and they also offer many apt objects of noninstrumental devotion. Virtuous devotion to the good of a country would be sensitive to these aspects of its ethical structure. It would also take a long view of the dependence of the new generations we create on the stability of both natural and institutional systems.[19] Virtuous patriotism would consequently be devoted to environmental preservation and sustainability, in the sense of preserving the country's natural basis of opportunity to live well, and it would be devoted to equal opportunity for *all* the diverse people who belong to it.

This is not to deny, but rather to clarify, the value of good institutions and what ethically appropriate responsiveness to the value of institutions would consist of. Good institutions matter to people's prospects of living well together, and some such institutions are unavoidably public. Others that are not public may nevertheless have fundamental constitutional significance, in the sense that they shape our activities and interactions with one another, thereby substantially determining the structure of opportunities to live well. An expansive constitutional patriotism or patriotism of real freedom for all would be devoted to collectively examining and improving upon all such institutions, in the interest of cooperation in living well together. They would include institutions of public knowledge, such as an independent press, research institutions, and intelligence services immune to political influence, educational institutions, and workplaces and other institutions that provide opportunities to engage in activities of lives well lived.

Yet, the present era is unfortunately one in which the value of public institutions and public constitutional oversight is too often not acknowledged, owing substantially to several decades of ideological discrediting of public institutions and government action in the public interest. The aim and effect of such denigration has often been to defund public institutions and enfeeble their capacity to protect and advance the public interest, making allegations of public sector inefficiency and incompetence more credible in the process. This is not to say that public institutions are the only good institutions or the best for every purpose, but a democratic public that is so demoralized as to believe it cannot act efficaciously together in its own interest is not a virtuously patriotic public.[20] It condemns itself and its children to suffering under the overbearing weight of institutions that are beyond its control and indifferent to its interests.

Sensitivity to the ethical structure of a country is an aspect of the contextual sensitivity of virtuous devotion to a country's good. The benefits of civic cooperation at different levels of organization, from local to global, comprise a second, overlapping context to which such devotion would be sensitive. These forms of contextual sensitivity ensure that virtuous patriotism would not be prejudicial to legitimacy and vigilant public oversight of public officials in the way that actual patriotism often is. There are also circumstances in which they would justify dissent and make it a requirement of devotion to the good of one's country. And they would make virtuous patriotism compatible with global justice and cooperation. Each of these claims deserves some elaboration.

Virtuous concern for one's country would not be loyalty to the state or a head of state, nor would it be an idolatrous regard for the letter of a written constitution or the specific historical form an institution might have taken. As we have said, it would be focused on the people, their well-being, and what is conducive to that well-being now and for future generations, and the impetus to act that it provides would be mediated by civic intelligence or judgment. As such, it should not blind the virtuously patriotic to the badness of bad government decisions, policies, laws, or specific institutional arrangements. An appreciative and intelligent responsiveness to what is valuable in a country should, indeed, do just the opposite. It should favor legitimacy, as well as dissent and other contributions to public reason that are reasonably calculated to protect and advance a country's good. It would be a civic-minded antidote to narrow self-interest, drawing the virtuously patriotic toward an *impartial* concern for the whole country. Such concern would not be *impersonal*, however, because it would be an expression of personal endorsement of ideals of justice "for all" and entanglement of the individual's identity and well-being in that of the country.[21]

Simon Keller has argued that, on the contrary, patriotism inherently involves bad faith or self-deception, because from a patriot's perspective, "The country's having certain virtues is a presumption of her very identity. To tell a patriot that she is wrong about the nature of her country is to throw into question her understanding of herself."[22] He acknowledges that "bad faith can be tempered by other traits . . . [that] a patriotic person might, as well as being patriotic, have a commitment to avoiding any kind of self-deception, and she might have a highly tuned capacity to respond appropriately to new evidence about herself and her country," but he suggests that "still, to the extent to which a patriot is not primed to be self-deceiving, that will be so in spite of her patriotism."[23] On this basis, Keller concludes that a nonpatriotic form of loyalty to country might be preferable—a "robust commitment to country that does not rely upon any sense that the country is a good country"—and better still would be loyalty to, or "fundamental concern" for, "things within" countries rather than countries themselves.[24]

It would be a problem for our conception of virtuous patriotism if Keller's arguments were compelling, but they are built on what he acknowledges are "psychological speculations" about patriotism conceived as a "complex psychological state."[25] First, it is not clear that a patriot's conception of herself is necessarily thrown into question by learning she is wrong about her country's nature. This would presumably depend on the details of why she perceives herself as Australian, say, and whether she has prior experience with disappointing discoveries about her country and has adopted the attitude that it is better to know the truth and not blindly endorse every aspect of the country, its history, and its policies. Second, we see neither definitional nor psychological grounds for holding that patriotism necessarily involves an all-things-considered judgment about the goodness of one's country, or for seeing patriotism as fundamentally in tension with a clear-eyed awareness of one's country's faults. Constitutional patriotism is, among other things, an attempt to frame a constructive national project to which Germans can commit themselves, without needing to reconcile a troubling past with a summary judgment of their country's goodness. The virtuous patriotism we have described is itself a concern for, and responsiveness to, what does have value in one's country, the "things within" the country that are worth protecting because they are intrinsically valuable or provide necessities for living well. Keller might object that what we defend is not patriotism because it does not involve loving the whole country or country itself, but we think it is sufficient for patriotism that there be loyalty or devotion to the country, in the form of a willingness to cooperate in preserving and strengthening its capacity to sustain a just and desirable collective existence, as long as there is any point in doing so.

If the psychic context of patriotic devotion to country is civic virtue that equips a person for civic responsibility in all the civic spheres to which she belongs, then patriotism should be compatible with global justice and cooperation. Civic virtue is not complete without motivational counterparts to caring about the good of one's country that are exhibited in acts of civic responsibility in other civic spheres—caring about the good of one's city and caring about the fate of global humanity, for instance. Nor is civic virtue complete without understanding and attunement to the requirements of just cooperation in all the civic spheres to which one belongs.

Recall Justice Robert Jackson's recognition that there are limits to loyalty entailed by the global scope of common ethical principles. Basic moral respect requires us to do no harm and to negotiate and honor fair terms of cooperation when our actions influence each other's well-being (as we saw in chapter 4). It is undeniable that those of us in the world's most affluent countries are influencing the well-being of everyone across the globe through the impact of our institutions on the terms of global trade and investment, the frequency and destructiveness of wars, and the global reach of the pollutants we emit into the atmosphere and oceans. The fair terms of cooperation we are morally bound to negotiate and honor would create special global civic obligations to everyone across the globe, in addition to the basic moral obligations that we already have. And in a world of global interdependence in which national governments cannot adequately protect their citizens' interests without wider cooperation, we also have reasons of prudence to be good global citizens. There are nevertheless more limited spheres of denser interaction than the global sphere, and these too call for enactment of just terms and institutional bases of cooperation governing the denser interactions. The current array of countries that are self-governing states is not isomorphic with the large-scale, subglobal patterns of dense human interaction, but state-level constitutional systems do regulate such interaction within territories, giving rise to special obligations and making civic virtue at the level of states or politically unified countries significant.

These special state-level obligations must be compatible with requirements of international and global justice. Because we cannot now determine what all of these requirements of a fully just world order would be, it is impossible to know how much legitimate discretion we may have to enact and accept special obligations at national and subnational levels. We can nevertheless assume that no terms of international cooperation could be regarded as just that did not leave room for projects of self-governance at national and subnational levels.[26] As we shall see in more detail in chapter 6, legitimate and effective governance is necessarily widely distributed and to some extent sustained by local rewards of participation. Such governance permeates the life of institutions that enable people to engage in the activities of lives well lived. These are the constitutionally significant institutions that an expansive constitutional patriotism would justly defend as a prerogative of legitimate patriotic partiality. The just and stable functioning of these institutions would require resources that the terms of international justice would permit, but the extent of such permitted resources might be far less than countries like the United States currently assume. Beyond this, it is not clear how much partiality can or need be claimed in the name of patriotism. One thing that does seem clear is that in interpersonal encounters, such as in saving innocent strangers from imminent danger, it would be morally reprehensible to favor compatriots over others on the basis of nationality (supposing one could discern nationality), just as it would be reprehensible to favor some over others on the basis of race.[27]

How widely applicable is this ideal of virtuous patriotism, and what good is it? We have defined a country as a geographic region within the jurisdiction of a common constitutional structure and the society of persons committed to living in that region within the terms of that constitutional structure. As such, all countries with the potential to provide their inhabitants with opportunities to live well would necessarily have value worthy of protection. There may be countries that are lost causes, such as countries hopelessly resistant to unitary self-rule because their borders were determined by departed colonial powers. However, even such countries may have the potential to provide all or many of their inhabitants with opportunities to live well, if they are subdivided—unless they have been made uninhabitable and can no longer support a population. Although patriotic devotion to a country's good would normally favor unified self-rule, it need not do so if devolving its parts would best preserve the valuable ways of life it may yet sustain. More difficult, perhaps, is the case in which the bad that must be opposed is so extensive and entrenched that devotion to the country's good would favor external humanitarian intervention. Our purposes here do not require that such questions be resolved, however. The claim we wish to make is simply that the patriotic devotion we envision is widely applicable. Wide applicability might be ruled out if patriotism were by its nature precluded from appealing to moral ideals that are not among a country's own ideals, but we have seen no reason to think that this is one of its inherent features. A patriot need only show that adoption of a new ideal would be good for the country.

Even if the ideal of virtuous patriotism is widely applicable, it is reasonable to ask what good may come of appealing to it and what hazards may accompany attempts to cultivate or encourage it. We suggested above, as Martha Nussbaum has, that virtuous patriotism may be a civic-minded antidote to narrow self-interest.[28] Because we define such patriotism as a kind of appropriate responsiveness to the objective value of one's country, where appropriateness is determined by that value and by commitments of membership consistent with requirements of global justice, it is reasonable to ask what appeals to patriotism would add to calling on someone to *do what is right*. The same question might be pressed against Maurizio Viroli, when he holds that what democracy needs is simply "a love of common liberty . . . to put it simply, patriotism."[29] The best answer we can give is that the force of a reference to patriotism is that it calls attention to what is at stake, namely, the country or some vital aspect of it. Whether this succeeds will depend on a variety of factors, including whether the listener cares about the country and shares a common understanding of what is consistent with its well-being. Consider that as we write this, Dan Rather has responded on Facebook to news that President Trump has fired Federal Bureau of Intelligence (FBI) director James Comey, who was leading an investigation of possible coordination between the Trump presidential campaign and Russian attempts to undermine Hillary Clinton's campaign. Rather writes, in part, that "it is incumbent upon everyone who claims to love this country to demand answers."[30] How much effect such calls to conscience have is not clear, but they won't persuade those who lack the constitutional perspective to share a common understanding of what is at stake.

As for the hazards that may accompany attempts to cultivate or encourage patriotic sentiment, we acknowledge their existence. Having identified virtuous patriotism, or appropriate responsiveness to the value of one's country, as a central motivational aspect of civic virtue with counterparts across the spectrum of civic spheres, we turn now to the educational cultivation of civic virtue generally. We will sketch some important aspects of the cultivation of the component virtues of civic intelligence, civic friendship, and civic competence, before returning to civic motivation itself. As noted previously, we will argue that love of country is a suitable goal of civic education only to the extent that it may be a product of an inclusive and enabling just school community that facilitates civic belonging and friendship, civic competence, and the accurately informed appreciation of the country's merits that is part of civic intelligence.

Cultivating Civic Intelligence

Civic intelligence is the intellectual basis for good citizenship and success in advancing the public interest. It entails not just a sound knowledge of government and the roles citizens may play in civic life, but a general education that enables students to understand diverse matters important to the public interest and to contribute to advancing that interest.[31] The problems that societies face are often complex and hard to manage, and the understanding we bring to them must be correspondingly nuanced and integrative. Students must learn how serious inquiry works and learn enough of diverse fields of study to bring the perspectives of relevant fields together in judgments about what is to be done.[32] They must also learn how to bring these analytical perspectives together with what they can learn of the society's needs through conversation with each other, because respect for free and equal citizenship requires public consultation and dialogue, and few social problems are ever solved without extensive consultation and widespread cooperation in a way forward. Good judgment is a product of not only relevant forms of disciplinary inquiry and knowledge, but also consultation, ethical perspective, critical thinking, and practice.[33]

The cultivation of good judgment could begin in forms of character education that orient children to thinking things through before acting, and it should include philosophical inquiries about justice and the merits of constitutional democracy. We wrote in chapter 4 that cooperative citizenship rests on a wide cultivation of understanding and discernment in matters of justice and the public interest, and this is all the more true of the expectations of citizenship beyond mere compliance with law. Immigrants and native-born citizens alike may lack such understanding and discernment, and there can be no objection to honest instruction and open-ended classroom debate that would enable students to think through the country's actual merits for themselves. Educational strengthening of judgment would involve instruction in critical thinking, analysis of case studies in decision making, and guided practice. It would use integrated curricula and cross-curricular inquiry-based learning that provide experience in bringing the resources of diverse disciplinary and analytical frameworks to bear on matters of importance to students' lives. The instruction in history that grounds judgments about the public interest should enable students to understand how societies work and how progress is made.[34]

An aspect of civic education that has been much discussed in recent years is practice in "public reason." Rawls argued that members of a society who are willing to accept fair terms of cooperation would ideally endorse both constitutional principles of justice and associated norms of public reason, which he described as a "shared basis for citizens to justify to one another their political judgments."[35] "Citizens must be able . . . to present to one another publicly acceptable reasons for their political views in cases raising fundamental political questions," and they must accept what Rawls called the "burdens of judgment" as conditions on "the use of public reason in directing the legitimate exercise of political power."[36] These burdens of judgment are factors that give rise to differences of judgment among reasonable people. An example is differences of life experience that lead reasonable people to weigh competing risks differently, such as the risks of greater government involvement in health care versus the risks of a system that is less equitable and cost effective. Rawls argues that acknowledging these factors when faced with beliefs and judgments different from one's own is fundamental to respectful and productive engagement in civic discourse.

Preparing students to engage in public reason is important but complicated. Public deliberations should adhere to norms of communicative respect in a multicultural setting, and progress in solving problems requires respect for authoritative standards of evidence and the values of free and equal citizenship enshrined in a nonsectarian constitution. Students will need to learn how evidence in different forms of inquiry works, they will need to engage in inquiry about justice, and they will need to engage in classroom dialogue, preferably with classmates whose diversity reflects that of the society itself.[37] Students will need to practice reasoning together with openness to the possibility that others with whom they disagree may be right, and they will need to discuss the kinds of controversies with which their society must grapple.[38] Whether or not practice in civic dialogue occurs in settings with diverse students, preparation for public debate and deliberation will be most effective if it also includes education about foreign and minority cultures.[39] Beyond the respectful engagement all of this implies, it is important that schools be places of cooperative learning and friendships that can bridge the cultural chasms that divide society. Without a foundation of friendly feeling and trust, it is doubtful how successful schools could be in nurturing lifelong habits of respectful engagement with diverse fellow citizens.

As important as it is to lay the educational groundwork for a society in which civic life is mediated by a give-and-take of reasons that respects free and equal citizenship, civic intelligence cannot be blind to reason-defying intransigence or be ill-equipped when it encounters such intransigence. "Useable" history lessons, in which students "can find values and projects to take as their own legacies . . . [and] build on what came before," must not only offer models of progress toward a "more perfect" union, but should honestly examine patterns of obstruction, strategies for overcoming injustice, and conditions for success in solving problems.[40] Responsible citizens will find themselves sometimes in cooperative civic exchanges and sometimes in uncooperative exchanges in which others do not listen to reason. In the latter circumstances, they should be prepared to protect their own rights and the public interest through forms of nonviolent resistance that reflect and defend the ideals of free, equal, and cooperative citizenship. "Activism oriented to social justice has [a] distinct claim on democratic life," and honesty about the realities of such activism and its role in the country's progress is not only a sensible investment in the country's health and well-being, but also something to which students—especially the most vulnerable—are *entitled.*[41] The basic function of just educational institutions is to promote personal development favorable to students living good lives in the world they will encounter as adults, and it is a world in which the integrity and well-being of both them and their country may require intelligent focus on overcoming obstacles to progress.

An educational focus on civic intelligence would both enable activism and favor responsiveness to reason and evidence in all aspects of active citizenship. Civic virtue is not blind. It is conscientious in the care it takes to grasp what is relevant, distinguish truth from falsehood, and judge wisely the civic affairs important to a people's well-being and a country's fate. To the extent that ideals and standards of inquiry are embraced by students as an aspect of civic responsibility, an education in these ideals and standards would also establish a basis of motivation favorable to advancing the country's good. Citizens motivated by such ideals and standards would be more likely than others to recognize and affirm neglected and suppressed truths important to the country's well-being.[42]

Cultivating Civic Friendship

We saw in chapter 2 that the idea of common schooling was an important aspect of the vision of public schools as institutions that would facilitate the integration of immigrant children into the social, civic, and economic life of American society. The creation of a shared "we" was to be achieved not simply through rituals of civic solidarity and aspects of the curriculum, but through children of diverse cultural backgrounds growing up together as schoolmates. The advantage of schooling a community's diverse children together as equals is twofold. It serves the inclusive and enabling roles noted at the opening of this chapter, and it enables children to know each other and have mutually formative experiences that result in them being more like one another than if they had been schooled in separate homogenous enclaves. In common schools, the specific friendships students form would sometimes bridge and overcome cultural divides, and those specific friendships would put friendly faces on the larger cultural groups to which the friends belong. In this way, the particular bonds formed at school might create a more vivid image of the country's whole people. They might also engender greater trust in the prospects for civic cooperation and a greater comfort and sense of belonging in sharing a common identity with a whole of many parts.[43]

If civic virtue involves appropriate responsiveness to the value of one's community, country, and world, and such value comes to rest most of all in the people and prerequisites of their well-being, then civic friendship would be a fundamental component of civic virtue. In this respect, civic friendship is simply the goodwill one should have toward the members of the communities to which one belongs and the friendly feeling one should often experience in face-to-face encounters within those communities.[44] From a relational standpoint, it is a feeling of positive relatedness or membership in a civic world where one belongs. It is a cognitive, emotional, and behavioral disposition to affirm the value and act for the good of the members of one's communities, in the policies one favors and in face-to-face encounters, together with a tendency to experience the successes, failures, and afflictions of the community as one's own. It is thus a central feature of the appropriate responsiveness to the value of one's country that we have identified as civic virtue.

Nurturing civic friendship in schools requires several things. It requires schools that approximate the common school ideal by enrolling students as diverse as the society itself. This is difficult, given the current patterns of residential segregation in the United States and the landscape of school choice, but steps can be taken to make enrollment in schools with diverse student bodies more attractive.[45] It also requires that students in schools with diverse student bodies not be separated in stratified ability groups that track the society's major social divides; students need to learn together as equals. It is helpful if the ethos of the school is dominated by cooperative learning and a mission more inspiring than individual competitive success.[46] And it is essential that schools be sized and structured to allow teachers and students to form substantial relationships. Students need time to play and form friendships. This may seem frivolous in an age of relentless focus on academic achievement and testing, but peer relationships are essential to children's well-being and a vital sphere of civic learning.[47] It is where children learn through experience the basics of what is and is not acceptable in the world of voluntary peer relationships, and it is in that sense a training ground for membership in a civic community of adults. We have said that classrooms should function as just communities, and this is often understood to mean that students will play a role in proposing and coming to agreement on some of the rules of classroom conduct.[48] Students typically take such opportunities very seriously, much as adults do when called upon to serve on juries, and we would expect the rules agreed upon to reflect the moral learning they have achieved through their firsthand experience of peer relationships.[49] The moral and civic language that students use will be acquired largely from adults and adult sources, such as children's literature, however. We noted in chapter 4 that the stories children encounter will and should portray what is good *as good*. This is entirely consistent with what children need, and it is an aspect of a just school community as we understand it, as long as students are free and encouraged to have open-ended discussions of the complexities of friendship, justice, and other aspects of moral and civic life when they are ready for it.[50]

Apart from what is learned in face-to-face peer interactions and literature, a basis for civic friendship can be established through the instruction about foreign and minority cultures mentioned above, including foreign language instruction and world literature. In order for civic friendship to have a global reach, students can be brought into friendly contact with distant others, as they were through the "international interschool correspondence" program of the Junior Red Cross, discussed in chapter 3.

Cultivating Civic Competence

President John F. Kennedy called upon Americans to ask what they can do for their country. So what *can* any of us do for our country? What does the good of the country require of us, and what are we good at doing? What civic capabilities or forms of civic competence can students acquire that would enable them to devote themselves to aspects of the good of their civic worlds?

Contemporary theorists of civic education tend to focus on such things as respectful and effective participation in democratic deliberation, but the activities of civic responsibility and corresponding forms of competence can take many forms. The community civics movement of the Progressive Era recognized this when it aimed to build cooperative problem-solving skills and dispositions, through hands-on, community-based projects. Done well, this might have developed a wide range of capabilities of communication, research, organization, leadership, teamwork, problem solving, experimentation, evaluation, and the like. We saw, similarly, that the Junior Red Cross engaged students in relief projects, food conservation, and other hands-on work. FFA clubs promoted competence in good farming practices, land preservation, and rural leadership—all of which were essential to the well-being of rural communities—and did so in ways that oriented students to finding evidence-based solutions to common problems.

We noted at the close of chapter 4 that it is always in specific ways that civic responsibility is enacted and that exercising the competence involved is one source of intrinsic motivation to serve in those ways. A recurring theme in scholarship on patriotic education is that abstract principles fail to motivate in the way that specific attachments can, but the specificity of acts of civic responsibility and the people, practices, and capabilities involved are routinely overlooked. The good soldier may be as motivated by the rewards of being good at what he does as by thoughts of the good of his country.[51] If the experience of competence is a fundamental human need and the inherent rewards of competence play an important role in motivating acts of civic responsibility, schools could profitably focus more attention on the civically valuable things students can be good at. Forms of community-based service learning in which students can experience making a valued contribution might be a good place to start.[52]

Cultivating Civic Motivation

We have said that love of country is a suitable goal of civic education only to the extent that it may be a product of an inclusive and enabling just school community that facilitates civic belonging and friendship, civic competence, and the accurately informed appreciation of the country's merits that is part of civic intelligence. While loving what is worthy of love may be admirable, it would be hard to defend the idea that love is obligatory in the civic sphere or any other. Love must be earned, but even then it is not something that can be owed, even if fulfillment of responsibilities *is* owed and should be undertaken without hesitation. This is one more reason why a lived experience of justice and the school's inclusive and enabling roles are foundational to the success of civic education. Justice and civic friendship in the society and the school community provide a rational basis of trust in each other and in the efficacy and value of civic cooperation, and these are fundamental prerequisites for sustaining civic responsibility. Against this background, teachers can anchor perceptions of the efficacy of civic efforts in exemplars of civic responsibility and progress, presenting the merits of the country's history and institutions without distortion. What we are imagining are case studies in civic responsibility and leadership, representing many kinds of civic contribution, diverse contributors to the public good, and enabling institutions. These should aim not to deify a select few, but to illustrate how progress is made and what we can all do within the context of our own lives. Teachers can also present and examine the case for citizens conceiving themselves as members of a public with the ability and need to identify and address common problems, and they can address hostility and indifference arising from misunderstandings.

We have argued that a sense of shared identity and wholehearted endorsement of ideals of justice can provide a core of civic motivation, while basic psychological needs for competence, mutually affirming relationships, and self-determination can play important roles in motivating specific acts of civic responsibility. We have also defended an ideal of virtuous responsiveness to the value of all a country entails, arguing that what *is* good should be presented *as* good in schools, but that students' understanding of the structure of value and their freedom to adopt values and goals on the basis of their own understanding requires value inquiry and reasoned discussion of civic affairs. The virtuous responsiveness to a country's value that may arise from such understanding, free endorsement of ideals, and sense of shared identity is a form of patriotic motivation that can play a role in civic virtue generally. Our position is that the legitimate role of education in inspiring such patriotic motivation is limited to providing an inclusive and enabling just school community that facilitates civic belonging and friendship, civic competence, and the informed appreciation of the country's merits that is part of civic intelligence. Societies must earn the affection of their members and cannot legitimately ask their schools to act as indoctrinating intermediaries.

An important matter to be elaborated upon is how teachers establish their authority with students. This is important as an aspect of habituation into the patterns of public life in a democracy, and because it mediates the satisfaction or frustration of students' autonomy needs and thereby the uptake and integration of civic norms and ideals that the school should stand for.

Leading students in the learning that is good for them and the society requires a moral vision made real and attractive to students. The focus of that vision must be the prospect of students' being self-determining in living well. Nurturing students' self-determination in living well is largely a matter of initiating them in the enterprise of self-reflective ethical inquiry. The attractiveness of the vision will be manifest more or less vividly in the dignity, competence, and autonomy it offers students, but also and necessarily in the norms of respectful engagement and human flourishing that the teacher must herself exemplify. In accepting the requirements of ethical inquiry in a group setting, students may enact a positive and motivating self-image as they engage in a form of cooperative learning—one that reinforces the teacher's moral authority while distributing responsibility throughout the learning community. In seeking to create a classroom community of ethical inquiry, teachers will necessarily aim toward a cooperative social enterprise governed by norms of reasonableness and rational exchange. The participation to which students are invited will be predicated on acceptance of the responsibility to respect others through attentive openness to learning and being persuaded by them. It will also confer a corresponding right to establish moral authority of their own through the ethical perceptiveness of their remarks.

This vision of classroom leadership assumes that a teacher needs to be not merely *in authority*—in a position of authority in her classroom, in the sense of having an institutionally conferred right to teach and manage her class—but to *have authority* with students, in the sense of being able to procure their cooperation through their belief that she knows what is best. Such authority will be perceived by students as noncoercive to the extent that they perceive her as having *moral* authority. And they are likely to perceive her as having such authority—as knowing what is for the best—if their experience of her is that she respects them, cares about them, and manages her classroom in a way that aims effectively at the good of them all.

Conclusion

We noted in chapter 4 that education has five distinct normative dimensions, corresponding to its aims, authority, responsibilities, manner, and content. What we have argued, in brief, is that civic education has the same *aim* as all good education: it should enable students to live well in a world in which living well requires cooperation at different levels of civic organization, from the local to the global. The *authority* to require students' and parents' cooperation in this education rests on a public responsibility to ensure every child receives the education they need. We also argued that a just constitutional system and rule of law rely on widespread voluntary compliance and are transacted as much as possible through rational persuasion. Moreover, we argued that this can only be achieved through a fulfillment of public *responsibility* to ensure the adequate and equitable provision of the education that is foundational to public reason and a rational appreciation of the goodness of good laws and norms of justice. This public responsibility should be understood to require reasonable efforts to provide educational settings whose student and teacher populations reflect the diversity of the society itself, and to provide civic education that resists the marginalization and persecution of racial, religious, and ethnic minorities. The *manner* of civic education should be noncoercive; supportive of students' needs for autonomy, competence, and mutually affirming relationships; discussion and inquiry focused; cooperative and project and community based when possible; and favorable to civic friendship in all civic spheres. The *content* of civic education should provide a basis of useable understanding of civic institutions and how progress has been achieved, and a strong general education focused on not just bodies of knowledge but also modes of inquiry and critical thinking about civic matters. These should come together in inquiry and judgment concerning matters of importance to students and their communities. Such matters would clearly include the health of the land, waters, climate, and ecosystems on which our communities and country depend.

The form of civic virtue we envision would involve patriotism, in the form of civic-minded proper responsiveness to the country's value, but also civic identities and motivation at different levels of organization, including a global one. Civic virtue would thus involve respecting others around the world as moral equals and seeking fair terms of global cooperation to solve the problems of a civilization that is now in important respects global and critically dependent on the health of an atmospheric and oceanic system that defies national borders. We conclude in chapter 6 with a defense of global civic education as a focus of higher education.

SIX

Global Civic Education

The Association of American Colleges and Universities (AAC&U) has advanced a vision of global learning as a focus of undergraduate education for all students. Its 2005 initiative, Shared Futures: General Education for Global Learning, offers this vision as a "timely framework through which to develop the four main categories of liberal education outcomes . . . knowledge, skills, responsibility, and integration," and calls for a "comprehensive renegotiation of the goals of undergraduate education."[1] Global learning is conceived as preparation "for citizenship in a world of global change and interdependence," and the unsolved global problems facing humanity are identified as the appropriate overarching focus of student learning. Opportunities to "engage—globally and locally—in civic practice" are recommended. In all of these respects, the AAC&U's vision of general education is a globalized version of Progressive educators' model of "community civics" that engaged students in community-based, problem-focused learning to nurture active, intelligent, and cooperative citizenship.[2] Such learning would necessarily draw upon a variety of disciplines and would develop as much through experiential learning, including global service learning projects, as in classrooms. Knowledge of global problems, peoples, and governance systems would ideally culminate in the forms of intercultural competence and skills required for progress in solving the problems in question.

Educating students in this way would require cooperation across entrenched disciplinary and program divides, at a time when college and university faculties are more narrowly specialized than ever and rarely think about their collective responsibility to provide a suitable undergraduate education. Fulfilling the AAC&U's vision would require cross-disciplinary cooperation not only to design and provide a coherent education for global citizenship, but to secure the future of liberal education itself a general education in the arts and sciences—at a time when American college students are more focused than ever on the urgency of securing gainful employment. The obstacles to strengthening the general education component of American baccalaureate education seem daunting, in short. Yet, in an age in which the future of civilization may be as precarious as that of liberal education, the logic of devoting the latter to securing the former is undeniable.

Step behind Rawls's veil of ignorance, knowing the basics of human well-being that we introduced in chapter 4 and knowing the current consensus of climatologists and ecologists on the planet's declining capacity to sustain a desirable quality of life.[3] Now ask yourself how rational people would define the mission of higher education. Consider that it is an open question whether it will be possible to keep Miami, New York City, New Orleans, London, and Venice above water to the end of this century, and that doing so would almost certainly require ongoing global cooperation to sharply reduce carbon emissions.[4] Consider also the evidence acknowledged by the US Department of Defense that climate change displaces populations, destabilizes governments, and threatens security, "because it degrades living conditions, human security and the ability of governments to meet the basic needs of their populations. . . . [We are] already . . . observing the impacts of climate change in shocks and stressors to vulnerable nations and communities, including in the United States, the Arctic, the Middle East, Africa, Asia and South America."[5] Americans seem to overwhelmingly define the mission of higher education as enabling young people to outdo each other in competing for the best jobs, but this makes little *collective* sense even in the best of times.[6] In an age in which the solutions to domestic problems often require global cooperation, what would make collective sense would be to define the mission of institutions of higher learning as equipping students to live well while working toward solutions to the pressing problems faced by their society and global humanity. The reciprocity of individual and collective well-being this implies is the ideal we advanced in chapter 4. We argued there that representatives behind the veil of ignorance would agree that the institutions of a society would exist to enable all of its members to live well and should (as far as possible) provide opportunities sufficient to enable all of them to do so and thereby provide each other such opportunities.

We will argue that global civic education is needed both to prepare students for global cooperation in a world of global interdependence and as a foundation for the legitimacy of the terms of international governance. We take its aim to be global citizens who (1) possess understanding, capabilities, and virtues conducive to living well together as members of a cooperative global community; (2) are engaged in global constitutional activity exhibiting such understanding, capabilities, and virtues (an idea we will explain shortly); and (3) are connected to one another by bonds of global civic friendship. We envision these personal attributes, activities, and bonds as grounded in a liberal arts curriculum and established largely through participation in forms of international cooperation.

Our focus will be the role in global civic affairs and collegiate experiential education of global constitutional activity that is simultaneously organizational and personal. We will hold that engagement in such activity is what makes someone a global citizen, understanding the word *makes* in both formative (educative) and constitutive (definitional) senses.

What we mean by "global constitutional activity" is activity through which people function and experience themselves as a global public that shapes and preserves the norms and constitutional principles that regulate the global order. The United States has a written constitution that defines a system of government and principles on which the system should operate, so Americans think of a constitution as a document. The word *constitutional* is thus used to refer to matters pertaining to that document. We would regard the participants in the Constitutional Convention of 1787 as having engaged in "constitutional activity." However, as we use the term, it would also apply to many others who were not present at the convention but contributed in other ways to its creation and enactment. From a more global and historical perspective, the principles that regulate a system of government may not be gathered together in a single document, and the principles that are announced in constitutional documents may play a smaller role in regulating how a system actually functions than implicit or customary norms. The actual patterns of governmental functioning are analogous to a person's state of health, which we sometimes refer to as a person's "constitution." It was in essentially this sense that political philosophers of the ancient Greek world understood a political constitution as the functional state of a political community: how its parts are actually constituted, arranged, and function together. The way we use the word *constitutional* in the phrase "constitutional activity" reflects this wider concern with the norms and principles that animate a system of governance and the way widely distributed activity can be directed to shaping and reinforcing patterns of governance. Constitutional activity shapes terms of cooperation and may only rarely be focused on the creation or amendment of a constitution in the modern sense.

Consider, for example, that reforming the grounding principles and policies of intergovernmental organizations (IGOs), such as the United

Nations, International Monetary Fund, and World Bank, is a goal of much transnational constitutional activity, as we understand it. The management of specific problems, such as sustainable sourcing of products or human trafficking, also qualifies as constitutional activity when efforts are directed toward reforming corporate and government policies and practices.[7] The constitutional activity that makes a person a global citizen might also be good or bad, which is to say more or less guided by and aspiring toward acceptable norms of global cooperation.

In referring to activity that is simultaneously organizational and personal, we have in mind activity through which individuals across the globe come to be not only engaged in global cooperation but experience motivationally significant value in that cooperation.[8] This would predictably involve relational, competence, and self-determination rewards associated with an emerging or developed global civic identity, as well as motivation to address specific problems or forms of injustice. A sense of efficacy, or ability to make a difference, will figure importantly in motivating acts of global citizenship. In present circumstances, such efficacy is most likely to be widely experienced through membership in transnational advocacy networks (TANs) and working with NGOs (nongovernmental organizations) embedded in TANs. TANs may be defined as networks of actors "working internationally on an issue, who are bound together by shared values, a common discourse, and dense exchanges of information and services."[9] Given our understanding of civic virtue, acts of transnational civic responsibility would qualify as manifestations of global civic virtue, if they display a suitable responsiveness to the value of what is at stake in the global sphere.

The Case for Global Civic Education

An early expression of the need for global civic education is Article 26 of the 1948 *Universal Declaration of Human Rights*. It holds that

> education shall be directed to the full development of the human personality and to the strengthening of respect for human rights and fundamental freedoms. It shall promote understanding, tolerance and friendship among all nations, racial or religious groups, and shall further the activities of the United Nations for the maintenance of peace.

Against the background of twentieth-century warfare and genocide, the insistence on respect for universal human rights, maintenance of peace, and "friendship among all nations" is understandable.

More ambitious goals for global civic education have emerged with the immense impact of global economic activity since World War II and recognition that states are not the only actors on the international stage or always the most influential. The resources and influence of transnational corporations now dwarf those of many countries, and individual people all over the world interact with each other indirectly through the supply chains that feed their daily activities and the upstream and downstream pollution associated with those activities. The ways we live connect each of us to nearly everyone else in the world, in a global system that is increasingly unsustainable. In these circumstances, the established terms of community life and national citizenship neither protect our long-term interests adequately nor fully capture the extent of our responsibilities to others. The ethic of universal respect introduced in chapter 4 implies that our unavoidable global interdependence and imposition of risk on one another entails a moral obligation to seek fair terms of global cooperation. This is a basic aspect of individual responsibility in our world, a responsibility of cosmopolitan or universal morality. It implies, at a minimum, that individuals have a responsibility to encourage their governments to negotiate the terms of such cooperation for them, and to hold their governments accountable for failure to do so. When those governments fail to act, personal responsibility to seek fair terms of global cooperation might also require participation in some forms of global constitutional activity, or global citizenship, when such participation has the potential to strengthen norms of international cooperation, shift the policies of state and corporate actors, and strengthen international platforms for the negotiation of international treaties favorable to global justice. Education should prepare people to live responsible lives, and the global impact of our activities and the importance of global cooperation for the future of life on this planet imply that schools and universities should provide "a good grounding for international cooperation."[10]

Another argument that can be made on behalf of global civic education is that there are forms of preparation for global cooperation that are also essential to the legitimacy of any institutions of transnational or global governance that may emerge. As we noted in chapter 4, legitimacy rests on transparency and understanding of what is at stake, hence a foundation of relevant education for all who may be directly or indirectly parties to the negotiation of terms of cooperation or may be subject to those terms. Voluntary cooperation based on understanding figures importantly in legitimate systems of governance, both ethically and practically. A corollary of this is that legitimate governance is necessarily distributed and largely informal; cooperative constitutional activity both prefigures and persists as an integral aspect of legitimate systems of government. The most promising and legitimate model for global citizenship is consequently neither that we would all just possess free-floating cosmopolitan sentiments of goodwill nor that we would all just comply with coercively imposed laws that are enacted to implement international treaties. Global citizenship should be conceived of, instead, as broadly participatory. An education suitable to nurturing virtues of global citizenship would engage students in the very kinds of global constitutional activities that require those virtues. These activities would include forms of self-organized governance. The next section is devoted to the role of such governance in solving common problems, using environmental problems as an example.

Self-Organized Governance and Global Environmental Problems

We cannot simply wait for solutions to global problems to materialize in the form of binding global treaties—not ethically and not practically, if progress is to be made in solving the problems we collectively face. Global climate destabilization is the most obvious case in point, but far from the only transnational environmental problem to be dealt with.[11] What we and our students can do, and many are already doing, is to participate in voluntary efforts to address the problems, encourage government and corporate reforms, and enlist others in respecting norms of cooperation that are not yet established in law. The work of Elinor Ostrom is helpful to understanding how such efforts can succeed.

A pioneer in the study of self-organized management of common resources, Ostrom identified the factors favorable to the success of such management and argued convincingly that there are advantages to organizing cooperatively on a variety of scales to address common problems. The research she and others conducted over several decades demonstrates that "a surprisingly large number of individuals facing collective action problems do cooperate. . . . Many groups in the field have self-organized to develop solutions to common-pool resource problems at a small to medium scale."[12] Sufficient assurance that others will cooperate does appear to be present in diverse settings in which there is no centralized enforcement of rules, so that individuals find it rational to cooperate by voluntarily complying with shared norms and participating in the enforcement of those norms through social networks. In light of this research and the failure of centralized governance that had replaced successful distributed management of common resources in developing countries, there has been a shift back to decentralized governance through common property arrangements in recent years.[13]

Ostrom identifies the following factors as among the most important that increase the likelihood of successful self-organization to manage common resources: individuals share an accurate understanding of the function of ecological systems and the costs and benefits of their own actions; they regard the system or resource as important and take a long-term view of its value in their decisions; it is important to each of them to have a reputation for being a "trustworthy reciprocator"; they can communicate with each other; they are able to engage in "informal monitoring and sanctioning" and consider it appropriate to do so; "social capital and leadership exist" and are associated with "previous successes in solving joint problems."[14] Two further factors of interest are that users who "share moral and ethical standards regarding how to behave in groups they form . . . and have sufficient trust in one another to keep agreements" are more likely to cooperate.[15] The implication of these findings for global civic education of the kind called for by the AAC&U is that accurate understanding, communication, shared norms, trust, and leadership are all important goals.

Having noted the feasibility of self-organization at local and regional scales, Ostrom makes three important arguments for proceeding with a distributed and multiscale approach to environmental governance, acknowledging that global agreements will be indispensable. The first is the relative speed of organization at subglobal levels. The second is the efficacy of distributed administration. The third is the importance of multiscale self-management to the legitimacy of any global regime of environmental governance that emerges.[16] There are competing theories of what is essential to the democratic legitimacy of global environmental governance, but the theories all regard three factors as important: accountability to those affected, representation of those affected, and participation by those affected in transnational spheres of public discourse.[17] From our point of view, wide participation in constitutional activity sufficient to create a global civil society is almost certainly a precondition for a global system of environmental governance that would be perceived as fair.

The argument that distributed and multiscale governance is efficacious rests on several well-grounded claims: that large units of government often lack the resources to effectively manage problems, reliance on local monitors is essential, adaptive tailoring of management to local circumstances is important, trust is more easily established in smaller-scale systems, local cooperation can be built on the local benefits it generates, and a multiscale approach permits experimentation that can inform subsequent efforts. From our perspective, the value in such experimentation is not only in the building of capacity or civic competence, but in the *experience* of civic competence and cooperation. What can plausibly motivate sustained civic effort is experience of competence, the relational rewards of joining with others in civic cooperation, trust established through incremental reciprocation, and valuing something of immense value: a desirable human future.

Constitutional Activity as the Culmination of Global Civic Education

Participation in multiscale self-organized governance is a form of constitutional activity, as we understand it. The constitutional activities in which global citizens engage could include the self-organized direct resource management that Ostrom has studied and many other forms of voluntary constitutional activities as well. Examples would be involvement in community and regional projects, developing advocacy networks, pursuing strategies to change corporate behavior, informing and shaping the policies of governments and IGOs, and encouraging and informing the negotiation of international treaties. Such forms of participation can be mediated by social networks, TANs, NGOs, and national or transnational social movement organizations. Whether or not such entities are involved, widespread participation in such forms of constitutional activity is essential to the formation of a global civil society that can hold international bodies accountable, provide representation for diverse global stakeholders, and engage in transnational public discourse that informs institutionalized global governance.[18] All of this is within the reach of college students, moreover, and already encouraged and facilitated by some colleges.[19] Participation in transnational cooperative constitutional activities would both prepare students for responsible global citizenship and contribute in useful ways to the emergence of a more cooperative and sustainable world order.

The very idea of global citizenship might be dismissed on the grounds that citizenship is a distinctive role, different from being a subject in a monarchy or dictatorship and more than just a social role. It is sometimes held, more specifically, that citizenship amounts to membership in a public or political community constituted as such under a system of government that provides fair and equal means to influence its policies. In response to this, we agree that "it is the *prospect* of influencing government policy according to reasonably fair rules and on a more or less equal basis with others that forms the distinguishing mark of the citizen," but we deny that it follows from this that the public in question must already be constituted as a whole under an existing government.[20] We take it to be sufficient for global citizenship that (1) the reform *or establishment* of such governance is a goal and

(2) the pursuit of that goal exhibits virtues of civic friendship and, accordingly, adopts means that are substantively consistent with establishing common systems of governance that provide equitable means for global citizens to influence policy. Both of these conditions are entailed by participation in global constitutional activity as we have defined it—activity through which people function and experience themselves as a global public and shape and preserve the norms and constitutional principles that regulate the global order. We have said that engagement in such activity makes a person a global citizen. An aspect of this we must now make explicit is the assumption that activities through which people function and experience themselves as a global public are necessarily ones in which they exhibit virtues of cooperation, goodwill, and fairness in pursuing civic goods—virtues we regard as aspects of civic friendship.

We have said that global civic education should culminate in global constitutional activity and that many forms of such activity are within the reach of college students. We offer the following illustration. The National Council for Science and the Environment (NCSE) hosts annual conferences in Washington, DC, bringing together prominent scientists, leaders from government and industry, and science journalists. Many universities are institutional affiliates of the NCSE and sponsor administrator, faculty, and student participants in the conferences. The aim is to facilitate the dissemination of actionable scientific understanding of the environment and stimulate the development of sound policy based on that understanding. The January 2011 conference, Our Changing Oceans, was convened not long after the catastrophic BP oil spill in the Gulf of Mexico and President Obama's call for the development of the first comprehensive ocean governance policy. The conference included a working session devoted to defining the guiding principles for such a policy.[21] This had been requested by the French ambassador to the United States, and it began with presentations by key players from recently developed regional ocean governance systems. The ambassador herself was a presenter and active participant in this group of about two dozen, but it was an American college student who volunteered and served as the scribe, as the group formulated and refined the basic principles of a comprehensive ocean governance framework to be sent on with the NCSE's recommendation to the Obama administration. At the conclusion of these sessions, participants from the US Environmental Protection Agency invited active participants in the session to a conference some weeks later at which their work on the framework would continue. Many such paths into continuing engagement in global constitutional activity can be imagined, and these sessions might have been only the first steps the student scribe was taking into continued involvement in such activity. Internships, fieldwork, and virtual conferencing might provide the basis for further steps.

Nurturing Global Civic Friendship

We take the aim of global civic education to be fostering global citizens who (1) possess personal attributes conducive to living well as members of a cooperative global community, (2) are engaged in global constitutional activity, and (3) are connected to one another by bonds of global civic friendship. We have focused on the idea of becoming a global citizen who is engaged in constitutional activities that seek solutions to global problems, and we have done so on the assumption that global problems are largely problems whose solution or management requires forms and norms of governance that do not yet exist. We shall conclude now with some remarks about global civic friendship as an intended product of such learning—what it could be and how it might be fostered by a liberal education for global citizenship.

The 1948 *Universal Declaration of Human Rights* states that education "shall promote . . . friendship among all nations," and it would presumably do so by cultivating in each student dispositions of basic moral respect and friendly goodwill toward the members of all national groups. It could begin in schools, as it did in the United States in 1917 through the Junior Red Cross, with "international interschool correspondence" designed to encourage "sympathetic appreciation" for children across the globe.[22] And it could continue in college through relationships formed in the experiential, collaborative, problem-based learning we envision as taking place through transnational networks, study abroad, internships, exchange programs, and the internationalization of American college and university student bodies. Yet, if liking a person on the basis of substantial firsthand acquaintance is a fundamental aspect of friendship, there will be few actual friendships between global citizens. How can the ideal of universal civic friendship be reconciled with the limited number of friends a person can actually have? One response to this is to hold that "it is not the emotions of friendship that are relevant to politics but rather its core practices."[23] This is predicated on the idea that there are practices through which friends manage conflict, express goodwill, build trust, and come to agreement; and the claim is that friendship of a politically valuable kind consists of people engaging in these practices in their encounters with others in the public sphere. Education that facilitates engagement in these practices with diverse others can lay the groundwork. We find this helpful, though without being persuaded that emotions of friendship such as goodwill and trust are, in the long run, functionally separable from practices that express them. It seems likely that persisting in the practices would normally engender the related emotions. It also seems likely, as an implication of BPNT, that *expressing* goodwill would be more intrinsically rewarding than simply enacting practices that would normally express goodwill.

Our own ideal of global civic friendship has two parts. The first is that not only individual people (natural persons) but collective and corporate actors in the public sphere would all display respect for global others and a commitment to establishing and accepting fair terms of global cooperation in the policies they advocate and adopt as their own. The second is that when there is contact between such individuals and actors it should exhibit friendliness or mutual goodwill.[24] The thought we shall close with is that the global learning the AAC&U and we commend might further the development of global networks of individuals who *are* genuinely friends with a significant number of diverse others, and the existence and successes of these networks may further the propagation and diffusion of the dispositions and practices of goodwill that are essential to civic friendship, so understood. Global citizens may make up a rather small proportion of the world's population for the foreseeable future, but they may in this way be connected to one another by bonds of global civic friendship that are both rewarding in themselves and vital to a desirable future—a future in which the opportunities for living well are more equitable and abundant than they are today.

Present knowledge of human motivation suggests that the rewards of such friendship, and of competence in freely protecting a world one values, could be motivationally powerful bases of global civic responsibility. Global civic virtue could incorporate such motivation and be consistent with virtuous patriotic motivation in the domestic sphere.

By contrast with views that see patriotism and global citizenship as fundamentally incompatible, we have argued that true civic virtue is manifested in responsibility across all of the civic spheres to which a person belongs. It combines cosmopolitan respect for people the world over with appropriate responsiveness to the good of one's country and communities. Such responsiveness may display a special devotion to one's country, but this is no more inherently incompatible with global civic virtue than a special devotion to one's city, town, or civic organizations is inherently incompatible with fulfilling one's civic responsibilities at a regional or national level. Recognizing this should lead institutions of higher learning to not only accept the AAC&U's globalized version of the Progressive Era's "community civics" model but also bridge the two with regional initiatives that address the problems of rural communities left behind by economic globalization. Colleges and universities should consider how they can direct some of their formidable imagination and resources to community outreach, partnerships, and projects that serve the public interest, even—or especially—in towns and regions where institutions of public knowledge are vilified as bastions of a corrupt liberal elite that has abandoned real Americans. How might such projects deploy the diverse forms of expertise cultivated and gathered together in these institutions? How might they bring multidisciplinary teams of faculty, administrators, and students together in work that is both intellectually rewarding and socially valuable? How might this strengthen the education of students at all levels and better prepare them for citizenship, work, and living well in the society and world that await them?

King invoked a cosmopolitan ethic in his speech at Riverside Church in 1967, and we have suggested how this ethic might be made real and motivationally potent through the friendships that reach across racial, national, and other divides. A world intent on cooperating to solve common problems will construct inspiring images of international unity, but to inspire effectively they must build on a foundation of achieved friendship, successes in working together, and global civic intelligence. Global civic education must evoke and illustrate the virtues of civic friendship, competence, and intelligence, and in doing so communicate the intrinsic rewards of global civic responsibility. It must also be honest about how progress actually occurs, and must equip students with the global civic understanding and competence required to succeed. We have argued that patriotism should be conceived as the motivational core of civic virtue with respect to one's own country, and we have identified such motivation as an appropriate responsiveness to the value of what is valuable in a country. Understood in this way, patriotic sentiment has a cosmopolitan counterpart that animates global civic virtue, and the two are compatible. Learning what is valuable in one's country and the world beyond it may be the journey of a lifetime, but it is a journey on which we can all make progress.

Realizing America in a Global Age

O, let my land be a land where Liberty
Is crowned with no false patriotic wreath,
But opportunity is real, and life is free,
Equality is in the air we breathe.

—Langston Hughes[1]

Margaret Gordon was just a student in need of answers when it happened. Many of her classmates at Kent State had returned the night before to a university that had been placed under martial law. A curfew had been imposed, and the Ohio National Guard was out in force and armed, on foot and in helicopters with searchlights overhead. Yet, little had been communicated by the university or its president, who did not return from his travels to manage the crisis. Buildings were locked down as students continued to arrive and make their way to their dorms, where—pursued by Guardsmen with bayonets drawn—they frantically tried to enter their buildings, as those inside struggled to help them, distressed that their campus was under siege and not knowing why. Other students and faculty returned the next morning, the fourth of May in 1970, the day it happened, and in classrooms across the university that Monday morning they asked each other why there were National Guardsmen on their campus. The professor in Margaret's 8:00 a.m. class was among those who suggested they all assemble on the commons— not knowing they had been forbidden to assemble there—a meeting place where antiwar protests had taken place. By noon, over two thousand students had gathered, some to protest the presence of National Guard on the campus, but most to hear from faculty and student leaders. Guardsmen fired tear gas and advanced on them with fixed bayonets, moving the students across Blanket Hill and into a practice field bordering the Prentice Hall parking lot. All but a few of the students remained sixty to seventy-five yards from the Guardsmen as they marched back up the hill. Why did the Guardsmen then stop, turn, and fire on the students? It is evident in photos of the event that some did not fire *at* the students but over their heads or at the ground.

When the Guardsmen opened fire, Margaret was 110 yards away from them in the parking lot, a few feet from Allison Krause, who was killed, and from Douglas Wrentmore, who was wounded. Margaret was knocked to the ground and shielded by a parked car, and Allison and Douglas were among the thirteen wounded and dying students felled by a thirteen-second hail of gunfire. "When I was able to stand up from between the two cars and from underneath the people on top of me . . . I looked around in disbelief and saw bodies . . . on the ground. I didn't know who was dead . . . [but] my life would be changed forever."[2] Having survived this horrific chapter in the history of American higher education, Gordon has often been asked to recount these experiences of an ordinary student pursuing her education on a day in the American "Heartland" that changed the way people across the world think about patriotism, war, and the militarization of schools.

Photos of the Kent State dead and wounded circled the globe and a strike by 4 million students shut down 450 universities, colleges, and high schools across the United States. On May 8, eleven people were bayoneted by Guardsmen at the University of New Mexico, and on May 15 city and state police fired on a crowd of student protesters at Jackson State University, in Mississippi, killing two students and injuring twelve. Richard Nixon, the president whose decisions had brought the country to war with itself, withdrew to Camp David as the nation's capital exploded in violent protest.

How we think about democracy and the imperatives of wartime discipline matters. Does democratic debate over the merits of a war "give comfort to our enemies"? Is dissent that is motivated by the good of one's country and consistent with norms of public reason not patriotic? What if the war is conducted by our own government in a way that is not only contrary to our own self-interest and ideals—the ideals on which the legitimacy of our own system of government rests—but contrary to international conventions whose authority the United States has formally recognized and relied upon? What happened at Kent State when many students were away for the weekend of May 2 and 3 was beyond dissent, beyond the give-and-take of reasons. In that season of dissent—of reiterations of reasons that never registered— what happened was that the ROTC building was torched. We saw in chapter 3 how the logic of "total war" has sometimes encouraged the militarization of schools and mobilization of students for both combatant and noncombat-ant roles in war. We saw how this has drawn students into meaningful and personally rewarding citizenship and public service, but we also saw how it has aligned with indoctrination and rituals of mass compliance that suppress independent thought and contributions to public reason, undermining the legitimacy of government authority and the wisdom of its decisions. The presence of ROTC units on college campuses has been controversial, and in the spring of 1970—when the US carpet bombing of Cambodia that had drawn it into the Vietnam War was in its second year and Nixon's announce-ment of a ground invasion of eastern Cambodia triggered massive protests across the United States—their presence was a flash point of frustration with an administration whose hubris seemed boundless.[3]

Many observers of the events at Kent State concluded that the Guardsmen knew before the events of May 4 that they would be ordered to fire on the students and had time to contemplate what they would do, allowing some to decide that they would disobey the orders by firing above the students' heads or at the ground. The possibility they would be given such orders would have been, in any case, self-evident; and they were, by all accounts, exhausted and ambivalent, at best, about being deployed to a campus to put students opposed to the war in their place. What were they doing there but enforc ing a conception of total war—of democracy itself—in which leaders are the "deciders" and the role of students and other citizens is to comply without question? They weren't protecting property or defending themselves when they fired on students in the Prentice Hall parking lot—a fact that would have been clear to them at the time. Even the fire in the ROTC building could eas-ily have been prevented by the police alone, if they had done their jobs; and investigating the arson as a criminal act after the fact would have sufficed and been far preferable to the indiscriminate use of lethal force that occurred.[4]

It bears emphasizing that many of those who fired upon the students will have suffered grievous moral wounds. They will have suffered guilt, shame, and maybe feelings of betrayal by those whose orders they obeyed, and their suffering will almost certainly have been compounded by the unjustified condemnation heaped on Guardsmen and US soldiers upon their return from Vietnam. Nancy Sherman describes "moral injury" as

> experiences of serious inner conflict arising from what one takes to be griev-ous moral transgressions that can overwhelm one's sense of goodness and humanity. The sense of transgression can arise from (real or apparent) trans-gressive commissions and omissions perpetrated by oneself or others, or from bearing witness to the intense human suffering and detritus that is a part of

the grotesquerie of war and its aftermath. In some cases the moral injury has less to do with specific (real or apparent) transgressive acts than with a generalized sense of falling short of moral and normative standards befitting good persons and good soldiers.[5]

Sherman writes tellingly of the "disconnect between those who wear the uniform and those who don't," of bridgeable chasms of understanding that are seldom bridged, and the importance of building those bridges to healing the moral injuries of those who serve and to greater wisdom in deploying them.[6] Patriotic responsiveness to all that is valuable in one's country would seek and embody this understanding, healing, and wisdom. It would repudiate the judgment of FBI director J. Edgar Hoover, and many residents of the communities near Kent State, that the student victims at Kent State deserved to die, and it would repudiate the related false assumption that requiring our youths to kill on our behalf does them no harm.[7]

The "elect us and stay out of our way" version of democracy is associated with the name Joseph Schumpeter, but expressions of it in American public life are not uncommon.[8] Public figures do not always know what they are doing, however, and disorderly protest and violent suppression of protest are predictable responses to perceptions that the give-and-take of reasoning together in the public interest is all give and no uptake. Weigh up the enormous, unredeemed human, material, and environmental costs of the Vietnam War and invasion of Iraq in the aftermath of the September 11 terrorist attacks, and add to those costs the immense strains they imposed on our national psyche.

How do we live together as a society governed by reason and laws above which no one stands, and not by force wielded by a few or many in their own interest? This ancient question, posed by Plato, is as important today as it was 2,400 years ago, and Plato's answer remains an essential point of departure for answering it. His view, as we have seen, is that the society must first be just and its laws and policies worthy of respect. Opportunity, freedom, and equality must be "real" and palpable, to paraphrase Langston Hughes. If the society is not just and its laws and policies are not worthy of respect, then people who reason together with insight will have reason to reform or abandon it. An aspect of the society being just is that it would provide all its children with an education that affirms their belonging and cultivates understanding, capabilities, and virtues foundational to them living well together, including the intellectual and civic virtues essential to them reasoning together productively and responding appropriately to reasons and evidence.

A goal in creating citizens is that they would accept the burdens of co-operation along with its benefits. Understanding the merits of their country and having grown up a part of it, they would predictably—but not invariably—acquire a form of patriotic attachment that could play a central motivating role in civic virtue. Whatever the norms of civic life might contribute to the prevalence of civic virtue and responsibility, schools have important roles to play in cultivating civic intelligence, friendship, and competence, and it is vital to our collective well-being that in war and peace alike they understand what virtues are and what virtuous patriotism would entail. War is enormously costly, and a public prepared to think about the prospect of it critically and intelligently will be one better able to protect its own interests and the interests of distant others whose fates are so often entwined with our own. Knowing what is actually at stake in policy debates and who is manipulating the terms of those debates can be hard to fathom, but an alert citizenry stands a better chance. We have also seen that it is in the nature of legitimate governance to be widely distributed. It is the limits of force itself—of a command-and-control model of democracy—that make justice, civic virtues, and distributed self-governance essential to a society being governable. As we saw in chapters 1 and 6, there is no legitimate or effective alternative to self-governance guided by broadly acceptable norms of cooperation.

Countries are works in progress, and in the age of global climate disruption and unsustainability unfolding before us, the fates of individual countries are inseparable from that of a global civilization in progress. Countries and civilizations are works in progress because they are essentially constellations of interacting systems: social, political, economic, and environmental. How they are constituted and function—their *constitutions* in the sense that matters most—are dependent on the ongoing, highly distributed observance of norms. These norms must be broadly acceptable to be broadly observed, and they must be compatible with the preservation of land and the diverse capacities of ecosystems on which we all ultimately depend for the opportunities we cherish.

Langston Hughes's poem "Let America Be America Again" ends with these lines:

> We, the people, must redeem
> The land, the mines, the plants, the rivers.
> The mountains and the endless plain—
> All, all the stretch of these great green states—
> And make America again!

The poem opens with a reference to "the pioneer on the plain seeking a home where he himself is free," and this and many other features of it suggest that when Hughes refers to redeeming the "land" he has in mind making America a place where all are free, equal, and have abundant opportunities. It is nevertheless striking that he invokes a wealth of geographical features of "these great *green* states" and suggestions of human reliance on those features in depicting the making or realization of America he has in mind. What is a "country," in the end, but a land we claim and make our home, its waters, climate, and the life and ways of life it sustains?

It is hard to overstate the challenges faced by global humanity and how far we are from believing in our capacity to face and solve these challenges collectively. A paradox of our collective existence as Americans is the extraordinary ideological dominance of competitive individualism wed to a doctrine of unregulated markets—of markets that are allegedly self-maintaining and optimally efficient in providing social well-being in the absence of any attempts by the public to act through its governments in the public interest. In the aftermath of the 2008 financial collapse that could not have happened if economic orthodoxy were sound, and in the face of overwhelming evidence that the land, the country we treasure, is endangered as never before, Americans continue to vest inordinate faith in the efficacy of market relations and remarkably little faith in its power as a democratic public to act efficaciously *as a public* through its democratic institutions. We have also largely failed to grasp that the problems we experience at home are also global and cannot be solved without global cooperation. The global expansion of humanity has closed every habitable frontier, and the economic expansion that continues without an expanding planetary base is overburdening and degrading the capacities of the natural systems on which we rely. If living sustainably means living in a way that preserves opportunities to live well that are as good as we have now into the future, then our way of life is unsustainable because it is destroying the land and the opportunities it offers.[9] Shall we insist, against all odds, that the present consumerist American way of life "is not negotiable," or must we realize a less opulent and more just version of an American dream?

Plato wrote against the background of the Peloponnesian War, the end of an Athenian empire of territories conquered to colonize with its poor, and we have seen how the idea of a closing of the American frontier and related problems of urban poverty stimulated an analogous rethinking of justice and citizenship by leading figures in the Progressive movement. The problems we now face and can only solve through global cooperation are similarly those of a global expansion of humanity that has overshot the planet's limits and has nowhere to go but turn back on itself. We resist but must surely embrace a domestic and global civic-mindedness and cultivate civic virtues of cooperative problem solving, loving this land, and *realizing* what is essential to preserving it—a realization of America in a global age, recognizing the importance of our ideals of freedom, equality, and opportunity to a just and sustainable world order.

NOTES

PREFACE AND ACKNOWLEDGMENTS

1. Starting points for a tour of the philosophical literature on patriotism would include Jürgen Habermas, "Citizenship and National Identity: Some Reflections on the Future of Europe," *Praxis International* 12, no. 1 (1992): 1–19; Stephen Nathanson, *Patriotism, Morality, and Peace* (Lanham, MD: Rowman and Littlefield, 1993); Maurizio Viroli, *For Love of Country: An Essay on Patriotism and Nationalism* (Oxford: Clarendon Press, 1995); Martha Nussbaum, *For Love of Country?*, ed. Joshua Cohen (Boston: Beacon Press, 1996); Robert McKim and Jeff McMahan, eds., *The Morality of Nationalism* (New York: Oxford University Press, 1997); George Kateb, "Is Patriotism a Mistake?," *Social Research* 67, no. 4 (2000): 901–24; Igor Primoratz, ed., *Patriotism* (New York: Humanity Books, 2000); Samuel Scheffler, *Boundaries and Allegiances: Problems of Justice and Responsibility* (Oxford: Oxford University Press, 2001); Kok-Chor Tan, *Justice without Borders: Cosmopolitanism, Nationalism, and Patriotism* (Cambridge: Cambridge University Press, 2004); Richard Arneson, "Do Patriotic Ties Limit Global Justice Duties?," *Journal of Ethics* 9, nos. 1–2 (2005): 127–50; Simon Keller, *The Limits of Loyalty* (Cambridge: Cambridge University Press, 2007); Jan-Werner Müller, *Constitutional Patriotism* (Princeton, NJ: Princeton University Press, 2007); Igor Primoratz and Aleksandar Pavkovic, eds., *Patriotism: Philosophical and Political Perspectives* (Aldershot: Ashgate, 2007); Stephen Macedo, "Just Patriotism?," *Philosophy and Social Criticism* 37, no. 4 (2011): 413–23; John Kleinig, Simon Keller, and Igor Primoratz, *The Ethics of Patriotism: A Debate* (Oxford: Wiley Blackwell, 2015).

2. Max Bearak, "Theresa May Criticized the Term 'Citizen of the World.' But Half the World Identifies That Way," *Washington Post*, October 5, 2016, https://www.washingtonpost.com/news/worldviews/wp/2016/10/05/theresa-may-criticized-the-term-citizen-of-the-world-but-half-the-world-identifies-that-way/; "Theresa May's Rejection of Enlightenment Values," *Guardian, US edition*, October 9, 2016, letters, https://www.theguardian.com/politics/2016/oct/09/theresa-may-rejection-of-enlightenment-values.

3. Bearak, "Theresa May Criticized the Term 'Citizen of the World.'"

4. Department of Defense, "DoD Releases Report on Security Implications of Climate Change," *DoD News*, July 29, 2015, http://www.defense.gov/News-Article-View/Article/612710; Joshua Hammer, "Is a Lack of Water to Blame for the Conflict in Syria?," *Smithsonian Magazine* (June 2013), http://www.smithsonianmag.com/innovation/is-a-lack-of-water-to-blame-for-the-conflict-in-syria-72513729/?no-ist.

INTRODUCTION

1. From Langston Hughes, "Let America Be America Again," in *The Collected Poems of Langston Hughes*, ed. Arnold Rampersad and David Roessel (New York: Vintage, 1995 [orig. pub. in 1938]), 189–91.
2. "A Time to Break Silence," in *Testament of Hope: The Essential Writings and Speeches of Martin Luther King, Jr.*, ed. James Melvin Washington (San Francisco: Harper, 1986), 231–44, at 231.
3. Ibid., 232.
4. Ibid., 233.
5. Quoted in C. Vann Woodward, *The Strange Career of Jim Crow*, 3rd rev. ed. (New York: Oxford University Press, 1974), 175–76.
6. Allan M. Jalon, "A Break-In to End All Break-Ins," *Los Angeles Times*, March 8, 2006.
7. In response to pressure from big business, the FBI and Department of Homeland Security's systematic surveillance of citizens' organizations, classification of legal political activity as security threats, and disruption of peaceful demonstrations is now focused especially on peaceful environmental activists. See Donald Gilliland, "Pennsylvania Homeland Security Office Engaged in Domestic Surveillance, Compared Political Groups to Al Qaeda," *Patriot-News*, November, 12, 2010, http://www .pennlive.com/midstate/index.ssf/2010/11/pennsylvania_homeland_security_1 .html; Nafeez Ahmed, "Pentagon Bracing for Public Dissent over Climate and Energy Shocks," *Guardian* June, 14, 2013, http://www.theguardian.com/environment /earth-insight/2013/jun/14/climate-change-energy-shocks-nsa-prism; Adam Federman, "We're Being Watched: How Corporations and Law Enforcement Are Spying on Environmentalists," *Earth Island Journal* 28, no. 2 (2013), http://www.earthisland .org/journal/index.php/eij/article/we_are_being_watched/.
8. "A Time to Break Silence," 234.
9. Cf. Alasdair MacIntyre, "Is Patriotism a Virtue?," in *Patriotism*, ed. Igor Primoratz (Amherst, NY: Humanity Books, 2002), 43–73; Habermas, "Citizenship and National Identity." MacIntyre conceives of patriotism as loyalty to a national project, some aspects of which are beyond critical scrutiny, because what is and is not virtuous is substantially a function of community membership (45, 49, and 50). By contrast, Habermas predicates his constitutional patriotism on a process of ongoing scrutiny of a country's values in light of universal norms. In developing this view, Habermas relied on the neo-Kantian idea of a postconventional identity "directly inspired by the 'stage five' [of moral development] identified by [Lawrence] Kohlberg in which universal rights take priority over specific laws," writes Justine Lacroix, in "Does Europe Need Common Values? Habermas vs. Habermas," *European Journal of Political Theory* 8, no. 2 (2009): 141–56, at 143. See also Jan-Werner Müller, *Another Country: German Intellectuals, Unification and National Identity* (New Haven, CT: Yale University Press, 2000), chap. 3; "On the Origins of Constitutional Patriotism," *Contemporary Political Theory* 5 (2006): 278–96; and *Constitutional Patriotism*.
10. King wrote in his "Letter from Birmingham City Jail" that "a just law is a man-made code that squares with the moral law or law of God. An unjust law is a code that is out of harmony with the moral law. . . . Any law that uplifts human personality is just. Any law that degrades human personality is unjust. All segregation statutes are unjust because segregation distorts the soul and damages the personality." In *Testament of Hope*, 289–302, at 293.
11. Readers who are concerned to place this conception of legitimacy within the scheme of contemporary philosophical theories of legitimacy should note that as we define

it, legitimacy pertains to the mediation of public life by truthful and reasoned persuasion. Governance is legitimate if it creates and respects the conditions for rational and informed cooperation. Legitimacy thereby makes ongoing general cooperation with acts of government likely, but *actual* consent is not a necessary condition for legitimacy, strictly speaking, and *hypothetical* consent is not a sufficient condition for it. The idea of hypothetical consent is a way of capturing the merits of cooperating, and such merits are among the conditions for rational and informed consent, but even in the face of such merits a system of governance might be imposed in illegitimately coercive, manipulative, or deceptive ways. In chapter 4 ("The Ethical Dimensions of Education"), we distinguish five ethical dimensions of governance. In the terms of that scheme, legitimacy is an aspect of governance being ethical with respect to its manner or mode of conduct (chapter 4, "Universal Respect for Persons").

12. "A Time to Break Silence," 241.

13. Ibid., 242, 233.

14. See Nathanson, *Patriotism, Morality, and Peace,* 34–35; Igor Primoratz, "Patriotism," in *The Stanford Encyclopedia of Philosophy* (Fall 2013 ed.), ed. Edward N. Zalta, http://plato.stanford.edu/archives/fall2013/entries/patriotism/. John Kleinig, Simon Keller, and Igor Primoratz write in the introduction to *The Ethics of Patriotism* that although they "do not agree on any straightforward definition of patriotism . . . there are three crucial defining features of patriotism they all accept" (4). What they agree on is that (1) "patriotism is a species of love or loyalty and that the object of patriotism . . . is a country"; (2) patriots have "special concern for" or "favor" their own country over others, "usually expressed as a concern for the country's interests" that can include "concern with the country's moral performance"; and (3) patriotism involves "identification with your country" in the sense that "you see your country as *yours*" (4–5). Primoratz is the only one of the three who relies on a specification of necessary and sufficient conditions for patriotism (6–7), and he follows Nathanson in defining it as "love of one's country, identification with it, and special concern for its well-being and that of compatriots" (74). This is essentially our definition.

15. Martha Nussbaum, "Teaching Patriotism: Love and Critical Freedom," *University of Chicago Law Review* 79, no. 1 (2012): 213–50, at 237–40.

16. Katherine Lee Bates (lyrics) and Samuel A. Ward (music), "America the Beautiful," https://en.wikipedia.org/wiki/America_the_Beautiful

17. Woody Guthrie, "This Land Is Your Land," http://www.woodyguthrie.org/Lyrics/This_Land.htm.

18. John Kleinig ("The Virtue in Patriotism," in Kleinig, Keller, and Primoratz, *The Ethics of Patriotism,* 37) notes similarly the significance of "landscapes and bushland" in Australian patriotism, exemplified by this verse from "My Country," a poem by Dorothea Mackellar "that many Australians learn in childhood":

> I love a sunburnt country, a land of sweeping plains,
> Of ragged mountain ranges, of droughts and flooded rains,
> I love her far horizons, I love her jewel-sea,
> Her beauty and her terror—the wide brown land for me!

19. A transcription of the lyrics as sung by Robeson in November 1947, available at https://www.youtube.com/watch?v=U3syulBjkng.

20. For recent defenses of forms of patriotism that include a valuing of and concern to protect the land and ecosystems that are fundamental to the well-being of a country, see Robyn Eckersley, "Environmentalism and Patriotism: An Unholy Alliance?," in Primoratz and Pavkovic, *Patriotism,* 183–200; Philip Cafaro, "Patriotism as an

Environmental Virtue," *Journal of Agricultural and Environmental Ethics* 23 (2010): 185–206. Igor Primoratz allows that love for a land and people is basic to patriotism when he writes that, "at least in the modern usage, the patriot's love of his country is not restricted to the land and those living in it, but also encompasses the state and its citizens," in "Patriotism and Morality: Mapping the Terrain," in Primoratz and Pavkovic, *Patriotism*, 17–35, at 18.

21. Brian Barry defined *nationalism* as an ideology according to which "all human beings should have one and only one nationality, which should be their primary focus of identity and loyalty." Nationalist movements call on their followers "to subbordinate the common interests . . . that they share with their fellow citizens to those that they share with other members of the national group" ("Nationalism," in *The Blackwell Encyclopedia of Political Thought*, ed. David Miller [Oxford: Basil Blackwell, 1987], 352–54, at 352, 353).

22. Maurizio Viroli defends "love of country understood . . . as love of common liberty and the institutions that sustain it," and refers to this as "patriotism of liberty," in *For Love of Country*, 12, 17, and 184. Viroli essentially endorses Habermas's form of constitutional patriotism, while disputing the latter's view of republicanism as Aristotelian and unsuitable for pluralistic societies (170–71). Habermas's constitutional patriotism is "a new version" of the republican tradition, he argues (171), and it involves "an attachment to the values of democracy as they are embodied in the political institutions and documents of the Federal Republic" (172). Fending off nationalist and communitarian arguments that civic virtue requires stronger cultural ties, Viroli insists that "a love of common liberty should be all that we need"—an attachment to political values "perceived and lived as cultural values" (174, 175).

23. Editorial Board, "Emmanuel Macron Mounts a Patriot's Challenge to Marine Le Pen," *New York Times*, April 23, 2017, https://www.nytimes.com/2017/04/23/opinion/france -election-emmanuel-macron-marine-le-pen-a-patriots-challenge.html?_r=0.

24. For an analysis of populism with many examples from contemporary Europe and observations about the 2016 US presidential election, see Jan-Werner Müller, *What Is Populism?* (Philadelphia: University of Pennsylvania Press, 2016). Müller's analysis is consistent with subsequent events, such as President Trump's tweet on and about the day of his inauguration: "January 20th, 2017, will be remembered as the day the people became the rulers of this nation again," quoted in Jessica Estrepa, "The First 100 Days: What Did Trump Tweet?," *USA Today—Democrat and Chronicle*, April 30, 2017, 5B. Müller's view that populism is antidemocratic is also borne out by evidence that authoritarianism is a growing force in American politics, with about one-third of Americans expressing a preference for "strong" authoritarian leadership over democracy ahead of the 2016 presidential election. See Amanda Taub, "The Rise of American Authoritarianism," *Vox*, March 1, 2016, http://www.vox .com/2016/3/1/11127424/trump-authoritarianism#change; Karen Stenner, *The Authoritarian Dynamic* (Cambridge: Cambridge University Press, 2005).

25. Jane Addams, *Peace and Bread in Time of War* (Urbana: University of Illinois Press, 2002 [1922]), 81.

26. Niraj Chokshi, "Muhammad Ali on Donald Trump: 'Muslims Have to Stand Up' to Anti-Islamic Speech," *Washington Post*, December 10, 2015, https://www.washing tonpost.com/news/acts-of-faith/wp/2015/12/10/muhammad-ali-on-donald-trump -muslims-have-to-stand-up-to-anti-islamic-speech/.

27. Ibid.

28. Quoted in Dave Zirin, *What's My Name, Fool? Sports and Resistance in the United States* (Chicago: Haymarket Books, 2005), 58.

29. Randy Roberts and Johnny Smith, *Blood Brothers: The Fatal Friendship between Muhammad Ali and Malcolm X* (New York: Basic Books, 2016), 14ff.

30. Zirin, *What's My Name, Fool?*, 63.

31. Roberts and Smith, *Blood Brothers*, 227–29.

32. Zirin, *What's My Name, Fool?*, 64.

33. Roberts and Smith, *Blood Brothers*, 307.

34. Zirn, *What's My Name Fool?*, 66.

35. Ibid., 65.

36. On belligerent citizenship, see Sigal Ben-Porath, *Citizenship under Fire: Democratic Education in Times of Conflict* (Princeton, NJ: Princeton University Press, 2006). On football and "savage confrontation" as an aspect of American identity, see Steve Almond, *Against Football: One Fan's Reluctant Manifesto* (Brooklyn, NY: Melville House, 2014).

37. Almond, *Against Football*, 142, and 116ff. and 144ff. generally, citing, among other sources, Ivan Hannel, Andrew Gartman, and Jason Karpel, "Chronic Traumatic Encephalopathy: The Developing Case against High School Football," *Entertainment, Arts and Sport Law Journal* 25, no. 1 (Spring 2014): 44–50.

38. Almond, *Against Football*, 136.

39. Ibid., 133.

40. Ibid., 145, 143.

41. Tzvi Freeman, "Courage or Cowardice: What Makes the 9/11 Hijackers Terrorists and Us Heroes?," Chabad.org, http://www.chabad.org/library/article_cdo/aid/1608824/jewish/Does-it-take-courage-to-be-a-terrorist.htm. For a debate on this, see "Six Views: Were the 9/11 Terrorists Cowards or Courageous?," *In Character: A Journal of Everyday Virtues*, posted January 1, 2009, http://incharacter.org/archives/courage/six-views-were-the-911-terrorists-cowards-or-courageous/.

42. "CIA's Final Report: No WMD Found in Iraq," NBC News, April 25, 2005, http://www.nbcnews.com/id/7634313/ns/world_news-mideast_n_africa/t/cias-final-report-no-wmd-found-iraq/.

43. Positive aspects of national pride are a central theme of Richard Rorty's book, *Achieving Our Country* (Cambridge, MA: Harvard University Press, 1998).

44. Simon Keller argues that bad faith or self-deception is an inescapable aspect of patriotism, in *The Limits of Loyalty* and "The Case against Patriotism," in Kleinig, Keller, and Primoratz, *The Ethics of Patriotism*, 48–72.

45. Maurizio Viroli notes in *For Love of Country*, a history of patriotism and its relationship to nationalism, that "until the 1840s the language of patriotism in England was used not only to debate constitutional and parliamentary issues but also to address problems of social justice that 'arose directly from urbanization and industrialisation,' as Hugh Cunningham has remarked ["The Language of Patriotism, 1750–1915," *History Workshop* 12 (1981): 16]. The new social conflict was described in terms of despotism: industrial workers and the urban poor were the new slaves; the capitalists and landlords the new despots. . . . Poverty and exploitation were denounced as incompatible with the values of citizenship that patriotism had been sustaining for centuries" (141–42).

46. Julie Turkewitz, "Knee by Knee, a Protest against Racism Spreads," *New York Times*, October 4, 2016, A11–12; Nancy Armour, "How National Anthem Protests Bring Out Worst in People," *USA Today*, Sports, September 27, 2016, http://www.usatoday.com

/story/sports/columnist/nancy-armour/2016/09/25/colin-kaepernick-anthem-pro
tests-backlash-social-media-emails/91076216/; Dave Zirin, "Colin Kaepernick is Winning," *Nation*, September 9, 2016, https://www.thenation.com/colin-kaepernick-is
-winning/.

CHAPTER ONE

1. "Making Good Citizens of the Foreign Born: How Public School Authorities and
    Mayor's Defense Committee Have Systemized Training in Our Language and Cus-
    toms," *New York Times*, October 28, 1917, SM5.
2. Ibid.
3. Paula Fass, *Outside In: Minorities and the Transformation of American Education* (New
    York: Oxford University Press, 1989), 16.
4. David Tyack, *The One Best System: A History of American Urban Education* (Cambridge,
    MA: Harvard University Press, 1974), 230.
5. Quoted in ibid., 132.
6. Fass, *Outside In*, 23.
7. Jacob Riis, *How the Other Half Lives: Studies among the Tenements of New York* (New
    York: Charles Scribner's Sons, 1914).
8. See, e.g., Diana Selig, *Americans All: The Cultural Gifts Movement* (Cambridge, MA:
    Harvard University Press, 2008).
9. Patricia Albjerg Graham, *Schooling America: How the Public Schools Meet the Nation's
    Changing Needs* (Oxford: Oxford University Press, 2005), 23.
10. Proceedings of the National Teachers Association afterward the National Education
    Association from its foundation in 1857 to the close of the session of 1870, compiled
    by Henry Barnard, LL.D., vol. 8 (Syracuse, NY: C. W. Bardeen, 1866), 605–6.
11. Nietzsche was himself ardently antinationalistic, but in the present context it is
    enough to know the book titles Orwell had in mind: *Beyond Good and Evil* and *Will to
    Power*. Both were published under Nietzsche's name, but the latter was a compilation
    of his writings published by his sister without his consent.
12. George Orwell, *England, Your England, and Other Essays* (London: Secker and War-
    burg, 1953), 41–42. John Lukacs echoes Orwell's understanding of patriotism,
    while contrasting it with a conception of nationalism closer to Müller's: "Patriot-
    ism is the love of a particular land, with its particular traditions; nationalism is the
    love of something less tangible, of the myth of a 'people,' justifying many things";
    Democracy and Populism: Fear and Hatred (New Haven, CT: Yale University Press,
    2005), 36.
13. Edmund Morris, *The Rise of Theodore Roosevelt* (New York: Ballantine Books, 1979),
    esp. chaps. 22–26.
14. Quote is drawn from Roosevelt's essay entitled "What 'Americanism' Means," in
    which he honors the quote's original author. Theodore Roosevelt, "What 'American-
    ism' Means," *Forum*, April 1894, 196.
15. See Jonathan M. Hansen, *The Lost Promise of Patriotism: Debating American Identity,
    1890–1920* (Chicago: University of Chicago Press, 2003).
16. Quoted in Robert D. Richardson, *William James: In the Maelstrom of American Modern-
    ism* (Boston: Houghton Mifflin, 2006), 358–59.
17. Hansen, *The Lost Promise of Patriotism*, 15.
18. See, e.g., Steven L. Schlossman, "Is There an American Tradition of Bilingual Educa-
    tion? German in the Public Elementary Schools, 1840–1919," *American Journal of
    Education* 91, no. 2 (1983): 143–45.

19. James Crawford, *Bilingual Education: History, Politics, Theory, and Practice* (Trenton, NJ: Crane Publishing Co., 1989), 19–20.
20. Amanda Kibler, "Speaking Like a 'Good American': National Identity and the Legacy of German-Language Education," *Teachers College Record* 110, no. 6 (2008): 1246.
21. Jonathan Zimmerman, "Ethnics against Ethnicity: European Immigrants and Foreign Language Instruction, 1890–1940," *Journal of American History* 88, no. 4 (2002): 1383–84.
22. Kibler, "Speaking Like a 'Good American,'" 1252–54.
23. Cynthia M. Koch, "Teaching Patriotism: Private Virtue for the Public Good in the Early Republic," in *Bonds of Affection*, ed. J. Bodnar (Princeton, NJ: Princeton University Press, 1996), 26–31.
24. Carl F. Kaestle, *Pillars of the Republic: Common Schools and American Society, 1780–1860* (New York: Hill and Wang, 1983), 81.
25. Joel Spring, *The American School, 1642–1985* (New York: Longman, 1986), 140. We will address the content of these readers in more detail in chapter 2.
26. Julie Reuben, "Beyond Politics: Community Civics and the Redefinition of Citizenship in the Progressive Era," *History of Education Quarterly* 37, no. 4 (1997): 406–16.
27. "The Teaching of Community Civics," US Bureau of Education Bulletin, No. 23, Whole Number 650 (Washington, DC: Government Printing Office, 1915), 9.
28. Julie Reuben, "Patriotic Purposes: Public Schools and the Education of Citizens," in *The Public Schools*, ed. S. Fuhrman and M. Lazerson, Institutions of American Democracy (Oxford: Oxford University Press, 2005), 13.
29. "The Teaching of Community Civics," 10.
30. Ibid., 17–18.
31. Ibid., 11–12.
32. Ibid., 20, emphasis in original.
33. Ronald W. Evans, *The Social Studies Wars: What Should We Teach the Children?* (New York: Teachers College Press, 2004), 10–15. Also see Thomas Fallace, "Did the Social Studies Really Replace History in American Secondary Schools?," *Teachers College Record* 110, no. 10 (2008): 2245–70.
34. Evans, *The Social Studies Wars*, 19.
35. Harold Rugg, *That Men May Understand: An American in the Long Armistice* (New York: Double Day, Doran and Co., 1941), 177–80.
36. Ibid., 181–93. On the development of Rugg's worldview and curricular program, see Ronald W. Evans, *This Happened in America: Harold Rugg and the Censure of Social Studies* (Charlotte, NC: Information Age Publishing, Inc., 2007), esp. chaps. 2 and 3.
37. Quoted in Peter F. Carbone, *The Social and Educational Thought of Harold Rugg* (Durham, NC: Duke University Press, 1977), 139, emphasis in original.
38. Rugg, *That Men May Understand*, 44–45; Carbone, *The Social and Educational Thought of Harold Rugg*, 28. On the series' development, see Marian C. Schipper, "Textbook Controversy: Past and Present," *New York University Education Quarterly* 14, no. 3 (1983): 31–32.
39. Herbert M. Kliebard, *The Struggle for the American Curriculum, 1893–1958*, 2nd ed. (New York: Routledge, 1995), 175.
40. Carbone, *The Social and Educational Thought of Harold Rugg*, 28.
41. "Board Clears 4 School Books of Red Charges," *Washington Post*, December 19, 1935, 1.
42. Carbone, *The Social and Educational Thought of Harold Rugg*, 26.
43. Schipper, "Textbook Controversy," 32. In 1941, Falk helped found the "Guardians of American Education, Inc.," a reactionary group that claimed it was "a completely

independent, non-profit, non-political, non-sectarian organization. . . . Alarmed by propaganda in school books designed to undermine patriotism and faith in American institutions and bring about radical changes in our form of society." The group dissolved in 1952. Yale University, Divinity Library Special Collections, Social Ethics Pamphlet Collection, Record Group No. 73, Series I: G, Box 16, Folder 16, "Guardians of American Education, Inc."

44. Bertie C. Forbes, "Treacherous Teachings," *Forbes*, August 15, 1939, 8.
45. Ibid.
46. O. K. Armstrong, "Treason in the Textbooks," *American Legion Magazine*, September 1940, 8.
47. C.A. Bowers, "Social Reconstructionism: Views from the Left and the Right, 1932–1942," *History of Education Quarterly* 10, no. 1 (1970): 39.
48. Armstrong, "Treason in the Textbooks," 8.
49. See, e.g., Diane Ravitch, *The Language Police: How Pressure Groups Restrict What Students Learn* (New York: Vintage Books, 2004); Joan DelFattore, *What Johnny Shouldn't Read: Textbook Censorship in America* (New Haven, CT: Yale University Press, 1992); Michael W. Apple and Linda K. Christian-Smith, eds., *The Politics of the Textbook* (New York: Routledge,1991); Frances FitzGerald, *America Revised: History Schoolbooks in the Twentieth Century* (Boston: Little, Brown and Co., 1979).
50. Roger Lotchin, *The Bad City in the Good War: San Francisco, Los Angeles, Oakland, and San Diego* (Bloomington: Indiana University Press, 2003), 231.
51. Jonathan Zimmerman, *Whose America? Culture Wars in the Public Schools* (Cambridge, MA: Harvard University Press, 2002), 79.
52. Allan Nevins, "American History for Americans," *New York Times Magazine*, May 3, 1942, 6; Benjamin Fine, "Ignorance of U.S. History Shown by College Freshman," *New York Times*, April 4, 1943, 1.
53. Quoted in Richard J. Paxton, "Don't Know Much about History—Never Did," *Phi Delta Kappan* 85, no. 4 (2003): 267.
54. Sam Wineburg, "Crazy for History," *Journal of American History* 90, no. 4 (2004): 1403–4.
55. See, e.g., Sam Wineburg, *Historical Thinking and Other Unnatural Acts: Charting the Future of Teaching the Past* (Philadelphia: Temple University Press, 2001).
56. Emphasis in original. Wineburg and Monte-Sano included this qualifier when pilot testing revealed that some students responded to the prompt by simply listing "the first five names that popped into mind." These, the researchers found, "turned out to be the usual suspects—George Washington, Thomas Jefferson, Abraham Lincoln, Bill and Hillary Clinton, or George W. Bush."
57. Sam Wineburg and Chauncey Monte-Sano, "'Famous Americans': The Changing Pantheon of American Heroes," *Journal of American History* 94, no. 4 (2008): 1189–91.
58. Sixty-seven percent of the respondents chose King, 60 percent Parks, and 44 percent Tubman.
59. David Tyack, *Seeking Common Ground: Public Schools in a Diverse Society* (Cambridge, MA: Harvard University Press, 2003), 43.
60. Zimmerman, *Whose America?*, 127.
61. See, e.g., Howard Zinn, *A People's History of the United States: 1492–Present*, 20th anniversary ed. (New York: Harper Collins, 1999); Ronald Takaki, *A Different Mirror: A History of Multicultural America* (Boston: Little, Brown and Co., 1993).
62. For a full accounting of these events, see Gary B. Nash, *History on Trial: Culture Wars and the Teaching of the Past* (New York: Alfred A. Knopf, 1998).

63. Raymond W. Smock, "In Conversation with Senator Robert C. Byrd," *Perspectives on History: The Newsmagazine of the American Historical Association* (January 2004), http://www.historians.org/publications-and-directories/perspectives-on-history/january-2004/in-conversation-with-senator-robert-c-byrd.

64. Margarita L. Meléndez, "Teaching American History," *Federalist: Newsletter of the Society for History in the Federal Government*, 2nd ser., no. 19 (Fall 2008).

65. Ibid.

66. Sandra Day O'Connor and Roy Romer, "Not Math Alone," *Washington Post*, March 25, 2006, A19.

67. US Department of Education, Office of the Deputy Secretary, Program Description: Race to the Top Fund (Washington, DC, June 2016), http://www2.ed.gov/programs/racetothetop/index.html.

68. "Literacy Wins, History Loses in Fiscal '12 Federal Budget," *Education Week*, January 11, 2012, 19.

69. Ellen Sorokin, "NEA Delivers History Lesson," *Washington Times*, August 19, 2002, A01.

70. Lynne Cheney, William J. Bennett, William Damon, and John Agresto, "September 11: What Our Children Need to Know," Thomas B. Fordham Foundation (Washington, DC, September 2002), https://edexcellence.net/publications/sept11.html.

71. Joppatowne High School: Homeland Security and Emergency Preparedness Program, Harford County Public Schools, Joppa, MD, https://www.edline.net/pages/JoppatowneHighSchool/Homeland_Security_Page.

72. Mimi Hall, "High School Course Aims for Better Citizens," *USA Today*, December 10, 2007, http://usatoday30.usatoday.com/news/nation/2007-12-10-homeland_N.htm; Sibile Morency, "How to Stop Terrorism? Begin in School," ABC News /Technology, January 11, 2008, http://abcnews.go.com/Technology/story?id=4117248&page=1.

73. Chris Colin, "Black Ops Jungle: The Academy of Military Industrial-Complex Studies," *Mother Jones* (September/October 2007), http://motherjones.com/politics/2007/09/black-ops-jungle-academy military-industrial-complex-studies.

74. Joppatowne High School: Homeland Security and Emergency Preparedness Program, Harford County Public Schools, Joppa, MD, https://www.edline.net/pages/JoppatowneHighSchool/Homeland_Security_Page.

75. Oakland Military Institute College Preparatory Academy, Oakland Unified School District, Oakland, California, http://www.oakmil.org.

76. Student Handbook, Oakland Military Institute College Preparatory Academy, Oakland Unified School District, Oakland, CA, p. 3, http://www.oakmil.org/apps/pages/index.jsp?uREC_ID=527646&type=d&pREC_ID=1042315.

77. Rachel Gottlieb, *Hartford Courant*, December 4, 2006, http://www.courant.com/news/education/hc-militaryschool1203.artdec04,0,4893652.story?page=1&coll=hc-headlines-education.

78. Delaware Military Academy: About Delaware Military Academy, Wilmington, DE, http://www.demilacad.org/about-us.htm.

79. NJROTC: What Is Navy Junior Reserve Officers Training Corps?, Pensacola, FL, http://www.njrotc.navy.mil/what_is_njrotc.html.

80. Democracy Prep Public Schools: About Democracy Prep, New York, NY, http://democracyprep.org/about/.

81. Schools That Can: Democracy Prep Public School, New York, NY, http://www.schoolsthatcan.org/schools/ny/democracy-prep/.

82. Democracy Prep Public Schools: Civic Education at Democracy Prep, New York, NY, http://www.democracyprep.org/about/civic.

CHAPTER TWO

1. "Letter, Billy Gobitas to Minersville, Pennsylvania, school directors, explaining why the young Jehovah's Witness refused to salute the American flag," November 5, 1935, William Gobitas Papers, Library of Congress. Cited in "Words and Deeds in American History," http://lcweb2.loc.gov/cgi-bin/query/r?ammem/mcc:@field(DOCID +@lit(mcc/016)).

2. Sarah Barringer Gordon, *The Spirit of the Law: Religious Voices and the Constitution in Modern America* (Cambridge: Belknap Press, 2010), 27. Frequently referred to in the literature as a twelve-year-old, Lillian was born on November 2, 1923, making her eleven years of age when she refused to recite the pledge and twelve when she was expelled.

3. Carl L. Bankston and Stephen J. Caldas, *Public Education: America's Civil Religion* (New York: Teachers College Press, 2009).

4. John H. Westerhoff, *McGuffey and His Readers: Piety, Morality, and Education in Nineteenth-Century America* (Nashville: Abingdon, 1978), 32; Harvey C. Minnich, *William Holmes McGuffey and His Readers* (New York: American Book Co., 1936), 8.

5. Dolores P. Sullivan, *William Holmes McGuffey: Schoolmaster to the Nation* (Rutherford, NJ: Fairleigh Dickinson University Press, 1994), 32–33.

6. Ibid., 44–45.

7. Sullivan, *William Holmes McGuffey*, 44, 63, 90–91.

8. Westerhoff, *McGuffey and His Readers*, 45.

9. Minnich, *William Holmes McGuffey and His Readers*, 7.

10. *McGuffey's Second Eclectic Reader*, rev. ed. (New York: Van Antwerp, Bragg and Co., 1879), 28.

11. Ibid., 7.

12. Ibid., 28.

13. Ibid., 38–39.

14. Richard D. Mosier, *Making the American Mind: Social and Moral Ideas in the McGuffey Readers* (New York: King's Crown Press, 1947), 40.

15. *New McGuffey Fourth Reader* (New York: American Book Co., 1901), 130.

16. David Glassberg, *American Historical Pageantry: The Uses of Tradition in the Early Twentieth Century* (Chapel Hill: University of North Carolina Press, 1990), 24.

17. Ibid., 225.

18. "American Independence Week" was celebrated from June 28 to July 5, 1926, when most schools were not in session. Cities around the country marked the occasion with a variety of festivities. See, e.g., "American Independence Week," *Pittsburgh Gazette*, June 11, 1926, 6.

19. "'Patriots' Week' in Schools to Be Observed Feb. 12 to 22," *New York Times*, February 7, 1926, 3.

20. Ibid.

21. Christopher N. Matthews, *An Archaeology of History and Tradition: Moments of Danger in the Annapolis Landscape* (New York: Springer, 2002), 108.

22. Mary Antin, *The Promised Land* (Boston: Houghton Mifflin, 1969), 199.

23. Ibid., 206.

24. Ibid., 222.

25. Ibid., 223.

26. Ibid., 224.

27. Ibid., 224–25.

28. Bankston and Caldas, *Public Education*, 46.

29. Ibid.

30. James W. Loewen, *Lies My Teacher Told Me: Everything Your American History Textbook Got Wrong* (New York: Simon and Schuster, 1995), esp. chap. 3. For a comprehensive history of Plymouth Colony, see Nathaniel Philbrick, *Mayflower: A Story of Courage, Community, and War* (New York: Viking Press, 2006).

31. For a comprehensive history of Jamestown Colony, see James Horn, *A Land as God Made It: Jamestown and the Birth of America* (New York: Basic Books, 2005).

32. "George Washington's Thanksgiving Proclamation, October 3, 1789," George Washington Papers, Library of Congress, http://lcweb2.loc.gov/ammem/GW/gw004.html. Noticeably absent from Washington's proclamation is any specific mention of the Pilgrims of Plymouth Colony or their Thanksgiving celebration. For a history of the Thanksgiving holiday, see James W. Baker, *Thanksgiving: The Biography of an American Holiday* (Hanover: University of New Hampshire Press, 2009).

33. Ibid., 71.

34. Stuart McConnell, "Reading the Flag: A Reconsideration of the Patriotic Cults of the 1890s," in *Bonds of Affection: Americans Define Their Patriotism*, ed. J. Bodnar (Princeton, NJ: Princeton University Press, 1996), 106.

35. Ibid., 107.

36. Glassberg, *American Historical Pageantry*, 11–12.

37. For comprehensive histories of the GAR and its predecessors, see Wallace E. Davies, *Patriotism on Parade: The Story of Veterans' and Hereditary Organizations in America, 1783–1900* (Cambridge, MA: Harvard University Press, 1955), and Mary R. Dearing, *Veterans in Politics: The Story of the G.A.R.* (Baton Rouge: Louisiana State University Press, 1952).

38. For a comprehensive history of the American flag, see Marc Leepson, *Flag: An American Biography* (New York: St. Martin's Press, 2005).

39. McConnell, "Reading the Flag", 110.

40. Ibid., 110.

41. George T. Balch, *Methods of Teaching Patriotism in the Public Schools* (New York: D. Van Nostrand Co., 1890), ix.

42. Ibid., vii.

43. Cecilia Elizabeth O'Leary, *To Die For: The Paradox of American Patriotism* (Princeton, NJ: Princeton University Press, 1999), 152.

44. Balch, *Methods of Teaching Patriotism in the Public Schools*, 12.

45. Of the staff, e.g., Balch wrote, "Of straight-grained, well-seasoned white maple, or other light, strong wood; three-eighths of an inch in diameter and thirty-six inches long; tipped with a wooden spear-head, covered with *silver* leaf." Ibid., 21.

46. Ibid., 23.

47. Ibid., 28, 32.

48. Ibid., 38.

49. Cody Dodge Ewert, "Schools on Parade: Patriotism and the Transformation of Urban Education at the Dawn of the Progressive Era," *Journal of the Gilded Age and the Progressive Era* 16, no. 1 (January 2017): 65–81.

50. Jeffrey E. Mirel, *Patriotic Pluralism: Americanization Education and European Immigrants* (Cambridge, MA: Harvard University Press, 2010), 58.

51. O'Leary, *To Die For*, 185.

52. "The Schoolhouse Flag," *Youth's Companion*, July 2, 1891, 376.

53. Ibid.

54. "The Flag and the Public Schools," *Youth's Companion*, January 9, 1890, 31.
55. Jeffrey Owen Jones and Peter Meyer, *The Pledge: A History of the Pledge of Allegiance* (New York: St. Martin's Press, 2010), 42.
56. Ibid., 44.
57. Ewert, "Schools on Parade," 70.
58. Jones and Meyer, *The Pledge*, 55–69.
59. "National School Celebration of Columbus Day: The Official Programme," *Youth's Companion*, September 8, 1892, 446–47.
60. "The Address for Columbus Day: The Meaning of the Four Centuries," *Youth's Companion*, September 8, 1892, 446.
61. Ibid.
62. Quoted in Jones and Meyer, *The Pledge*, 71.
63. Francis Bellamy, "The Story of the Pledge of Allegiance to the Flag," *University of Rochester Library Bulletin* 8, no. 2 (1953): http://rbscp.lib.rochester.edu/3418.
64. "Salute to the Flag," *Youth's Companion*, September 8, 1892, 446.
65. Bellamy, "The Story of the Pledge of Allegiance to the Flag."
66. Jones and Meyer, *The Pledge*, 110.
67. Ibid., 87, 109.
68. O'Leary, *To Die For*, 231.
69. Richard J. Ellis, *To the Flag: The Unlikely History of the Pledge of Allegiance* (Lawrence: University Press of Kansas, 2005), 65–67.
70. Ibid., 129–37.
71. For a sourcebook on these cases, see Michael Kent Curtis, ed., *The Constitution and the Flag: The Flag Salute Cases*, 2 vols., vol. 1 (New York: Garland Publishing Co., 1993).
72. Jones and Meyer, *The Pledge*, 122.
73. Ellis, *To the Flag*, 99–102; Gordon, *The Spirit of the Law*, 30.
74. *Gobitis v. Minersville School Dist.*, 24 F. Supp. 271 (E.D. Pa. 1938).
75. *Gobitis v. Minersville School Dist.*, 24 F. Supp. 271 (E.D. Pa. 1938).
76. *Minersville School Dist. v. Gobitis*, 108 F.2d 683 (3d Cir. 1939).
77. Gordon, *The Spirit of the Law*, 31.
78. *Minersville School Dist. v. Gobitis*, 310 U.S. 586 (1940).
79. On the violence following the ruling, see Shawn Francis Peters, *Judging Jehovah's Witnesses: Religious Persecution and the Dawn of the Rights Revolution* (Lawrence: University Press of Kansas, 2002), chap. 3.
80. Ellis, *To the Flag*, 109–10.
81. Quoted in Melvin I. Urofsky, "The Flag Salute Case," *OAH Magazine of History* 9, no. 2 (Winter 1995): 31.
82. Jones and Meyer, *The Pledge*, 132.
83. Peters, *Judging Jehovah's Witnesses*, 245–46.
84. Kern Alexander and M. David Alexander, *American Public School Law*, 5th ed. (Belmont, CA: Thompson/West, 2005), 240–43.
85. *West Virginia State Board of Education v. Barnette*, 319 U.S. 624 (1943).
86. Ellis, *To the Flag*, 140–43.

CHAPTER THREE
1. The commission consisted of representatives of the NEA and American Association of School Administrators.
2. *Education and the Defense of American Democracy* (Washington, DC: Educational Policies Commission of the National Education Association and the American

Association of School Administrators, 1940), 21; *A War Policy for American Schools* (Washington, DC: Educational Policies Commission of the National Education Association and the American Association of School Administrators, 1942), 3.

3. The significance of this being a *transformation* should be noted: Although the deployment of US military forces on foreign soil has been a frequent occurrence, Americans typically resist conceiving of their country in militaristic terms, and schools in the United States have avoided the totalitarian practice of employing schools to prepare future generations for war. Americans responded with bewilderment at the United States' sudden involvement in a war against Japan following the 1941 Japanese attack on Pearl Harbor, a response that mimicked their reaction to the US declaration of war against Germany twenty-four years earlier. See Horace M. Kallen, "The War and Education in the United States," *American Journal of Sociology* 48, no. 3 (1942): 335–36.

4. Thomas J. Morgan, *Patriotic Citizenship* (New York: American Book Co., 1895), 10.

5. Robert W. Tucker, *Woodrow Wilson and the Great War: Reconsidering America's Neutrality, 1914–1917* (Charlottesville: University of Virginia Press, 2007), esp. chap. 5.

6. John Milton Cooper, *Woodrow Wilson: A Biography* (New York: Alfred A. Knopf, 2009), 308–15.

7. David Esposito, "Political and Institutional Constraints on Wilson's Defense Policy," *Presidential Studies Quarterly* 26, no. 4 (1996): 116.

8. *The Statutes at Large of the United States of America from December, 1915, to March, 1917*, vol. 39, Sixty-Fourth Congress, Session I, chap. 134, 1916 (Washington, DC: Government Printing Office, 1917), 191–92.

9. History of Military Training at Bangor High School, WCSH.com, Portland, ME, March 14, 2011, http://bangor.wcsh6.com/news/news/history-military-training-bangor-high -school/58747.

10. Leavenworth High School: JROTC History, Leavenworth Unified School District, Leavenworth, KS, http://lhs.usd453.org/apps/pages/index.jsp?uREC_ID=216724&type=d &pREC_ID=745203.

11. Cecilia Elizabeth O'Leary, *To Die For: The Paradox of American Patriotism* (Princeton, NJ: Princeton University Press, 1999), 179–86.

12. Ibid., 30

13. Journal of the Thirty-First Annual Encampment, Department of Michigan, Grand Army of the Republic, held at Kalamazoo June 22–24, 1909 (Lansing, MI: Wynkoop Hallenbeck Crawford, Co., 1909), 110.

14. O'Leary, *To Die For*, 183.

15. "Report of the Adjutant General of the State of California for the Period November 17, 1914, to June 30, 1920" (Sacramento: California State Printing Office, 1922), 51.

16. "California Rules and Regulations for the Government of the High School Cadets" (Sacramento: California State Printing Office, 1911), 27–28. The program's official title remained "California High School Cadets" until 1947, when the state legislature adopted the popular name "Cadet Corps." For a detailed curriculum of the wartime Cadet Corps program, see *California High School Cadets: A Manual for Period Instruction* (Sacramento: Adjutant General, State of California, 1944). Also see *California Cadet Corps: The Cadet Manual* (Sacramento: California State Printing Office, 1953), 3–5.

17. Quoted in Jonathan Zimmerman, "Storm over the Schoolhouse: Exploring Popular Influences upon the American Curriculum, 1890–1941," *Teachers College Record*, 100, no. 3 (1999): 609–10.

18. Ibid.
19. See, e.g., Frederick Rand Rogers, "The Amazing Failure of Physical Education," *American School Board Journal* 109, no. 6 (1944): 17–19; William P. Uhler, "Military Training in Secondary Schools," *American School Board Journal* 102, no. 2 (1941): 28–29.
20. "No High School Cadet Corps," *Daily Palo Alto Times*, September 13, 1940; "Education Board Suggests Course to 'Harden' Boys," *Daily Palo Alto Times*, October 11, 1940.
21. "Toughen Up: Ray to Enlarge, Improve Program of Physical Fitness at High School," *Daily Palo Alto Times*, July 10, 1942, 5; Howard C. Ray, "School Adapts 'Physical Ed' to Wartime," *Daily Palo Alto Times*, October 1, 1942.
22. Mary Katherine Hays and Frank Greenfield, "Uniforms Appear in Paly Halls as Cadet Corps Gets Started," *Daily Palo Alto Times*, October 5, 1944.
23. "Cadet Corps to Be Part of P.A. High School Life," *Daily Palo Alto Times*, September 6, 1944.
24. "Cadets to Collect Tin May 7," *Berkeley Jacket*, May 3, 1944, 1.
25. "First Military Ball Tonight," *Berkley Jacket*, June 2, 1944, 1.
26. California Cadet Corps: F.A.Q., Camp San Luis Obispo, CA, https://cacadets.org /about/faq.
27. "Report of the Adjutant General of the State of California for the Period November 17, 1914, to June 30, 1920" (Sacramento: California State Printing Office, 1922), 52.
28. History of Military Training at Bangor High School, WCSH.com, Portland, ME, March 14, 2011, http://bangor.wcsh6.com/news/news/history-military-training -bangor-high-school/58747; Leavenworth High School: JROTC History, Leavenworth Unified School District, Leavenworth, KS, http://lhs.usd453.org/apps/pages/index .jsp?uREC_ID=216724&type=d&pREC_ID=745203.
29. Jill Tucker, "S.F. School Board to Vote on JROTC," *SF Gate*, May 13, 2009, http://www .sfgate.com/bayarea/article/S-F-school-board-to-vote-on-JROTC-3161996.php.
30. Jill Tucker, "S.F. School Board Grants Junior ROTC 2 More Years," *SF Gate*, June 14, 2011, http://www.sfgate.com/bayarea/article/S-F-school-board-grants-Junior-ROTC -2-more-years-2368152.php.
31. On the history of the American Red Cross, see Julia F. Irwin, *Making the World Safe: The American Red Cross and a Nation's Humanitarian Awakening* (Oxford: Oxford University Press, 2013); Foster Rhea Dulles, *The American Red Cross: A History* (New York: Harper and Brothers, 1950).
32. Woodrow Wilson quoted in "Junior Red Cross," *Journal of Education* 125, no. 12 (1917): 319.
33. Dulles, *The American Red Cross*, 169.
34. Julia F. Irwin, "Teaching 'Americanism with a World Perspective': The Junior Red Cross in the U.S. Schools from 1917 to the 1920s," *History of Education Quarterly* 53, no. 3 (2013): 269.
35. Ibid., 258.
36. Quoted in ibid., 271.
37. Dulles, *The American Red Cross*, 250–51.
38. Ibid., 254.
39. American Red Cross: Contributions of Young Americans, Washington, DC, http:// www.redcross.org/about-us/who-we-are/history/contributions-young-americans.
40. "Red Cross Collections Go over the Top," *Campanile*, November 19, 1943.
41. "Girls' League War Projects Successful," *Campanile*, October 29, 1943.
42. Sally Maycock, "Join the Junior Red Cross," *Campanile*, November 10, 1942.

43. "Trooper Reeves: 'It's Rugged'; Field Enlists in Nurse Corps," *Campanile*, October 15, 1943.

44. Ronald D. Cohen, "Schooling Uncle Sam's Children: Education in the USA, 1941–1945," in *Education and the Second World War: Studies in Schooling and Social Change*, ed. R. Lowe (Bristol: Falmer Press, 1992), 50.

45. Richard M. Ugland, "'Education for Victory': The High School Victory Corps and Curricular Adaptation During World War II," *History of Education Quarterly* 19, no. 4 (1979): 435.

46. "High-School Victory Corps Announced," *Education for Victory* 1, no. 15 (1942): 1.

47. Ugland, "Education for Victory," 438.

48. David E. Hanson, "Home-Front Casualties of War Mobilization: Portland Public Schools, 1941–1945," *Oregon Historical Quarterly* 96, nos. 2–3 (1996): 197.

49. Ugland, "Education for Victory," 438.

50. I. L. Kandel, *The Impact of the War upon American Education* (Chapel Hill: University of North Carolina Press, 1948), 92.

51. Sue Maxwell, "A Birmingham High School Meets the Challenge of War," *American School Board Journal* 107, no. 1 (1943): 20–21.

52. Ibid., 21–22.

53. Phillip W. Perdew, "The Secondary School Program in World War II," *History of Education Journal* 3, no. 2 (1952): 44; Frank B. Lindsay, "Preflight Aeronautics in California Schools," *California Journal of Secondary Education* 18, no. 1 (1943): 139.

54. For participation rates in various states, see Timothy DeWitt Connelly, "Education for Victory: Federal Efforts to Promote War-Related Instructional Activities by Public School Systems, 1940–1945" (PhD diss., University of Maryland, 1982), 239–43.

55. Ugland, "Education for Victory," 440–41.

56. Cohen, "Schooling Uncle Sam's Children," 50.

57. Andrew Spaull, "World War II and the Secondary School Curriculum: A Comparative Study of the USA and Australia," in *Education and the Second World War: Studies in Schooling and Social Change*, ed. R. Lowe (Bristol: Falmer Press, 1992), 164.

58. E. B. White, "One Man's Meat," *Harper's Magazine*, April 1943, 500.

59. Spaull, "World War II and the Secondary School Curriculum," 164.

60. Quoted in Connelly, "Education for Victory," 221.

61. Ibid., 219.

62. William O'Neill, *A Democracy at War: America's Fight at Home and Abroad in World War II* (New York: Free Press, 1993), 79–80; Robert W. Kirk, *Earning Their Stripes: The Mobilization of American Children in the Second World War* (New York: Peter Lang, 1994), 79.

63. "Sharing America: A Defense Savings Program for Schools" (Washington, DC: Government Printing Office, 1941).

64. "Songs for Schools at War," published for the Music Educators National Conference by Education Section, War Savings Staff, Treasury Dept. (Washington, DC: Government Printing Office), 1943.

65. Ibid., 11.

66. "Queens, Varieties, Ambulances Are Featured in Bond Drive," *Berkeley Jacket*, June 4, 1943.

67. Jean Hutton, "War Stamp Contest Launched," *Daily Palo Alto Times*, October 27, 1942.

68. "Sequoia High Accepts Paly's Challenge; War Stamp Purchasing Duel Underway," *Campanile*, October 29, 1942.

69. Joan Paulin (Manning), interview with author, Palo Alto, CA, September 15, 2000.

70. Peter Edmondson, interview with author, Palo Alto, CA, September 25, 2000.
71. Paula Berka (Minard), interview by author, Palo Alto, CA, August 7, 2000.
72. "Pursuit Plane: First Day of School Drive Nets $14,750," *Daily Palo Alto Times*, April 8, 1943.
73. "Picture of Paly's B-25 Bomber Here," *Campanile*, October 15, 1943.
74. "Keep It Burning," *Berkeley Jacket*, April 10, 1942.
75. "You Can Do Your Part," *Berkeley Jacket*, April 24, 1942.
76. "P-30 to Spark BHS War Bond Drive," *Berkeley Jacket*, January 6, 1944.
77. "Students, Teachers Purchase $60,000 Worth of Bonds," *Berkeley Jacket*, June 11, 1943.
78. William M. Tuttle, *Daddy's Gone to War: The Second World War in the Lives of America's Children* (New York: Oxford University Press, 1993), 125–26.
79. "Cover Art," *American School Board Journal* 109, no. 3 (1944).
80. Richard Lingeman, *Don't You Know There's a War On? The American Home Front, 1941–1945* (New York: G. P. Putnam's Sons, 1970), 265–66.
81. Ira T. Miller, "Seattle Schools Are in the War," *American School Board Journal* 107, no. 4 (1943): 19.
82. I. C. Johnson, "A Township High School Helps War Effort," *American School Board Journal* 104, no. 6 (1942): 41.
83. "Local Farmers Hit by Labor Shortage; Depend on Students," *Campanile*, September 24, 1942, 1.
84. Sally Edmondson (Allen), interview with author, Palo Alto, CA, September 25, 2000.
85. Peter Edmondson, interview with author, Palo Alto, CA, September 25, 2000; Paula Berka (Minard), interview by author, Palo Alto, CA, August 7, 2000.
86. Charles W. Lockwood, "Palo Alto's Students Work in the Harvests," *California Journal of Secondary Education* 18, no. 4 (1943): 236.
87. B. Allen, "No Gym for War-Working Students?," *Campanile*, April 9, 1943.
88. "Berkeley High Students Go to Work," *Berkeley Jacket*, May 15, 1942, 3.
89. National FFA Organization, "FFA History," https://www.ffa.org/about/what-is-ffa/ffa-history.
90. Bradley W. Bryant, "History of the Virginia FFA Association" (doctoral diss., Virginia Polytechnic Institute and State University, 2001), 24.
91. Philip M. Fravel, "A History of Agricultural Education in South Carolina with an Emphasis on the Public School Program" (doctoral diss., Virginia Polytechnic Institute and State University, 2004), 28.
92. Bryant, "History of the Virginia FFA Association," 26.
93. Larry Cuban, "Enduring Resiliency: Enacting and Implementing Federal Vocational Education Legislation," in *Work, Youth, and Schooling: Historical Perspectives on Vocationalism in American Education*, ed. H. Kantor and D. B. Tyack (Stanford, CA: Stanford University Press, 1982), 48.
94. Herbert M. Kliebard, *The Struggle for the American Curriculum, 1893–1958*, 2nd ed. (New York: Routledge, 1995), 111–22.
95. On the social efficiency movement, see, e.g., Raymond Callahan, *Education and the Cult of Efficiency: A Study of the Social Forces That Have Shaped the Administration of the Public Schools* (Chicago: University of Chicago Press, 1962).
96. "Roosevelt Talks on 'The Man Who Works with His Hands,'" *Spokesman-Review*, June 1, 1907, 2.
97. Kliebard, *The Struggle for the American Curriculum*, 124.
98. *The Statutes at Large of the United States of America from December, 1915, to March, 1917*, vol. 39, Sixty-Fourth Congress, Session II, chaps. 113, 114, 1917 (Washington,

DC: Government Printing Office, 1917), 929–36. For a contemporary accounting of federal aid to vocational education, see Charles A. Prosser and Charles R. Allen, *Vocational Education in a Democracy* (New York: Century Co., 1925), esp. chap. 16.

99. D. Barry Croom, "The Development of the Integrated Three-Component Model of Agricultural Education," *Journal of Agricultural Education* 49, no. 1 (2008): 114.

100. Another important national organization, 4-H, grew out of the club movement of the late nineteenth and early twentieth centuries, just as the FFA did. See Franklin M. Reck, *The 4-H Story: A History of 4-H Club Work* (Ames: Iowa State College Press, 1951); Thomas Wessel and Marilyn Wessel, *4-H: An American Idea, 1900–1980* (Chevy Chase, MD: National 4-H Council, 1982).

101. Bryant, "History of the Virginia FFA Association," 70.

102. Fravel, "A History of Agricultural Education in South Carolina with an Emphasis on the Public School Program," 200.

103. On the New Farmers of America, see Cecil L. Strickland, *New Farmers of America in Retrospect: The Formative Years, 1935–1965* (Prarie View, TX: Prarie View A&M University, 1994).

104. A. Webster Tenney, *The FFA at 50* (Alexandria, VA: Future Farmers of America, 1977), 21.

105. W. H. Garrison, "The Future Farmers of America," *South Carolina Education* 14, nos. 4 and 5 (1933): 136–37.

106. National FFA Organization: FFA History, Indianapolis, IN, https://www.ffa.org /about/what-is-ffa/ffa-history.

107. *Future Farmers of American in Action* (Washington, DC: Future Farmers of America, 1945).

108. Agnes Harrigan Mueller, *That Inspiring Past: The Future Farmers of America in Minnesota, 1930–1955* (Saint Paul, MN: Webb Publishing Co., 1955), 53–54.

109. J. A. Linke, "Past, Present, and Future of F.F.A.," *Agricultural Education* 5, no. 4 (1932): 61.

110. W. A. Ross, "Meeting the Needs of Rural Youth," *Phi Delta Kappan* 25, no. 8 (1943): 145.

111. Croom, "The Development of the Integrated Three-Component Model of Agricultural Education," 114–15.

112. *United States Statutes at Large, 1950–1951*, vol. 64, Eighty-First Congress, Session II, Chap. 823, 1950 (Washington, DC: Government Printing Office, 1952), 563–67.

113. National FFA Organization Records, 1916–2008, http://www-lib.iupui.edu/special/ffa.

114. National FFA Organization, "FFA History."

CHAPTER FOUR

1. William Galston, *Liberal Purposes: Goods, Virtues and Diversity in the Liberal State* (Cambridge: Cambridge University Press, 1991), 243–44.

2. Ibid., 244.

3. David Archard, "Should We Teach Patriotism?," *Studies in Philosophy and Education* 18, no. 3 (1999): 157–73; Harry Brighouse, "Should We Teach Patriotic History?," in *Citizenship and Education in Liberal-Democratic Societies*, ed. Kevin McDonough and Walter Feinberg (Oxford: Oxford University Press, 2003), 157–75; Michael Hand, *Patriotism in Schools* (London: PESGB, 2011).

4. Robert Fullinwider, "Patriotic History," in *Public Education in a Multicultural Society*, ed. R. Fullinwider (Cambridge: Cambridge University Press, 1996), 203–27; Eamonn Callan, *Creating Citizens* (Oxford: Clarendon Press, 1997); Sigal Ben-Porath,

Citizenship under Fire: Democratic Education in Times of Conflict (Princeton, NJ: Princeton University Press, 2005). The quote is from Ben-Porath, *Citizenship under Fire*, 103. While seeing a role for mythic history, she also offers criticisms of it at 51–54, and calls for "supplementing . . . patriotic teachings with a more complex view of the relational history of the nation," at 103.

5. Randall Curren, "Indoctrination," in *International Encyclopedia of Education*, ed. Gary McCulloch and David Crook (London: Routledge, 2008), 310–11; Eamonn Callan and Dylan Arena, "Indoctrination," in *The Oxford Handbook of Philosophy of Education*, ed. Harvey Siegel (Oxford: Oxford University Press, 2009), 104–21.

6. Marcia Baron, "Loyalty," in *Encyclopedia of Ethics*, 2nd ed., ed. Lawrence Becker and Charlotte Becker (New York: Routledge, 2001), vol. 2, 1027–29; Keller, *The Limits of Loyalty*.

7. David Walker, Randall Curren, and Chantel Jones, "Good Friendships among Children: A Theoretical and Empirical Investigation," *Journal for the Theory of Social Behaviour* 46, no. 3 (2016): 286–309.

8. A consequence of superior orders being viewed as absolutely binding was that they were also viewed as precluding punishment in US military tribunals when war crimes were committed in following orders. As pressure mounted to prosecute Nazi war criminals, the US Law of Land Warfare was revised in November 1944 to remove this barrier to punishment, and it was revised again in 1956 to say more explicitly that pursuing a superior's order is "not a defense." See William F. Fratcher, "The New Law of Land Warfare," *Missouri Law Review* 22, no. 2 (Apr. 1957): 143–61, 145–46.

9. *West Virginia State Board of Education v. Barnette*, 319 U.S. 624 (1943), 641; Robert Jackson, "Opening Statement before the International Military Tribunal," Nuremberg Trials, https://www.roberthjackson.org/speech-and-writing/opening-statement -before-the-international-military-tribunal/.

10. Albert Speer, *Spandau: The Secret Diaries*, trans. Richard and Clara Winston (New York: Macmillan, 1976), 192.

11. For examples based on a sampling of contemporary textbooks, see Brighouse, "Should We Teach Patriotic History?" For a contrasting view of the extent of actual distortion of history in these texts, see Fullinwider, "Patriotic History."

12. See Ian MacMullen, "Doing without Love: Civic Motivation, Affection, and Identification," *Journal of Politics* 76, no. 1 (2014): 73–85, which argues that cultivating identity is a better way to motivate civic responsibility than cultivating love.

13. On the role of love in patriotism, see Eamonn Callan, "Love, Idolatry, and Patriotism," *Social Theory and Practice*, 32, no. 4 (2006): 525–46; Martha Nussbaum, "Teaching Patriotism: Love and Critical Freedom," *University of Chicago Law Review* 79, no. 1 (2012): 213–50.

14. See Robert Fullinwider, "Moral Conventions and Moral Lessons," in *Philosophy of Education: An Anthology*, ed. Randall Curren (Oxford: Blackwell, 2007), 498–506; Randall Curren, "Judgment and the Aims of Education," *Social Philosophy and Policy* 31, no. 1 (2014): 36–59; Randall Curren, "Virtue Ethics and Moral Education," in *Routledge Companion to Virtue Ethics*, ed. Michael Slote and Lorraine Besser-Jones (London: Routledge, 2015), 459–70.

15. "The Teaching of Community Civics," 9.

16. Harold Rugg, quoted in Carbone, *The Social and Educational Thought of Harold Rugg*, 139.

17. "Berkeley High Students Go to Work," 3.

18. See Randall Curren, "A Neo-Aristotelian Account of Education, Justice, and the Human Good," *Theory and Research in Education* 11, no. 3 (2013): 232–50; *Philosophy of Education: An Anthology*.

19. John Dewey, *Democracy and Education* (New York: Macmillan, 1916), 98.

20. Eamonn Callan argues in "Love, Idolatry, and Patriotism" that patriotism and some partiality toward compatriots is compatible with cosmopolitan justice if it is nonidolatrous, and Harry Brighouse responds in "Justifying Patriotism" (*Social Theory and Practice* 32, no. 4 [2006]: 547–58) that (1) it is hard to justify such partiality to those made worse off by it (555–56) and (2) it may be very difficult to educationally and socially construct a "morally apt" patriotism that is not an obstacle to domestic and global justice (558). Martha Nussbaum attempts a reconciliation of patriotism and cosmopolitanism in "Toward a Globally Sensitive Patriotism," *Daedalus* 137, no. 3 (2008): 78–93, reversing her earlier view, in *For Love of Country?*, that patriotism and cosmopolitanism are fundamentally opposed. Richard Miller rejects any such reconciliation in "Unlearning American Patriotism," *Theory and Research in Education* 5, no. 1 (2007): 7–21. Other notable works on patriotic partiality and universal or cosmopolitan morality and justice include David Miller, *On Nationality* (Oxford: Oxford University Press, 1995); Richard Miller, "Cosmopolitan Respect and Patriotic Concern," *Philosophy and Public Affairs* 27 (1998): 202–24; Daniel Weinstock, "National Partiality: Confronting the Intuitions," *Monist* 82, no. 3 (1999): 516–41; Arneson, "Do Patriotic Ties Limit Global Justice Duties?"; Viet Bader, "Reasonable Impartiality and Priority for Compatriots: A Criticism of Liberal Nationalism's Main Flaws," *Ethical Theory and Moral Practice* 8 (2005): 83–103; David Miller, "Reasonable Partiality toward Compatriots," *Ethical Theory and Moral Practice* 8 (2005): 63–81; Stephen Nathanson, "Patriotism, War, and the Limits of Permissible Partiality," *Journal of Ethics* 13 (2009): 401–11; Macedo, "Just Patriotism?"

21. For other defenses of limited patriotic partiality, see Marcia Baron, "Patriotism and 'Liberal' Morality," in Primoratz, *Patriotism*, 59–86; Stephen Nathanson, "In Defense of Moderate Patriotism," in Primoratz, *Patriotism*, 87–104; Nathanson, *Patriotism, Morality, and Peace*, Kwame Anthony Appiah, *The Ethics of Identity* (Princeton, NJ: Princeton University Press, 2005), chap. 6; Tan, *Justice without Borders*; John Kleinig, "The Virtue of Patriotism," in Kleinig, Keller, and Primoratz, *The Ethics of Patriotism*, 19–47, Primoratz, "Patriotism: A Two-Tiered Account," in Kleinig, Keller, and Primoratz, *The Ethics of Patriotism*, 73–122.

22. The word *rational* in the phrase "rational agent" signifies that the person's self-determination makes enough sense in the context in which it occurs that others can see the person as responding to evidence and acting for reasons.

23. Immanuel Kant, *Grounding for the Metaphysics of Morals*, trans. J Ellington (Indianapolis: Hackett, 1981); Barbara Herman, "Mutual Aid and Respect for Persons," in *Kant's Groundwork of the Metaphysics of Morals*, ed. Paul Guyer (Lanham, MD: Rowman and Littlefield, 1998), 133–64; Onora O'Neill, "Consistency in Action," in Guyer, *Kant's Groundwork of the Metaphysics of Morals*, 103–31; Onora O'Neill, "Constructivism in Rawls and Kant," *The Cambridge Companion to Rawls*, ed. Samuel Freeman (Cambridge: Cambridge University Press, 2003), 347–67.

24. Immanuel Kant, *The Metaphysics of Morals*, trans. M. Gregor (Cambridge: Cambridge University Press, 1991), § 6.

25. *Republic* I 327c, emphasis added; from the Grube and Reeve translation, *Plato, Complete Works*, ed. John Cooper (Indianapolis: Hackett Publishing, 1997).

26. Randall Curren, *Aristotle on the Necessity of Public Education* (Lanham, MD: Rowman and Littlefield, 2000).

27. On the developmental immaturity of prison populations and what actually deters people who contemplate criminal activity, see A. Reiss et al., *Understanding and Preventing*

Violence (Washington, DC: National Academy Press, 1993); Tom Tyler, *Why People Obey the Law* (Princeton, NJ: Princeton University Press, 2006).

28. Tyler, *Why People Obey the Law*.

29. *West Virginia State Board of Education v. Barnette*, 319 U.S. 624 (1943), 644.

30. John Rawls, *Justice as Fairness: A Restatement* (Cambridge, MA: Harvard University Press, 2001), 5–7.

31. Ibid., 85–89; Rawls, *A Theory of Justice*, rev. ed. (Cambridge, MA: Harvard University Press, 1999), 119.

32. This approach is developed in greater detail in Randall Curren, "Aristotelian Necessities," *Good Society* 22, no. 2 (2013): 247–63; "Judgment and the Aims of Education"; and Randall Curren and Ellen Metzger, *Living Well Now and in the Future: Why Sustainability Matters* (Cambridge, MA: MIT Press, 2017), chap. 3.

33. For a concise overview of the theory of basic psychological needs and four decades of supporting research, see. Edward L. Deci and Richard M. Ryan, "Motivation, Personality, and Development within Embedded Social Contexts," in *The Oxford Handbook of Human Motivation*, ed. Ryan (New York: Oxford University Press, 2012), 85–107. See also Valery I. Chirkov, Richard M. Ryan, and Kennon M. Sheldon, eds., *Human Autonomy in Cross-Cultural Context: Perspectives on the Psychology of Agency, Freedom, and Well-Being* (Dordrecht: Springer, 2011).

34. See Richard M. Ryan, Randall Curren, and Edward L. Deci, "What Humans Need: Flourishing in Aristotelian Philosophy and Self-Determination Theory," in *The Best within Us: Positive Psychology Perspectives on Eudaimonia*, ed. Alan S. Waterman (Washington, DC: American Psychological Association, 2013), 57–75. The definitive overview of SDT as of 2017 is Richard M. Ryan and Edward L. Deci, *Self-Determination Theory: Basic Psychological Needs in Motivation, Development, and Wellness* (New York: Guilford Press, 2017).

35. For the evidence of cross-cultural validation, see Chirkov, Ryan, and Sheldon, *Human Autonomy in Cross-Cultural Context*.

36. Edward L. Deci, Jennifer G. La Guardia, Arlen C. Moller, Marc J. Scheiner, and Richard M. Ryan, "On the Benefits of Giving as Well as Receiving Autonomy Support: Mutuality in Close Friendships," *Personality and Social Psychology Bulletin* 32 (2006): 313–27.

37. In Rawls's theory, what makes a conception of a good life reasonable is that it is compatible with his fundamental principles of justice and the free and equal citizenship of others.

38. This claim about the basic function of education places our approach within a recent wave of ones that focus on flourishing as the chief aim of education. Representative works include Harry Brighouse, *On Education* (London: Routledge, 2005); John White, *Exploring Well-Being in Schools: A Guide to Making Children's Lives More Fulfilling* (New York: Routledge, 2011); Doret De Ruyter, "Well-Being and Education," in *Education, Philosophy and Well-Being: New Perspectives on the Work of John White*, ed. Judith Suissa, Carrie Winstanley, and Roger Marples (London: Routledge, 2015), 84–98. For an overview, see Kristján Kristjánsson, "Recent Work on Flourishing as the Aim of Education: A Critical Review," *British Journal of Educational Studies* 65, no. 1 (2017): 87–106. The most relevant counterpoints to such approaches are those that give priority to civic education. Exemplars would include Amy Gutmann, *Democratic Education* (Princeton, NJ: Princeton University Press, 1987); Eamonn Callan, *Creating Citizens* (Oxford: Oxford University Press, 1997); and Stephen Macedo, *Diversity and Distrust: Civic Education in a Multicultural Democracy* (Cambridge, MA: Harvard

University Press, 2003). Our view is distinctive in arguing that just institutions enable individuals to engage in the activities of good lives in ways that enable others to do the same. That is, we posit a form of eudaimonic reciprocity that reconciles educating children for others with educating them for themselves.

39. It would take us too far afield to discuss the many ramifications of defining the basic function of educational institutions in this way, but to say this is the function or basic function implies that the design of the institutions and whatever happens in them should be in the service of this function.

40. On the idea of learning as initiation pertaining to forms of goodness and not just skills or knowledge, see R. S. Peters, "Education as Initiation," in Curren, *Philosophy of Education: An Anthology*, 55–67; Kenneth Strike, "The Ethics of Teaching," in *A Companion to the Philosophy of Education*, ed. Randall Curren (Oxford: Blackwell, 2003), 509–24.

41. Curren, "Judgment and the Aims of Education."

42. National Research Council Institute of Medicine, *Engaging Schools: Fostering High School Students' Motivation to Learn* (Washington, DC: National Academies Press, 2004), 17–18.

43. See *Theory and Research in Education* 7, no. 2 (2009), for a wide-ranging overview of the relevant research up to the time of its publication, and Ryan and Deci, *Self-Determination Theory*, 351–81.

44. See Kenneth Strike, *Small Schools and Strong Communities: A Third Way of School Reform* (New York: Teachers College Press, 2010).

45. Randall Curren, "A Virtue Theory of Moral Motivation," http://www.jubileecentre.ac.uk/userfiles/jubileecentre/pdf/conference-papers/Varieties_of_Virtue_Ethics/Curren_Randall.pdf.

46. Julia Annas, *Intelligent Virtue* (Oxford: Oxford University Press, 2011); Randall Curren, "Motivational Aspects of Moral Learning and Progress," *Journal of Moral Education* 43, no. 4 (2014): 484–99; Curren, "Virtue Ethics and Moral Education."

47. Richard M. Ryan, "Psychological Needs and the Facilitation of Integrative Processes," *Journal of Personality* 63 (1995): 397–97; Kennon M. Sheldon and Tim Kasser, "Coherence and Congruence: Two Aspects of Personality Integration," *Journal of Personality and Social Psychology* 68, no. 3 (1995): 531–43; Deci and Ryan, "Motivation, Personality, and Development within Embedded Social Contexts."

48. Edward L. Deci, Haleh Eghrani, Brian C. Patrick, and Dean R. Leone, "Facilitating Internalization: The Self-Determination Theory Perspective," *Journal of Personality* 62, no. 1 (1994): 119–42.

49. Christopher P. Niemiec, Martin F. Lynch, Maarten Vansteenkiste, Jessey Bernstein, Edward L. Deci, and Richard M. Ryan, "The Antecedents and Consequences of Autonomous Self-Regulation for College: A Self-Determination Theory Perspective on Socialization," *Journal of Adolescence* 29 (2006): 761–75, at 763.

50. Deci and Ryan, "Motivation, Personality, and Development within Embedded Social Contexts," 89.

51. Deci, Eghrani, Patrick, and Leone, "Facilitating Internalization," 124.

52. Deci and Ryan, "Motivation, Personality, and Development within Embedded Social Contexts," 86, 93.

53. E. Deci and R. Ryan, "The 'What' and 'Why' of Goal Pursuits: Human Needs and the Self-Determination of Behavior," *Psychological Inquiry* 11 (2000): 227–68; Netta Weinstein and Richard Ryan, "When Helping Helps: Autonomous Motivation for Prosocial Behavior and Its Influence on Well-Being for the Helper and Recipient," *Journal of Personality and Social Psychology* 98, no. 2 (2010): 222–44.

CHAPTER FIVE

1. Adrienne Clarkson, *Belonging: The Paradox of Citizenship* (Toronto: House of Anansi Press, 2014), 179–80.
2. Ibid., 112.
3. *West Virginia State Board of Education v. Barnette*, 319 U.S. 624 (1943), 644.
4. Rick Jervis, "Candidates Talk Tough on Muslims: Rights Groups Horrified by Calls for Restricted Entry and Patrols," *USA Today*, March 26, 2016, reporting Ted Cruz's unconstitutional proposal to "patrol and secure Muslim neighborhoods before they become radicalized."
5. Max Wind-Cowie and Thomas Gregory, *A Place for Pride* (London: Demos, 2011), quoted in Doug Saunders, *The Myth of the Muslim Tide: Do Immigrants Threaten the West?* (New York: Vintage Books, 2012), 70, emphasis added.
6. Saunders, *The Myth of the Muslim Tide*, 70.
7. Ibid., 71–72; *French Muslims Favor Integration into French Society* (Washington, DC: Department of State, Office of Research, Opinion Analysis M-58-05, 2005).
8. Jacob L. Vigdor, *Comparing Immigrant Assimilation in North America and Europe* (New York: Center for State and Local Leadership, May 2011), http://bydo.ug/87.
9. Saunders, *The Myth of the Muslim Tide*, 76, 81.
10. In *The Muslim Question in Canada: A Story of Segmented Integration* (Vancouver: UBC Press, 2014), Abdolmohammad Kazemipur concludes that the economic challenges faced by Muslims in Canada are largely a consequence of their social isolation, and that mutual comfort between rooted Canadians and Muslim immigrants will likely grow with greater social interaction and a commitment to equal economic opportunity. He notes the important roles of integrated neighborhoods and schools in creating "the right milieu for the development of emotional bonds and common identities," and advises collaborative, project-based learning to foster friendly interaction (184). Another recent study by Claire L. Adida, David D. Laitin, and Marie-Anne Valfort, *Why Muslim Integration Fails in Christian-Heritage Societies* (Cambridge, MA: Harvard University Press, 2016), is focused largely on France and finds that overcoming anti-Muslim discrimination in labor markets and education will be important to the integration of Muslims. Employing some unusually sophisticated research methods, the authors were able to show that anti-Muslim sentiment and discrimination is largely nonrational but has engendered a pattern of mutually reinforcing hostility—a "discriminatory equilibrium" (9). A third recent study by Jonathan Laurence, *The Emancipation of Europe's Muslims: The State's Role in Minority Integration* (Princeton, NJ: Princeton University Press, 2012), does not address schools as such, but shows that as European countries have developed offices and institutions that constructively engage Muslim populations and leaders, Islamic activism, leaders, and federations "have responded positively to the government outreach" and increasingly accepted the consultative and procedural norms of Western democracies (270).
11. None of this is to say that there is an easy answer to how many immigrants a given country can successfully integrate within a given stretch of time or how countries should weigh the prospects of successful integration into their calculations of how many refugees and other immigrants they should accept out of humanitarian concern and to fulfill their international treaty obligations.
12. Ian MacMullen argues that patriotic love is a fundamental threat to legitimacy, in "Doing without Love: Civic Motivation, Affection, and Identification," *Journal of Politics* 76, no. 1 (2014): 73–85.
13. E.g., MacIntyre, "Is Patriotism a Virtue?"

14. *Compact Edition of the Oxford English Dictionary* (Oxford: Oxford University Press, 1971), vol. 1, 580.
15. *Compact OED*, vol. 2, 2099.
16. For a history of the term, see Mary G. Dietz, "Patriotism: A Brief History of the Term," in Primoratz, *Patriotism*, 201–15.
17. See, e.g., Eamonn Callan, "Love, Idolatry, and Patriotism," *Social Theory and Practice* 32, no. 4 (2006): 525–46. Following George Orwell, Callan defines the country a patriot loves as "a particular place and the community that resides there and stretches across many generations into the past and future" (532–33). Cf. Ajume Wingo, "To Love Your Country as Your Mother: Patriotism after 9/11," *Theory and Research in Education* 5, no. 1 (2007): 23–40. Wingo writes vividly of land as a traditional object and basis of patriotic attachment (along with kin relationships and a common religion), but he assumes none of these can play a significant role in patriotism in mobile, urbanized, and pluralistic societies like the United States. He says civic education needs to particularize the universal principles by telling *our* story of devotion to them. In lumping land, blood, and religion together, he overlooks the fact that "this land" *can* be "our land" in a way that one religion or ethnicity cannot be. Americans can and have particularized the land and diverse people comprising the country in many ways, including the one Wingo implies we can only use to concretize universal principles. Robyn Eckersley makes much the same point in arguing in a different context that "attachment to the national environment would supply the particularistic loyalties that are missing from Habermas's constitutional patriotism, but without the dangers associated with an uncritical allegiance to the state or to a particular ethnic grouping within the state" ("Environmentalism and Patriotism," 192). For background on the view that patriotism is properly focused specifically on a constitutional tradition and the principles that animate it, see Habermas, "Citizenship and National Identity"; Müller, *Constitutional Patriotism*.
18. See Habermas, "Citizenship and National Identity"; Müller, *Constitutional Patriotism*.
19. For a systematic exploration of the ethics of this long-term dependence, see Curren and Metzger, *Living Well Now and in the Future*.
20. In saying this, we do not mean to deny that at present only Americans who fall within the top three socioeconomic deciles have *any* influence on policy, and that those at the extreme upper end of the wealth and income distribution have far and away the greatest political influence. See Martin Gilens, *Affluence and Influence: Economic Inequality and Political Power in America* (Princeton, NJ: Princeton University Press, 2012); Larry M. Bartels, *Unequal Democracy: The Political Economy of the New Gilded Age* (Princeton, NJ: Princeton University Press, 2010); Michael Tomasky, "The Dangerous Election," *New York Review of Books* 62, no. 5 (March 24, 2016): 4–6.
21. Cf. MacIntyre, "Is Patriotism a Virtue?," which runs the impartial and impersonal together.
22. Keller, "The Case against Patriotism," in Kleinig, Keller, and Primoratz, *The Ethics of Patriotism*, 48–72, at 62.
23. Ibid., 67.
24. Ibid., 68, 70.
25. Ibid., 59, 69.
26. Kok-Chor Tan makes much the same point in the following way: "Cosmopolitans accept the ideal of impartiality . . . as a . . . claim about institutional arrangements. . . . Accordingly, the aim of cosmopolitan impartiality is not to eliminate all forms of national and other associative concerns, interests, and pursuits, but to determine

the global context and rules within which such concerns and interests may be legitimately pursued. . . . [So] individuals [may] pursue particular ends and ties, including the commitment of patriotism, within the limits of a just global institutional arrangement" (*Justice without Borders*, 157).

27. See Brighouse, "Justifying Patriotism," 547.

28. Nussbaum, "Teaching Patriotism."

29. Viroli, *For Love of Country*, 174.

30. Dan Rather, May 9, 2017, at 5:22 p.m., https://www.facebook.com/theDanRather/.

31. On what students in the United States know about civics and government, see Richard Niemi, "What Students Know about Civics and Government," and Peter Levine, "Education for a Civil Society," in *Making Civics Count*, ed. David E. Campbell, Meira Levinson, and Frederick M. Hess (Cambridge, MA; Harvard Education Press, 2012), 15–35 and 37–56.

32. Amy Gutmann and Denis Thompson, *Democracy and Disagreement* (Cambridge, MA: Harvard University Press, 1996), 14–15; Randall Curren, "Judgment and the Aims of Education." For guidance on how to teach multidisciplinary critical and deliberative thinking, see Gerald Nosich, *Learning to Think Things Through: A Guide to Critical Thinking across the Curriculum*, 4th ed. (Upper Saddle River, NJ: Pearson, 2011).

33. Curren, "Judgment and the Aims of Education."

34. Brighouse, "Should We Teach Patriotic History?"

35. Rawls, *Justice as Fairness*, 27, 89–94.

36. John Rawls, *Political Liberalism* (New York: Columbia University Press, 1993), 54; *Justice as Fairness*, 35–36, 91.

37. Eamonn Callan, *Creating Citizens* (Oxford: Oxford University Press, 1997); James Youniss, "How to Enrich Civic Education and Sustain Democracy," in Campbell, Levinson, and Hess, *Making Civics Count*, 115–33.

38. Diana Hess and Paula McAvoy, *The Political Classroom: Evidence and Ethics in Democratic Education* (New York: Routledge, 2015); Emily Robertson and Jonathan Zimmerman, *The Case for Contention: Teaching Controversial Issues in American Schools* (Chicago: University of Chicago Press, 2017).

39. Nussbaum, "Toward a Globally Sensitive Patriotism."

40. Fullinwider, "Patriotic History," 222.

41. The quote is from Emily Robertson, "Public Reason and the Education of Democratic Citizens: The Role of Higher Education," in *Education, Democracy, and the Moral Life*, ed. Michael S. Katz, Susan Verducci, and Gert Biesta (Dordrecht: Springer, 2008), 113–26, at 123. For an illuminating case study in how schools fail to teach the truth about the role of activism in overcoming injustice, see Herbert Kohl, *She Would Not Be Moved: How We Tell the Story of Rosa Parks* (New York: New Press, 2005). On meaningful civic education for the marginalized, see Meira Levinson, *No Citizen Left Behind* (Cambridge, MA: Harvard University Press, 2012).

42. Curren, "Motivational Aspects of Moral Learning and Progress."

43. The civic impact of common schooling would be greater, of course, in societies in which the membership of various neighborhoods, churches, interest groups, and associations are diverse and overlapping, so that the networks of sympathetic connection begun in schools could propagate and be reinforced through richer social connections. In such societies it would presumably also be easier to *create* a semblance of common schools.

44. See Curren, *Aristotle on the Necessity of Public Education*, 131ff.

45. See, e.g., Meira Levinson and Sanford Levinson, "'Getting Religion': Religion, Diversity, and Community in Public and Private Schools," in *School Choice: The Moral Debate*, ed. Alan Wolfe (Princeton, NJ: Princeton University Press, 2003).
46. Joan Goodman, "Student Authority: Antidote to Alienation," *Theory and Research in Education* 8, no. 3 (2010): 227–47.
47. Judy Dunn, *Children's Friendships: The Beginnings of Intimacy* (Oxford: Blackwell, 2006), 5–7, 38–40, 42–44; Walker, Curren, and Jones, "Good Friendships among Children."
48. F. Clark Power, Ann Higgins, and Lawrence Kohlberg, *Lawrence Kohlberg's Approach to Moral Education* (New York: Columbia University Press, 1989).
49. Brian J. Bigelow, Geoffrey Tesson, and John H. Lewko, *Learning the Rules: The Anatomy of Children's Relationships* (New York: Guilford Press, 1996): Walker, Curren, and Jones, "Good Friendships among Children."
50. Such discussion may, indeed, use children's literature as a point of departure. See Gareth Matthews, *Philosophy and the Young Child* (Cambridge, MA: Harvard University Press, 1980); Michael Pritchard, *Reasonable Children: Moral Education and Moral Learning* (Lawrence: University Press of Kansas, 1996).
51. The movie *The Hurt Locker* ends with a vivid depiction of the motivational power of being good at a military specialization.
52. Youniss, "How to Enrich Civic Education and Sustain Democracy."

CHAPTER SIX

1. Kevin Hovland, *Shared Futures: Global Learning and Liberal Education* (Washington, DC: AAC&U, 2006), 24, 27, and 28.
2. Ibid., 24 and 28.
3. UN Foundation, *The Millennium Ecosystem Assessment* (Geneva: UN Foundation, 2005), http://www.unfoundation.org/features/millenium_ecosystem_assessment .asp; Worldwatch Institute, *Vital Signs*, vol. 22, *The Trends That Are Shaping Our Future* (Washington, DC: Worldwatch Institute, 2015); UNEP, *Summary of the Sixth Global Environment Outlook, GEO-6, Regional Assessments: Key Findings and Policy Messages* (Nairobi: UN Environmental Programme, 2016), http://www.unep.org/publica tions/; Potsdam Institute for Climate Impact Research and Climate Analysis, *Turn Down the Heat: Why a 4°C Warmer World Must be Avoided* (Washington, DC: World Bank, 2013); World Wildlife Fund, *Living Planet Report 2014: Species and Spaces, People and Places* (Gland, Switzerland: WWF International, 2014), http://wwf.panda.org /about our_earth/all_publications/living_planet_report/.
4. James Hansen et al., "Ice Melt, Sea Level Rise and Superstorms: Evidence from Paleoclimate Data, Climate Modeling, and Modern Observations that 2°C Global Warming Could Be Dangerous," *Atmospheric Chemistry and Physics* 16 (March 22, 2016): 3761–812, http://www.atmos-chem-phys.net/16/3761/2016/acp-16-3761-2016 .html; David Pollard and Robert M. DeConto, "Contribution of Antarctica to Past and Future Sea-Level Rise," *Nature* 531, no. 7596 (March 31, 2016): 591–97, http://www .nature.com/nature/journal/v531/n7596/full/nature17145.html.
5. Department of Defense, "DoD Releases Report on Security Implications of Climate Change." See also Joshua Hammer, "Is a Lack of Water to Blame for the Conflict in Syria?"
6. For an analysis of the patterns of hierarchical educational systems shaped by competition for employment, see Randall Curren, "On the Arc of Opportunity: Education,

Credentialism, and Employment," in *Fair Work: Ethics, Social Policy, Globalization*, ed. Kory Schaff (London: Rowman and Littlefield International, 2017), 59–77.

7. See Margaret E. Keck and Kathryn Sikkink, *Activists beyond Borders: Advocacy Networks in International Politics* (Ithaca, NY: Cornell University Press, 1998); Kate Nash, "Towards Transnational Democratization?," in *Transnationalizing the Public Sphere*, ed. Kate Nash (Cambridge: Polity Press, 2014), 60–78; Jan Aart Scholte, ed., *Building Global Democracy? Civil Society and Accountable Global Governance* (Cambridge: Cambridge University Press, 2011); Sidney Tarrow, *The New Transnational Activism* (Cambridge: Cambridge University Press, 2005).

8. The idea of a global public (demos) or publics (demoi) has received attention in such recent works as James Bohman, *Democracy across Borders: From Demos to Demoi* (Cambridge, MA: MIT Press, 2007); Christian List and Mathias Koenig-Archibugi, "Can There Be a Global Demos? An Agency-Based Approach," *Philosophy and Public Affairs* 38 (2010): 76–110; David Miller, "Democracy's Domain," *Philosophy and Public Affairs* 37 (2009): 201–28.

9. Keck and Sikkink, *Activists beyond Borders*, 3.

10. Martha Nussbaum, *Not for Profit: Why Democracy Needs the Humanities* (Princeton, NJ: Princeton University Press, 2010), 80.

11. For comprehensive catalogs, see World Wildlife Fund, *Living Planet Report 2014*; Curren and Metzger, *Living Well Now and in the Future*.

12. Elinor Ostrom, "A Multi-Scale Approach to Coping with Climate Change and Other Collective Action Problems," *Solutions* 1, no. 2 (2010): 27–36, at 29.

13. Much of the research is summarized in Elinor Ostrom et al., eds., *The Drama of The Commons* (Washington, DC: National Academies Press, 2002), esp., chap. 2. See also Paul Stern, Thomas Dietz, and Elinor Ostrom, "Research on the Commons: Lessons for Environmental Resource Managers," *Environmental Practice* 4, no. 2 (2002): 61–64.

14. Elinor Ostrom, "A General Framework for Analyzing Sustainability of Social-Ecological Systems," *Science* 325 (July 24, 2009): 419–22.

15. Ibid., 420–21. The discussion of leadership in these pages notes that "entrepreneurial skills" and "the presence of college graduates" have a "strong positive effect."

16. Ostrom's understanding of legitimacy is similar to our own. See Ostrom, "A Multi-Scale Approach," 29.

17. Karin Bäckstrand, "The Democratic Legitimacy of Global Governance after Copenhagen," in *The Oxford Handbook of Climate Change and Society*, ed. John S. Dryzek, Richard B. Norgaard, and David Schlosberg (Oxford: Oxford University Press, 2011), 669–84.

18. See Ronnie Lipschutz and Corina Mckendry, "Social Movements and Global Civil Society," in Dryzek, Norgaard, and Schlosberg, *The Oxford Handbook of Climate Change and Society*, 369–83; Keck and Sikkink, *Activists beyond Borders*; Scholte, *Building Global Democracy?*

19. For profiles of AAC&U-sponsored initiatives, see https://www.aacu.org/shared-futures/previous-projects.

20. Richard Bellamy, *Citizenship: A Very Short Introduction* (Oxford: Oxford University Press, 2008), 4, emphasis added.

21. What follows is Curren's participant observations.

22. Irwin, "Teaching 'Americanism' with a World Perspective.'"

23. Danielle Allen, *Talking to Strangers* (Chicago: University of Chicago Press, 2004), 120.

24. For the detailed account of political friendship on which this is based, see Curren, *Aristotle on the Necessity of Public Education*, 123–39.

CONCLUSION

1. From Hughes, "Let America Be America Again," 189–91.

2. Unpublished March 2003 interview. Other details of the foregoing account are based on an interview with Gordon conducted by Curren in October 2003. For a chronology and further accounts and commentary, see William A. Gordon, *Four Dead in Ohio: Was There a Conspiracy at Kent State?* (Rancho Mirage, CA: North Ridge Books, 1995); Jerry M. Lewis and Thomas R. Hensley, "The May 4 Shootings at Kent State University: The Search for Historical Accuracy," *Ohio Council for the Social Studies Review* 34, no. 1(1998): 9–21 (available in draft at http://dept.kent.edu/sociology /lewis/LEWIHEN.htm); James Michener, *Kent State: What Happened and Why* (New York: Random House, 1971); I. F. Stone, *The Killings at Kent State: How Murder Went Unpunished* (New York: Review Books, 1971); Philip K. Tompkins and Elaine V. B. Anderson, *Communication Crisis at Kent State: A Case Study* (New York: Gordon and Breach, 1971).

3. For background on Nixon's decision to bomb Cambodia, see Edward Jay Epstein, *Agency of Fear* (New York: Putnam, 1977). Cambodia had remained neutral while tolerating the transit of North Vietnamese forces (much as Switzerland had remained neutral during World War II while tolerating the transit of fascist forces), and the intent of saturation bombing was to destroy every village in order to deny those forces safe haven and provisions in eastern Cambodia. Epstein recounts the flimsy assurances Nixon procured for believing that Cambodian society could be reconstructed by the United States at the conclusion of the war.

4. Gordon, *Four Dead in Ohio.*

5. Nancy Sherman, *Aftermath: Healing the Moral Wounds of Our Soldiers* (Oxford: Oxford University Press, 2015), 8.

6. Ibid., 18.

7. Gordon, *Four Dead in Ohio;* Michener, *Kent State.*

8. "Democracy is the rule of the politician," Schumpeter wrote in his influential classic, *Capitalism, Socialism, and Democracy,* first published in 1942 (London: Allen and Unwin, 1976), 285. For a lucid historical survey of competing conceptions of democracy, see David Held, *Models of Democracy,* 3rd ed. (Stanford, CA: Stanford University Press, 2006).

9. See Randall Curren, "Defining Sustainability Ethics," in *Environmental Ethics,* 2nd ed., ed. Michael Boylan (Oxford: Wiley-Blackwell, 2014), 331–45; Curren and Metzger, *Living Well Now and in the Future.*

INDEX

Muhammad, Elijah, 8
Müller, Jan-Werner, 144n24, 146n12
multiculturalism (diversity, inclusiveness, unity), 5–7, 29–30, 54, 63, 80, 91, 98–99, 105, 112, 113–14, 115, 118, 124, 132, 162n10, 164n43
Murphy, Frank, 54–55
music, 6–7, 67
Muslims, 8, 12, 162n4; black, 8–9; immigrant experience of, 98–99, 162n10
mythologizing, 77–79, 146n12, 158n4. See also religion, civil

Nathanson, Stephen, 143n14
national anthem, 5–6
National Center for History in the Schools, 30
National Council for Science and the Environment (NCSE), 129
National Education Association (NEA), 22–23, 24, 25, 32, 48, 50, 66, 152n1
National Endowment for the Humanities, 30
National FFA. See Future Farmers of America (FFA)
National Grange of the Patrons of Husbandry. See Grange
nationalism: definition of, 19, 144nn21–22; forms of, 7–8, 19; French, 7–8; German, 7; vs. patriotism, 7, 18–20, 146n12; US, 7–10, 18–20, 25, 52. See also populism
Nation of Islam, 8–9
NCSE. See National Council for Science and the Environment (NCSE)
NEA. See National Education Association (NEA)
needs: basic human, 88–89, 122; basic psychological, 88–89, 91–94, 95, 100, 116, 160n33. See also competence (efficacy); relatedness; self-determination
New Farmers of America, 73, 74
NGOs. See nongovernmental organizations (NGOs)
Nietzsche, Friedrich, 19, 146n11
Nixon, Richard M., 134, 135, 167n3
No Child Left Behind, 31
nongovernmental organizations (NGOs), 124, 128
Nuremberg Trials, 79–80
Nussbaum, Martha, 109, 159n20

Oakland Military Institute (OMI), 33–34
oaths. See pledges (oaths)
Obama, Barack, 8, 31, 129–30
obedience, 25, 77, 79; of deity, 37; of law, 45, 60; military, 79, 135, 158n8; by students, 21
O'Connor, Sandra Day, 31
O'Leary, Cecilia, 60
OMI. See Oakland Military Institute (OMI)
Orwell, George, 19, 25, 146nn11–12
Ostrom, Elinor, 126–28
Owens, G. W., 73

pageants, 42, 46
Parks, Rosa, 29, 148n58
partiality (favoritism), 84, 101, 108–9, 159n20, 143n14. See also impartiality
patriot, definition of, 103
patriotic education. See education: civic
patriotism: and civic virtue, 102–3; constitutional, 7, 104, 105, 107, 108, 142n9, 144n22; definition of, 19, 142n9, 143n14, 144n20; forms of, 8, 143n20; and ideals, 3; language of, 145n45; and love of country, 80, 104, 144n22; and morality, 3; vs. nationalism, 7–8, 18–20, 146n12; and philosophy, 141n1; virtuous, 4, 10, 11–12, 15–16, 79–80, 82–83, 84, 99–110, 117, 131, 137, 142n9
Patriot's Pledge of Faith, 42–43
Patriot's Week (New York City), 42–43
Patterson, Floyd, 9
PE. See school subjects: physical education
pen pals, 63
physical education. See under school subjects
Pilgrims, 44, 45, 151n32
Plato, 13, 40, 85–87, 136, 138
Pledge of Allegiance, 14, 37–38, 43, 50–52, 78, 81, 150n2; challenges to, 37, 52–55
pledges (oaths), 1–2, 10, 38; refusal to make, 37, 52–53, 55. See also Patriot's Pledge of Faith; Pledge of Allegiance
Plymouth Colony, 44–45
political correctness. See multiculturalism (diversity, inclusiveness, unity)
populism, 7–8, 72, 144n24. See also nationalism
pride, national, 11–12, 42, 80, 82, 145n43; language of, 9–10
Primoratz, Igor, 143n14, 144n20